He Said...

He Was...

Sorry...

Developed by: Joanna Johnson, MSW, CAC, MAC, CCFC

Dedication

This book is dedicated to the friendship between Brenda Mackee and Joanna Johnson. Their friendship began in a very unhealthy but spiritual place. They met when Brenda was renting her a house on Inerarity Point.

This was a close and personal friendship, which began when my mom came from Canada to heal from a very unhealthy and sometimes abusive marriage. Brenda and Joanna were like Thelma and Louise. They certainly loved each other.

About the Author

Joanna Johnson is the co-owner and clinical developer of Avalon Treatment Centers. She has been in the field of social work for 30 years. She has worked a very intricate and extraordinary recovery program for the same 30 years, which has helped with her personal journey from addiction to recovery. Her recovery story is one of honesty and integrity. It started when she was 18 years old with no boundaries and developed into a love affair. Her success of 30 years sober is the base of most of the work she has been involved in, both here in the United States and in Canada.

Mrs. Johnson was one of the first 10 women to be licensed in the State of Florida as a *Batterers Intervention Program Specialist.* Prior to that, she was the cofounder of Samuel's House; a shelter for women in Key West, Florida. She was also an original board member of family in Woodstock, New York. This program became infamous directly after the Woodstock Festival. The program that Mrs. Johnson created called the Soft Landing Machine is now a part of the Woodstock experience and has been for many years. Mrs. Johnson was the director and founder of The Recovery Center, which merged with Avalon Treatment Centers.

Mrs. Johnson's passion for Canada is expressed in all of her work and in everything she does. Her journey began at the Frog Lake Indian Reservation and has brought her to where she is now. She has completed thousands of assessments and facilitated thousands of groups. At the age of 71, she is still passionate about recovery. Mrs. Johnson has made it her personal mission to see that the courts are accurately given assessments to aid and educate through the legal process.

...Why do men batter? ...Why do women batter?

This is a question that complexes counselors, families, attorneys, social systems and every other professional and nonprofessional that is trying to understand the violence that is perpetrated in households today!

Years of working with men and women who have been sentenced by the courts to 26 weeks of Batterers Intervention program in the state of Florida; incline me to believe in four categories (excluding the psychopaths and sociopaths). The categories that I see, are learned behaviors and you control the key medication.

I want to share a personal story to make my point.

I had a boyfriend in Cripple Bush, New York in the early 60's. Three months pregnant with my fourth child, my partner and I got into an argument over something I can't even remember. He was driving and he spit in my face! I said, "Stop the car!" As he did I got out and began hitchhiking back home, which was longer than three miles from where he put me out on the road. I was picked up by a man, fairly well-dressed, who preceded to beat me and again I was put out on the road. This time I was found on the side of the road by a friend named Joe, who lived with my best friend Marcie. He contacted Marcie and my significant other. They proceeded to the hospital where Joe took me. The baby was not hurt and I was not hurt. I left with my boyfriend! He told me when I got into the truck that I had made him angry but because I was pregnant, *he said he was sorry*, and I was okay with that. Our relationship just went on.

This manual and all this material is a group process proven through 10 years of experience!

Thousands of men in Leon, Liberty, Wakulla, Gadsden, Franklin and Jefferson counties in the state of Florida have gone through this program created By Mrs. Joanna Johnson.

Personal Message: Good luck to all of you who are willing to use this tough manual to improve you and your family's lives. Numerous years of experience and many other teachers have prepared this material with warm feelings. - Joanna Johnson

Assessment

1. Do you call your partner names? ☐ Yes ☐ No
2. Do you keep your partner from participating in activities he or she wants to do that does not include your participation? ☐ Yes ☐ No
3. Do you control your partner's money? ☐ Yes ☐ No
4. Do you make decisions with little or no discussion? ☐ Yes ☐ No
5. Do you push, shove, block, threaten or intimidate your partner? ☐ Yes ☐ No
6. Do you put down her family or her friends? ☐ Yes ☐ No
7. Do you mimic or joke about her choices? ☐ Yes ☐ No
8. Do you tease, humiliate or ridicule them for their body style? ☐ Yes ☐ No
9. Do you accuse that he or she gives other people more attention than you? ☐ Yes ☐ No
10. Do you give your partner an allowance and or control all the money? ☐ Yes ☐ No
11. Do you use your children as threats? ☐ Yes ☐ No
12. Do you become rigid easily? ☐ Yes ☐ No
13. Do you become enraged when chores are not done in a timely way or to your liking? ☐ Yes ☐ No
14. Do you invade your partner's privacy? ☐ Yes ☐ No
15. Do you drive recklessly to intimidate? ☐ Yes ☐ No
16. Do you pick, pinch or punch? ☐ Yes ☐ No

17. Do you block passages such as in and out of rooms or in and out of the home? ☐ Yes ☐ No
18. Do you refuse to participate in the care of the children or maintain maintenance in the home?   ☐ Yes ☐ No
19. Do you demand that you be in all conversations? ☐ Yes ☐ No
20. Do you demean her in front friends? ☐ Yes ☐ No
21. Do you use putdowns to them as a person, parent or even as a friend? ☐ Yes ☐ No
22. 22. Do you throw or smack things or even create holes in the walls with the sole purpose of intimidation? ☐ Yes ☐ No

If you answer "yes" to any of the above, there is a problem. More than one "yes" becomes a dangerous situation that needs to be stopped immediately and interventions put in place.

Chapter 1

Why it Matters

Domestic violence consists of willing and compulsive behaviors, excessive intimidation and action. It is a mental, physical and spiritual act by one intimate partner to another. Today it is an epidemic. It affects every aspect of every economic class of partnerships in every community and in all societies. This is regardless of race, religion, economics, education or personal history.

One out of every four women will experience domestic violence in their lives at some point. It is estimated that 1.3 million women are victims of physical assault by an intimate partner. This is not even considering same-sex partnerships. History teaches us that physical assaults are usually by someone you know intimately.

It was recorded by the national coalition against domestic violence that the average age of a woman who is being assaulted is 20 to 24. This percentage is growing into girls who are abused by teen boyfriends.

The Agency for the Protection of the Elderly shows that women over 60 who reported being abused also reported that it started at around age 20.

Witnessing violence between one's parents, siblings or caregivers is the strongest learned behavior of physical violence to be generationally continued.

Boys who witnessed their fathers or brothers hitting, kicking, punching or controlling their partners have a strong tendency of becoming abusive themselves. This statistic is clear and is supported in relationships when they become abusive.

30% to 60% of men reported being abused or who are abusers have reported they were also abused as children. One out of every 66 women and one out of every 33 men have experienced an attempted or completed rape.

7.8 million Women reported that they've been sexually assaulted or raped by a colleague or their intimate partner.

Sexual assault is in approximately 40% to 45% of battering relationships. This statistic is supported by the assessments over the years by Joanna Johnson.

One out of every twelve women and one out of every 45 men have been stalked at some point in their life. 81% of the women reported that the stalker was a current or former partner.

Intimate partner violence results in more than $18.5 million in mental health care over each year. $4.1 billion, which is for direct medical care.

Estimates which are as low as 16,800 homicides and $2.2 million in medically treated injuries are due to a committed partner. This has cost an approximate $37 billion. These statistics come from the National Coalition of Domestic Violence.

It is also important to note that only one quarter of all physical assaults, and one fifth of rapes are only one half of what we have stated here, because they are rarely reported.

Common Myths of Domestic Violence – Why they are wrong!

1. Domestic Violence is not a problem in my community.
    a. In 2010, 113,378 crimes of domestic violence were reported to Florida law enforcement agencies resulting in 67,810 arrests. During fiscal year 2010-2011, Florida's certified domestic violence centers provided 477,489 nights of emergency shelter to 15,789 survivors of domestic violence and their children. Advocates created 87,474 tailored safety plans, provided a total of 484,950 hours of outreach and counseling services and answered 130,393 domestic violence hotline calls from individuals seeking emergency services, information and safety plan assistance. Many survivors of domestic violence are not reporting their abuse to the police or accessing services at domestic violence centers due to reasons such as shame, fear or being prevented from doing so by their abuser. For this reason we may never know the true extent of abuse in our country and in our state. Source: FCADV – Florida Coalition against Domestic Violence.
2. Domestic Violence only happen to poor women and women of color.

a. Domestic violence happens in all kinds of families and relationships. Persons of any class, culture, religion, sexual orientation, marital status, age and sex can be victims or perpetrators of domestic violence.

3. Some people deserve to be hit.
   a. No one deserves to be abused. Period. The only person responsible for the abuse is the abuser.
   b. Physical violence, even among family members, is wrong and against the law.

4. Alcohol, drug abuse, stress and mental illness cause domestic violence.
   a. Alcohol use, drug use and stress do not cause domestic violence; they may go along with domestic violence, but they do not cause the violence. Abusers often say they use these excuses for their violence.
   b. Generally, domestic violence happens when an abuser has learned and chooses to abuse.
   c. Domestic violence is rarely a cause by mental illness, but it is often used as an excused for domestic violence.

5. Domestic violence is a personal problem between a husband and wife.
   a. Domestic violence affects everyone.
   b. About 1 in 3 American women have been physically or sexually abused by a husband or boyfriend at some point in their life.

    c. In 1996, 30% of all female murder victims were killed by their husbands or boyfriends.

    d. 40% to 60% of men who abuse women also abuse children.

6. If it were that bad, she would just leave.

    a. There are many reasons why women may not leave. Not leaving does not mean that the situation is okay or that the victim wants to be abused.

    b. Leaving can be dangerous. The most dangerous time for a woman who is being abused is when she tries to leave.

    c. Many victims do leave and lead successful, violence free lives.

My Support Map

Although you may be thinking a lot about your relationships with "romantic" or "intimate partners", first let's take a look at some of the other relationships in your life. This is important, because sometimes we focus so intensely on one relationship that we lost sight of the importance of our other relationships, like with friends, family and other people who can help us reach our goals. Remember no one relationship can ever meet all your needs.

Below you can create a map of your support system. In the center circle, put your name. In the boxes connected to you, write the names and telephone numbers of the people or organizations who are or could be a part of your support system. This means anyone you could call on for help or support in any area of your life from a serious personal problem, to health care, to help at work. Feel free to draw in extra boxes if needed!

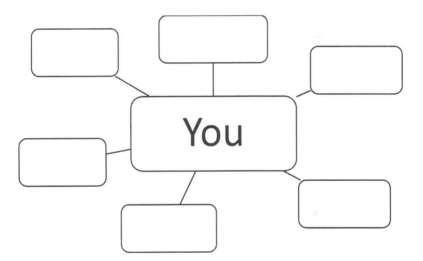

Examples of people and places your have in your support system:

Parents, brothers or sisters, other family members, close friends, teacher your can trust, your counselor or therapist, your church temple or place of worship, your dating partner, crisis hotline, co-workers, health clinic, a club, team or group you belong to, your school.

As you continue to work on developing healthy relationship, strong or confusing feelings may come up. Who in your support system can you talk to about these feelings?

Evaluating My Relationships

The purpose of this exercise is to help you start thinking about different aspects of your relationship. If you are not in a relationship right now, focus on a past relationship or a present relationship with a friend or family member. Ask yourself the following questions about that person and your relationships with him or her.

Can you name five things about this person that you really like?

_____

_____

_____

_____

_____

_____

_____

_____

_____

_____

_____

_____

Can you name five things about this person that you really dislike?

_____

_____

_____

_____

_____

_____

Do you think this person's relationship with family and friends are healthy? Why or why not?

_____

_____

_____

_____

_____

_____

Does this person encourage you to have friends, or discourage other friendships? In what way?

_____

_____

_____

_____

_____

_____

Can you name three things this person in interested in besides you?

_____

_____

_____

_____

_____

_____

Can you name three activities that you participate in without this person?

_____

_____

_____

_____

_____

Do you both have equal decision-making power in your relationship?

_____

_____

_____

_____

_____

How do the two of you usually handle conflict?

_____

_____

_____

_____

_____

Since you have been in the relationship, do your generally feel better about yourself, worse about yourself or about the same?

_____

_____

_____

_____

_____

How Healthy Is My Relationship

Following are two lists one of health relationship characteristics and one of unhealthy traits. Many relationships have a combination of both. The point of this exercise is to figure out what things in your relationship are healthy or unhealthy, so your can gain appreciation for the best things and decide what you want to change. Read both lists, and check the box next to every statement that is true about your relationship.

I am evaluating my relationship with: _____

Is It Healthy?

Check the circle if you and this person…

- o Have fun together more often than not
- o Each enjoy spending time separately, with your own friends, as well as with each other's friends
- o Always feel safe with each other
- o Trust each other
- o Are faithful to each other if you have made a commitment
- o Support each other's individual goals in life, like employment or school

- Respect each other's opinions, even when they are different
- Solve conflicts without putting each other down, cursing at each other or making threats
- Both accept responsibility for your actions
- Both apologize when you're wrong
- Have equal decision-making power about what you do in your relationship
- Each control your own money
- Are proud to be with each other
- Encourage each other's interests – like sports and extracurricular activities
- Have some privacy – your letters, diary, personal phone calls are respected as your own
- Have close friends and family who like the other person and are happy about your relationship
- Never feel like you're being pressured for sex
- Communicate about sex, if your relationship is sexual
- Allow each other space when you need it
- Always treat each other with respect

Is It Unhealthy

Check the circle if one of you…

- ○ Gets extremely jealous or accuses the other of cheating
- ○ Puts the other down by calling names, cursing or making the other feel bad about him or herself
- ○ Yells at and treats the other like a child
- ○ Doesn't take other person, or things that are important to him/her, seriously
- ○ Doesn't listen when the other talks
- ○ Frequently criticizes the other's friends or family
- ○ Pressures the other for sex, or makes sex hurt or feel humiliating
- ○ Has ever threatened to hurt the other or commit suicide if they leave
- ○ Cheats or threatens to cheat
- ○ Tells the other how to dress
- ○ Has ever grabbed, pushed, hit or physical hurt the other
- ○ Blames the other for your behavior ("If you hadn't made me mad, I wouldn't have…")
- ○ Embarrasses or humiliates the other
- ○ Smashes, throws or destroys things

- o Tries to keep the other from having a job or furthering his/her education
- o Makes all the decisions about what the two of you do
- o Tries to make the other feel crazy or plays mind games
- o Goes back on promises
- o Acts controlling or possessive – like you own your partner
- o Uses alcohol or drugs as an excuse for hurtful behaviors
- o Ignores or withholds affection as way of punishing the other
- o Depends completely on the other to meet social or emotional needs.

This list is a way of identifying some of the healthy and unhealthy characteristics of your relationship – it does not cover every possible situation. You may want to share this list with someone in your support system, and talk about where you want to make changes in your relationship and how you can begin to do this.

How my Relationship Affects my Life

Ask yourself the following questions about how your relationship is affecting important areas in your life. Then think about any areas where you want to make changes, and talk with someone in your support system about how you can do this.

I am evaluating my relationship with: _____

School:

Does this person encourage me to do well in school?

_____

Have my grades improved, fallen or stayed the same since I've been in this relationship?

_____

Does this person pressure me to skip school?

_____

Have I ever missed or been late to school because of a fight with this person?

_____

Have I ever quit a school group or club so I could spend time with this person?

_____

If I want to go to college, does this person support this goal?

_____

Work:

Does this person support me in my job/career?

_____

Have I ever missed or been late to work because of a fight with this person?

_____

Does this person pressure me to miss work?

Do I talk to this person on the phone so much while at work that it gets in the way of my job?

Has this person ever shown up at my job to check up on me because of jealousy?

If so, has this caused me embarrassment or questions from co-workers or boss?

My Physical Health:

Have I ever had cuts, bruises or other injuries as a result of a fight with this person?

_____

Have I ever gained or lost a significant amount of weight since I've been in this relationship?

_____

Have I ever contracted a sexually transmitted disease from this person?

_____

Have I had any unplanned pregnancies from this relationship?

_____

Have I ever been so upset about a fight with this person that I became physically ill?

_____

Does this person ever threaten me physically or do dangerous things, like driving recklessly with me in the car?

_____

My Emotional Health (Level of Stress, Feeling of Self-Worth):

Do I feel better about myself or worse about myself since I've been in this relationship?

_____

Do I ever think that "I am nothing" without this person – that I couldn't go on without him or her?

_____

Do I feel more or less stressed, depressed or anxious?

_____

Do I cry more or less frequently since I've been in this relationship?

_____

Do I have more trouble sleeping at night or sleep more than usual since I've been in this relationship?

_____

Use of Drugs/Alcohol:

Have I started/increased or stopped/decreased smoking, drinking or using drugs since I've been in this relationship?

_____

Does this person pressure me to use drugs or alcohol?

_____

Do I ever use drugs/alcohol to help myself calm down or feel better after a fight?

Do I ever use drugs/alcohol because I feel it will "loosen me up" or make me less inhibited around this person or around his/her friends?

My Family & Friendships:

How so my friends and family feel about this person? How does this person feel about them?

Have I grown apart from friends & family since I've been in this relationship or gotten closer?

Does this person ever act jealous of my friends/family and try to keep me away from them?

_____

Has this person ever threatened or gotten into a physical fight with a friend or family member?

_____

Has this person pressured me to quit a club, group or team?

_____

Do I find myself lying to my friends and family to cover up for this person?

_____

Do we spend time separately with our own friends?

_____

My Ability to Function Independently:

Do I have control of my own money?

Have my living arrangements become dependent on this person?

Do I ever feel that I could not make it without this person?

In what other ways, positive or negative, do I think this relationship has affected my life?

Balancing You, Me and Us

It's a romantic idea that when two people are in love they become one – but in reality, that way of thinking can sometimes be unhealthy. Another way to look at relationships is that two people, ME and YOU, overlap to create a third part of a relationship – US. If one of those three parts dominates, the other parts get neglected.

For example, if the relationship is all about ME, then I am focused on getting my need met and expect you to make my needs your priority too – but your needs suffer.

If the relationship's all about YOU, then I might spent all my energy trying to please you, but I do not take care of my own needs.

If the relationship is all about US, then we are both focused so intensely on the relationship that we each lose our individual identities.

In a healthy relationship, the ME, YOU and US are in balance most of the time. There might be days when I am having a problem so we focus on me, or you are celebrating a special accomplishment so we focus on you. But as a whole, we are able to achieve a balance between ME, YOU and US.

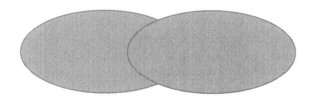

_____	_____	_____
Me	**Us**	**You**

The overlapping circles above represent the three parts of a relationship – ME, YOU and US. Write your name and the name of your partner under the left and right circles. In the pasty of the circle that represents only you, write the things that are part of you as an individual – for example, your close friends, family members, activities you enjoy by yourself, your education or career goals, talents and hobbies that are uniquely yours. Then do the same for your partner. In the center, where the two circles overlap to represent US in your relationship, write things that you and your partner share together: special feelings, activities you enjoy together, friends that you have in common, special memories or future plans.

Now ask yourself: Are the ME, YOU and Us in your relationship in balance?

_____

_____

If not, which part(s) need more attention?

_____

_____

WHAT DID YOU LEARN FROM THIS CHAPTER?

_____

_____

_____

_____

_____

_____

Chapter 2

AFFECTS ON CHILDREN

The reported long-term effects are frightening as we long to understand the effects on our families, especially on women and children. One reason for the critically important attention to this is simply that the home should be a safe haven, not a hostile environment, and half of all minors in these homes witness this turmoil. The environment, which at best is always changing, is not consistent and has no boundaries. It is rooted in fear and makes up the lives in the homes of so many of our children who witness this distorted reality of what a home should be. They are also victimized mentally. As statistics show they become fear-based and suffer debilitating illnesses, severe emotional problems, serious nurturing issues and severe anger issues. These children live in constant fear, being asked to pick sides, never getting enough sleep and never being sure of their next meal. It is not surprising that these homes create children who are slow learners, disappear and create the future ADDICT. They also experience severe early trauma in their learning process.

The effects on women of domestic violence, goes far beyond the immediate physical injuries. The mental, emotional and spiritual effects are everlasting. Domestic violence survivors report eating disorders, insomnia, fear-based anxiety, uncontrolled rage, battered women's syndrome, chronic pain and addiction or chemical dependency. The use of pills, barbiturates and opiates are prescribed to more women than men seeking some way of coping these unbearable situations. Mental health disorders such as posttraumatic stress disorder, migraines, personality disorders, bipolar disorders, sexual dysfunctions and trust issues are prevalent from the long-term effects of domestic violence. This is a far-reaching and devastating for victims because most often they are women and children who live in fear. They withdrawal and have very serious issues in personal relationships. Unfortunately, in so many cases they suffer silently.

The effects of domestic violence on women go far beyond the immediate physical injuries they suffer at the hands of their abuser. Many abused women find it difficult to function in their daily lives because of the inconsistency and fear that they live with. They are afraid to get away and yet are afraid to stay. They find themselves absent from work due to injuries or embarrassments. They don't visit doctors, so it causes them to lose their jobs making it even more difficult to leave these abusive situations.

Many women feel ashamed that their partners feel so little for them that they would physically, mentally, spiritually and emotionally hurt them. They feel unworthy of love because of the way love is being returned to them. Their self-perception is completely distorted. Priority thinking becomes something that they can't phantom. They develop low self-esteem, low self-worth and find themselves isolating themselves from friends and families because of their self-shame. This is exactly what their abusers want them to do. They don't participate in activities unless it is approved by the abuser. They see themselves as weak in their children's eyes and in some cases see themselves as unable to protect their children. Their physical injuries represent domestic violence and yet, their constantly making excuses for the children who witnessed this type of violence.

The children suffer consequences just as the parent. In some cases they are also physically battered. In most cases our study shows that it is a mental debilitation that they are dealing with.

Studies show that children who witnessed their father abusing their mother are themselves battered. These children suffer from the most pronounced behavioral and emotional disorders. Children who grow up in violent houses run their own houses as adults the same way. They exhibit negative behavior and they also learn how to use violence as power and control. The following comes as a result of the violent experiences: suicidal tendencies, use of drugs and alcohol, eating disorders, cutting and abusing themselves, gaining and losing extensive amounts of self, anxiety and depression, limited social skills, an inability to communicate anger and low self-esteem. All of these things are taken into their next relationships.

Domestic violence affects every member of the family including children. Family violence creates a home environment which children live in constant fear as we talked about earlier. Children who witness family violence are affected and are similar to children who are physically abused themselves. They are unable to establish nurturing bonds, even with their own children and are greatest at risk.

Even though there are parents who are nurturing the child and they never learn this behavior, statistics showed that over 3 million children that witness violence in their home suffer physically and emotionally. Children, who witness or hear the domestic violence, know that the control of the family is by one dominant member and they need to protect the family secret. Children react to their environment in different ways and reaction can depend on the child's age or gender. Children exposed to family violence are more likely to develop social, emotional and/or psychological behavior problems. Very early recent research indicates that children who witnessed the domestic violence show more anxiety, low self-esteem, depression, anger temperaments, tantrums, slow learning and developmental problems. Some of the potential effects are emotional. The children grieve for the family and the personal loss. They feel the shame and guilt then they blame themselves for what is happening in the family.

The confusion about conflicting parents, conflicting feelings towards parents and the feeling of abandonment create feelings and emotions that are unknown to them or even age inappropriate. They don't know how to express themselves in a healthy manner or just what to do with the emotion.

They feel anger, depression, embarrassment, helplessness and powerlessness as to how to help their parents. Through the eyes of the child they believe that they did something wrong to make mommy or daddy lose control. They want to run and hide because the pain is so bad and they don't know what they could've done. They feel it is all their fault: "If I weren't bad, if I weren't fat, if I weren't ugly, if I didn't listen, if I did everything you told me then you would you not be so angry. If I went somewhere else, would you be happy then?"

Behavioral Effects of Children

- Acting out
- Withdrawing
- Becoming aggressive or even becoming passive
- Refusing to go to school or acting out in school
- Caretaking and becoming the parent substitute- especially for the older siblings
- Lying to avoid confrontation
- Rigid defenses
- Excessive attention seeking
- Bedwetting and nightmares
- Out-of-control behaviors – especially exhibited at school
- Reduced intellectual capacities
- Manipulation
- Dependency
- Severe mood swings.

These are some of the social reactions of children who witness and are a part of physical, mental and emotional abuse exhibited by the intimate partner, parents, stepparents and guardians. Isolation from friends and relatives

- Difficulty in trusting – especially adults
- Passive with peers
- Physically acting out
- Psychosomatic complaints
- Short attention span
- Poor personal hygiene
- Regression in development – socially, emotionally and academically

- Anger towards their siblings
- Poor anger management and problem solving skills
- Bullying
- Somatic complaints
- Headache, stomach aches, nervous anxiety
- Frequently ill
- Self-abuse
- High Risk Play

Educate, Don't Punish

What is corporal punishment?

We have all experienced incidents of corporal punishment: when a mother smacks her son, trying to stop his tantrum because she doesn't want to buy him something; when a father shakes his daughter because she had hit another child; when an adolescent is hit for answering back.

It is not unusual to see smacking or blows to the neck. Most people in Spain don't see corporal punishment as something strange, something to be questioned and yet it does make us feel uncomfortable. Even people who think there are good reasons for corporal punishment often cannot avoid feeling slightly uneasy. They do not feel good about it.

The term corporal punishment can be understood in various ways; we therefore propose the following definition:

"Corporal punishment is the use of physical force causing pain, but not wounds, as a means of discipline."

Spanking, rapping on the head or slapping are forms of corporal punishment, which we do not classify as abuse. There are two factors to be taken into consideration when distinguishing between corporal punishment and physical abuse:

Intensity: The extent in which injuries have resulted from the use of violence.

Intention: the extent to which the intention is to teach/discipline.

Corporal punishment is just one the wrong ways to discipline a child. The aim is not to substitute corporal punishment with psychological abuse but to discipline without use violence.

Many people have been submitted to corporal punishment without being traumatized by it, however, the risk of it causing emotional harm to children requires us as parents and as a society to seek alternatives.

The use of corporal punishment is strongly rooted in our society and is passed on through generations, however, this doesn't mean that corporal punishment is justified. We just have to consider the treatment of women years ago, which was as different from today, accepting it was wrong and unfair. However, we don't want to lay blame; rather we want to bring about constructive changes.

Parents resort to corporal punishment for different reasons:

- Because they consider it appropriate to children's education.
- Because it relieves tension.
- Because they lack sufficient resources to tackle a situation or don't have strategies for achieving what they want.
- Because they are not skilled at interpreting the social situation in which they are using corporal punishment.
- Because they cannot control their emotions.

But whichever justification is given for corporal punishment, the effects are the same. Corporal punishment harms everyone.

Putting an end to corporal punishment is an ethnical duty. Corporal punishment is a means of discipline that relies on fear and submissiveness and diminishes a child's capacity to grow up as an autonomous and responsible person.

Effects of Corporal Punishment

On children:

- It lowers their self-esteem, teaching them poor self-control and promoting negative expectations of themselves.
- It teaches them to be victims. There is a broadly held belief that people who are submitted to corporal punishment are made stronger by it; it "prepares them for life." Today we know that corporal punishment doesn't make people stronger; rather is makes them more prone to becoming repeat victims.
- It interferes with the learning process and with their intellectual, sensory and emotional development.
- It discourages the use of reasoning. By precluding dialogue and reflection, it hampers the capacity to understand the relationship between behavior and its consequences.
- It makes children feel lonely, sad and abandoned.
- It promotes a negative view of other people and of society as a threatening place.
- It creates barriers that impede parent-child communication and damages the emotional links established between them.
- It stimulates anger and desire to run away from home.
- Violence begets violence. It teaches that violence is an acceptable way of solving problems.
- Children who have been subjected to corporal punishment may manifest difficulties with social integration.
- It doesn't teach children to cooperate with authority; it teaches them to comply with the rules or to infringe them.

- Children can suffer from accidental physical injuries. When someone hits a child, the situation can get out of hand and result in more harm than expected.

On Parents:

- Corporal punishment can produce feelings of anxiety or guilt, when the use of this kind of punishment is considered appropriate.
- Violence tend to escalate. The use of corporal punishment increases the probability that parents will show aggressive behavior in the future with growing frequency and intensity and also in other contexts.
- Corporal punishment inhibits communication and damages the relationships between parents and their children.
- When parents use corporal punishment because they lack alternative resources, they feel the need to justify their behavior to themselves and to society. So the unease derived from using corporal punishment on children is exacerbated by confused feelings arising from an incoherent and unfounded rationale.

On Society:

- Corporal punishment increases the use of violence in society and legitimizes it in the eyes of succeeding generations.
- It promotes a double standard: there are two categories of citizens – children and adults. It's acceptable to assault children, but not adults.
- Corporal punishment contributes to broken family patterns:

- Families where there is no communication between members become divided into assailants and the assaulted.
- Families that aren't integrated into society are in conflict with the equality advocated by democracy.
- Corporal punishment makes protection of the child difficult. Because the practice of corporal punishment is tolerated, children lose faith in society as a protective environment.
- Corporal punishment contributes to a society characterized by submissive citizenship, where individuals have learned from their earliest years that being a victim is a natural condition.

Further Information about Corporal Punishment

Smacking children is a socially accepted practice, regardless of the interviewed social level and gender:

- 47% of adult Spaniards interviewed affirm that smacking a child is indispensable "sometimes."
- 2% of people living with their children under 18 years old believe that it is "often" indispensable to slap a child.
- Women show more acceptance of corporal punishment. They smack more, because they probably spend more time with their children.
- Young people (18-19 years old) reject the use of corporal punishment more than adults (30-60 years old) do.
- Social classes do not influence this practice.

- 27% of parents recognize having smacked their children in the last month, with an average of three times a month, and 2.7% of parents recognize having severely smacked their children. The higher the degree of the person's authoritarianism, the more he/she justified different kinds of violence.

Incidence figures are similar or even higher in difference European countries (80% of adult Irish people remember having been smacked at home). Also, the acceptance of this violent practice is similar. This is why awareness campaigns have been developed aiming at the explicit prohibition of corporal punishment to be included in relevant legislation.

Sweden was the first country to include the prohibition of corporal punishment in families in its legislation, after an awareness campaign was developed in which 53% of Swedish considered at the beginning of the campaign that slapping was an "indispensable instrument" for education of children, turned into fighting kinds of corporal punishment. At present, campaigns aimed at abolishing this phenomenon in different countries as different as Greece, Ireland, Sweden and Norway have been developed. Public awareness of this problem has made its abolition an urgent task in the social policy of several countries.

Social acceptance of corporal punishment is a fact. Men and women use violence. As do people from different social or economic levels. Religious, political and judicial authorities have been in favor of corporal punishment at different times.

This social acceptance is also reflected in language. All languages have words like "spanking", Spanish has "zurrar." Phases such as "a smack in time" or "a good spanking" show that people resort to it as something good. From this we can see that it is not only the preserve of the lower class.

Common arguments vary from considering that "we all have gone through this and nothing has happened to us" to suggest that it is something inherent to certain cultures.

Assaulting adults is considered a crime but assaulting children is accepted as a parent's right, a way to legitimize their authority, teach and "make their children stronger."

We have already commented on the weakness of these arguments.

Although corporal punishment is part of our tradition, this does not mean it is good or makes it unchangeable.

Fortunately, it will take only parents' conviction and commitment in one generation to radically change this scene. It should be enough to stop the use of corporal punishment.

What does it mean to be a parent? Perfect father, perfect mothers?

Warning 1: There are no magic wands.

Nor is there one right way of doing things. This is why we want to discourage readers who are keen to find formulas and prescriptive recommendations. We can't give them because don't have them. We cannot literally put ourselves in any particular father or mother's position. But that doesn't mean the contents of this section of book are not useful. On the contrary, it offers possibility to think about what we are doing, learn from our experiences and reflect on the consequences of how we, as parents, behave towards our children.

Warning 2: It is not possible to be perfect

Clearly, wanting to do the right thing and actually doing it are related issues. But we must not believe we can do everything right. It would be difficult for our children if they had perfect parent who did everything right and could enter completely into the inner world of their children, anticipating their every difficulty, always saying the right thing and guessing what is going on in their minds. Contemporary rhetoric about parenting is certainly paradoxical. It demands a great deal and causes its own distress. We should not be asking ourselves to do the impossible.

Warning 3: Things are not that bad

A certain defeatist attitude towards the family seems to have entered many people's minds. This fundamental pessimism has also touched families themselves at a time when children are more frequently abused, hitting is becoming more common in families and parents have less power and more problems to face. We need to take a step back and look at a country where families still provide an important arena for social life and are a major source of contentment.

What is it to educate?

When talking about education, we must accept, from the outset, that humans are unfinished beings who must dynamically realize themselves throughout their lives. Education is the result of many agents and factors that converge in the act of educating, a task of the greatest complexity because of the many contributions and implications that are required in the harmonious development of person's personality.

Comprehensive Education:

As can be assumed, we refer here to the individuals' comprehensive education to the greatest degree he may achieve and which not only pays attention to academic knowledge but also, and fundamentally, to the emotional and social components. These three dimensions lay the foundation for the child to grow harmoniously with himself or herself, and will adjust to and evolve successfully in various interpersonal and work environments.

Thus understood, the prime objectives of the educational process are for the child to gradually learn to become independent and self-sufficient; to act with self confidence in the exercise of his or her own conduct and the rules that govern him or her; and for the child to internalize values including respect for the rights and freedoms of others, training to participate in cultural and social life, the attainment of peace, solidarity, cooperation and tolerance.

Educating, Parents First

Parents are their children's natural educators and also their first educators because theirs is, in the first place, the unavoidable responsibility of their children's education. First and foremost, children need to be loved by their parents, to be raised in a spirit of understanding and freedom. This is the basic assumption of all education because the future is written with a smile, with security, balance, affection and love that is transmitted to each child.

From birth children have rights. In addition to physical care they need respect, attention (time and listening), stimulation, support and encouragement (for them to know their parents will always be there when they need them).

Communication in Education

The psychological processes that make up the subject's development are that consequences of his or her relationship with the cultural environment. Consequently, education – basically seen as a communication process, is a socially required dialogue (underscoring the contrast of monologue) between children and the educational environment. In order of importance, this environment includes parents, other household members, teachers, friends and the social environment where the child lives.

We live, without a doubt, in the era of communication. Today as never before we have the opportunity of very rich and complex channels of communication. These include the printed press, radio, television and the Internet. Simultaneously it may be just as appropriate to hold that we live in the era of isolation and lack of communication. The potential for communication is huge, in the context of globalization. However the specific "I" may be deleted in this enormous world and where it loses its objective identity before "you," who also experiences similar lacks. Man has such as great capacity to communicate (or rather receive information) that he feels totally isolated for the same reason. He establishes relationships with databases and but not with other individuals. Ironically while this increasing wealth of technology makes communication easier, it also radically prevents it and makes individuals who live in multitudes effectively isolated beings.

What is Communication?

We have a better understanding of the nature of communication by examining the theory of information Shannon put forward a half century ago.

According to this theory of information, implies transmitting contents from a sender to a receiver by way of a message inserted in a physical channel or "medium." Communication occurs only when the sender and receiver share a repertoire of signs. Informative contents make up a message that has been coded as a set of signs organized within the repertoire. The message can be subject to interference or "noise" such that the receiver may or may not get the message or receive a blurred message. This depends on his or her ability to distinguish noise from relevant information signals.

The theory of information is complemented by cybernetic theory, which introduces the notion of feedback between senders and receivers. This allows for easier exchange of information, which is the ultimate purpose of communication.

Information is only the first stage of communication. From this viewpoint, television informs but does not lead to communication because there is no interaction between senders and receivers. Communication requires a message, a sender and a receiver, a shared code, an appropriate channel and a context that favors the whole process.

This scheme can be profitably transposed to the field of psychology of communication. It will therefore lead to the question whether in a family, school and social context, there is real communication or just information, or perhaps not even the latter (Is there dialog? If there is, is it the parent, teacher….who imposes his or her reasoning?); is there a shared repertoire between parents-children, teacher-students, adolescents-adults ("You don't understand me. I can't talk to you anymore", or "aren't you listening son?"). Is there a uniform message? Is "noise" making transmission difficult and to what extent? (Are there other different or contradictory messages that create interference and prevent capturing the original message?). Is there effective interrelationship and dialog ("shut up!"). These are just some of the questions that reflect the troubles of cross-generational communication.

A Different Way of Understanding Communication

From the standpoint of social psychology and pedagogy, communication is subject to a different approach and it is understood as a tool to show feelings and emotions, and as a privileged instrument to permit for coexistence and for solving our conflicts of interest with others.

Communication is a social act aiming at making the other participation in our own experiences and, simultaneously participating in the experiences of the other, thus becoming a factor for personal development and growth for the "I" and the "You" simultaneously. It implies mutual enrichment for all participants because they feel accepted and share the contributions of the others.

Communications requires acknowledging the other and being recognized by him/her. It naturally opens not only to the challenge of knowledge, but also those of affection, understanding, emotions, sympathy, and love, which makes a favorable climate for existential communication. If conducted within these parameters, communication will be a source of freedom and democracy.

Concept of Self and Self-Esteem

The concept of self and self-esteem are the fundamental basis for people to fully develop their potential. Those concepts perform an inevitable function in structuring personality, motivation and mental health.

Every human being's problem is to make sense of his or her life, reach self-realization to the point that the deepest human drive is the effort to become himself or herself, achieve improved self-esteem and build an appropriate image of their own self. We all possess the basic need to be positively valued, to feel loved, protected and accepted. Consequently, there is a manifest relationship between affection, self-esteem and the concept of the self.

The Concept of One's Self

The concept of the self-comprises the set of perceptions, feelings, images, and value judgment that individuals have about themselves including the image others may have of them and the person they would like to be. Thus understood, the concept of the self is the whole set of attitudes, thoughts and feelings, that individuals have about themselves.

What Are Values?

We must understand the concept of value. Values can be taken in two different ways. Values as the appraisal of physical goods, and values as conduct-guiding criteria. Psychology has been mainly interested in studying values as they appear as valuable goods in themselves and as behavior a guiding criteria. Thus understood, they are objective and remain beyond time and space, thus do not depend on subjective appreciations. The main values may be peace, love, justice, responsibility, dialogue, freedom, life, itself, ect. They are related to the existence of person's themselves, shape their behavior, mold their ideas and condition their feelings.

The nature of values includes three components:

1. **Intellectual Component:** We cannot value what we do not know or do not think we know. Value is given to a certain reality and depends on multiple factors. Sources contributing to our values are family, the school and society at large, and the media.

2. **Emotional Component:** The intellectual element is fundamental through not a sufficient condition needed to establish and internalize a value. The emotional component must be present as well. Things are valued depending on the strength and signs of emotional response they spur in the individuals who value them. The affection expressed toward an object depends on the extent to which it satisfies the need for self-satisfaction and self-esteem. A high unsatisfied individual will undervalue the world around him or her and behave either aggressively or be inhibited towards it.

3. **Behavioral Component:** A value belongs within the realm of the individual when it systematically guides

his or her behavior, thus demonstrating that it has been truly internalized. This process must take place in total freedom. What is imposed, will not be experiences as a value nor will it be assumed as an intrinsic rule of behavior. Additionally, an excess of rules can undermine the child's self-affirmation and self-esteem, and subsequently impede his or her capability to open up to more important values. Likewise, the absence of rules and controls lead to the absence of points of reference, to an attitude of indifference because nothing is worth anything at all.

What are Attitudes?

Attitudes fill a principle position in the field of social life and in the general structure of personality because they act as variables for or against the object at which they aim.

Attitudes are learned through social experience and interaction, they predispose us to action, to behave in a given way, and they are provided with an emotional weight.

The Family as a Source of Attitudes for Children

Families are the first and foremost agents in creating the attitudes that will prevail among their younger members. As can only be expected, family training should aim at creating in children the greatest number of positive attitudes. We will list below those that are considered fundamental for appropriate personal and social development.

- **Development of motivational attitudes**: Children must be shown the road to self-improvement and self-satisfaction for things well done. They must be persuaded they are able to reach the proposed goals, thus strengthening their self-esteem and image. They must also taught to be realistic and live with their own limitations.

- The family must provide a **context of responsibility** where children learn to comply with certain obligations and commitments. Through this they develop a set of attitudes that will allow them to respond to personal and social demands, since responsibility embraces both an individual and a collective component. Likewise children are capable of understanding they have not only rights but also duties. Families are assisted in this task by the school. In this case it is particularly important to prevent the divergence between teachers, otherwise a conflict will appear that may be hard for children to overcome.

- Children need their **parents' guidance and support** in achieving their projects. If parents do so they will help their children develop attitudes of cooperation and participation.

- **Building of willpower** through the reinforcement of self-control as a fundamental key for personal and professional success. This requires overcoming the self and recognizing the importance of long term effort and gratification.

Our Attitude towards Conflict

When we talk about conflict, we usually do so in negative terms: a conflict is a problem, an inconvenience, something that disrupts the normal flow of things. Something we are not certain we can solve. However, it is indicative to stop for a moment, and look back at the course of our life. If we consider the conflicts we have been through, how things have changed since then, how we are now and how we experience that conflict…. We may realize the following:

- We feel a conflict is a problem when it is actually an opportunity.
- We think conflict is exceptional when it really is part of our daily lives and the natural flow of human relations.
- We perceive conflict as a threat because it pushes us towards change, to question things that have already been established and that we took for granted.
- We feel conflicts are the products of ideas or interests in the present when actually they have an impact on the needs that come from our personal family background.
- We are under the impression that conflicts don't change when actually they are part of every group's life, family is no exception. We feel insecure because we know the solution to a conflict does not depend on the type of conflict we are facing or the topic it views but rather the way we deal with it.

Conflict within families is an opportunity for parents and children to get to know each other better. Conflict helps emotional relationships to get stronger, and to build new communication bridges. Obviously, however, there is a risk. Sometimes conflict seems to stagnate, to grow so big and so serious we no longer know what to do. It overwhelms us.

Among other things, the following pages aim to providing assistance in facing these situations.

A conflict may emerge because....

Conflict is part of natural life cycle of relations. Therefore, there are as many reasons as there are individuals. Conflicts may emerge because of:

- A conflict of interest
- Acting without thinking
- Lack of communication among people
- The emotional repercussions on a group member
- Underlying aggression
- The conflict's own spiral

Who is Involved in A Conflict?

Anybody may, at some point in time, be involved in one or even several conflicts.

A conflict evolves in a given situation among individuals with their own their own personal backgrounds, presenting a range of attitudes toward that problem and a given perception of it. People have their own goals to pursue. To achieve those goals they choose a way to face the problem. They develop a style to handle conflict.

Personal factors may condition conflict resolution, including preferences of style when facing problems, assumptions about the reasons for other people's behavior, our own perception of the problem or our prior experience when we deal with an issue.

We undertake an assessment of the skills we think we have to deal with the problem, in a sort of subconscious internal examination. In this, however, we are conditioned by our own experiences of success and failure in other conflicts, our expectations of the results we have at that point in time and our expectations for the outcome at a given point in time. All these personal factors come together to form a framework of decision. This framework will guide each one of us in what to do when facing a conflict.

What are the Stages of a Conflict?

A conflict is an event that takes place among given personal relations. As such, it is dynamic, since it evolves and changes. We now know that almost every conflict will go through some general stages at which the degree of difficulty to solve the issue at hand will vary.

1. Potential Opposition: The parties evidence the conflict through a confirmation in which they seemingly hold opposing and irreconcilable positions.

2. Conflict cognition and personalization by each of the involved parties. Personalization is determined by each individual's own perception of the problem and the involved feelings. In families, this valuation of things is always particularly colored by emotional factors.
3. Each individual will develop patterns of behavior that reveal a conflict management style.
4. Competition: open opposition, confrontation between the parties, firm and repetitive arguments and control of personal behavior.
5. Cooperation: holding one's own position but also inviting others to show their viewpoints; accepting differences, finding additional information together and examining the weakness and strengths of each individual involved.
6. Commitment: a moderate viewpoint is adopted and the will is expressed to find a point of convergence among the parties.
7. Denial: withdrawing, delaying or avoiding answers, shifting the focus of attention or suppressing personal feelings. Faced with a conflict, withdrawal is a smart choice when the problem is not of our concern, but not when we withdraw to punish the other party.
8. Adapting: Agreeing, yielding accepting one's own mistakes, surrendering, accepting the problem's lack of importance and calming down.

9. Results: the group, the family in our case, grows and gets stronger, to varying degrees.

What Kinds of Conflicts can Emerge?

As we already mentioned, the reasons for the emergence of conflict are many but they can affect different areas. We can thus establish the following classification:

- Relational conflict
- Informational conflict
- Value conflict
- Structural conflict
- Interest conflict

The Effects of Relationship Abuse on Children

If you are in an abusive relationship and have children or are thinking about having a baby, there are some things you should know about how your relationship will affect your child. First of all, your child is much more likely to be abused him or herself. About 70% of men who abuse their female partners also abuse their children. Even if you partner doesn't abuse your child, the emotional effects of being in an abusive relationship might make YOU more likely to abuse or neglect your child.

Here are just some of the characteristics that are common among children who witness relationship abuse (see or hear the abuse, or see the aftereffects of the abuse.)

Many children who witness relationship abuse

- Suffer from depression, sadness, stress and anger
- Refuse to go to school
- Act out sexually (are very promiscuous or sexually active)
- Run away
- Suffer from low self-esteem have few expectations for success
- Have troubled relationships with peers
- Are in constant fear for their own lives or parents lives
- Lie, cheat and steal
- Believe that violence is normal
- Begin hitting as a way of solving problems at a very young age
- Become involved in abusive relationships as teens
- Use violence in school, with peers and with family members
- Are at risk for suicide
- Have thoughts of murdering their parents
- Feel constantly confused and insecure

Children who witness relationship abuse are affected in these ways because they learn certain things from their environment. Below are some of the things children learn from violence. Next to each item, write what you want to teach your children.

What Violence Often Teach Children … What I Want to Teach my Children by Role-Modeling Healthy Relationships…

- It's OK to hurt others in order to control them
- They should be ashamed of their families
- They are powerless and incompetent (which leads to low self-esteem)
- People cannot be trusted
- The world is a scary place, it is never safe
- Love and violence go together
- Males/Females are cruel, controlling and violent
- Males/Females are weak and powerless

Are you ready to role model a healthy enough relationship to teach your child all the things you want to teach them? Or will they learn the things that violence teach?

_____

_____

_____

_____

_____

Is My Relationship Ready for a Baby? Am I?

People choose to have children for a number of reasons, and it is important to be clear about what those reasons are before making that decision. The purpose of this activity is to get you thinking about how ready you and your partner are for a baby.

1. Are you ready for a lifelong commitment to your partner? Even if you break up, a child means a permanent relationship as co-parents. On a scale of 1-10, how certain are you that you will want to have a relationship with this person for at least the next 18 years? Circle.

Not very Certain 1 2 3 4 5 6 7 8 9 10 Very Certain

2. Do you think having a child will change your relationship? List the changes you expect.

Positive Changes:

_____

_____

_____

_____

Negative Changes:

_____

_____

_____

_____

3. Having a children is sure to be the greatest source of
    conflict in your relationship. If you have experienced
    any form of abuse in your current relationship
    (physical, emotional or sexual) it is most likely that that
    abuse will escalate (get worse) during pregnancy and
    when you have a child. In other words, an emotionally
    abusive relationship often escalates into physical abuse
    during pregnancy; a physically abusive relationship
    often gets more violent, more often.

What is the worst conflict or abuse you've ever experienced
with your partner?

_____

_____

What would it look like if the conflict or abuse were twice as bad?

Are you concerned that your child might be affected by violence between you and your partner?

---

4. Think about your reasons for wanting to have a baby. Many people want to have a baby to fill something that's missing in their own life or their relationship – they want to feel loved or have someone to love, or they think caring for a baby will make them feel like a capable adult. When you think about being a parent, what the most positive ways you can imagine it will make you feel?

Are there other ways, besides having baby, you could get to have those feelings?

_____

_____

What are the most negative ways you imagine it will make you feel?

_____

_____

How will you cope with those feelings when they arise?

_____

_____

5. List some of you goals in life around school, career, family, social life

_____

_____

_____

How do you think having a baby will affect those goals?

_____

_____

_____

_____

_____

_____

Based on your thoughts answering the last five questions, do you think you ready to have a baby now? ____yes ____no

If yes, do the next exercise for issues to discuss with your partner before making a final decision.

Self –Esteem, Depression and Other Illnesses

Most People feel bad about themselves from time to time. Feelings of low self-esteem may be triggered by being treated poorly by someone else recently or in the past, or by a person's own judgments of him or herself. This is normal. However, low self-esteem is a constant companion for too many people, especially those who experience depression, anxiety, phobias, psychosis, delusional thinking, or who have an illness or a disability. If you are one of these people, you may go through life feeling bad need about yourself needlessly. Low self-esteem keeps you from enjoying life, doing the things you want to do, and working toward personal goals.

You have a right to feel good about yourself. However, it can be very difficult to feel good about yourself when you are under the stress of having symptoms that are hard to manage, when you are dealing with a disability, when you are having a difficult time, or when others are treating you badly. At these times. It is easy to be drawn into a down word spiral of lower and lower self-esteem. For instance, you may begin feeling bad about yourself when someone insults you, you are under a lot of pressure at work, or you are having a difficult time getting along with someone in your family. Then you begin yourself negative self-talk, like "I'm no good". That may make you feel so bad about yourself that you do something to hurt yourself or someone else, such as getting drunk or yelling at your children. We are going to discuss ideas and methods to help raise one's self esteem to help avoid engaging in negative activities, making poor choices, and gaining strength as an individual.

Before you begin to consider strategies and activities to help raise your self-esteem, it is important to remember that low self-esteem is a symptom of depression. To make things more complicated, the depression may be a symptom of some other illness.

Have you felt sad consistently for several weeks but don't know why you are feeling so sad, nothing terribly bad has happened, or maybe something bad has happened but you haven't been able to get rid of the feelings of sadness? If this accompanied by other changes, like wanting to sleep all the time or waking up very early and not being able to get back to sleep?

If you answered yes to either question, there are two things you need to do –

- See a doctor for a physical examination to determine the cause of your depression and to discuss treatment choices.
- Do some things that will help you to feel better right away like eating well, getting plenty of exercise and outdoor light , spending time with good friends, and doing fun things like going to a movie, painting a picture, playing a musical instrument, or reading a god book.

Things You Can Do Right Away- Every Day- To Raise Your Self-esteem

Pay attention to your own needs and wants. Listen to what your body, your mind, and your heart are telling you. For instance, if your body is telling you that you have been sitting down too long, stand up and stretch. If your heart is longing to spend more time with a special friend, do it. If your mind is telling you to clean up basement, listen to your favorite music, or stop thinking bad thoughts about yourself, take those thoughts seriously.

Take very good care of yourself. As you were growing up you may not have learned how to take good care of yourself. In fact, much of your attention may have been taking care of others, on just getting by, or on "behaving well". Begin today to take good care of yourself. Treat yourself as a wonderful parent would treat a small child or as one very best friend might treat another. If you work at taking good care of yourself, you will find you feel better about yourself. Here are some ways to take good care of yourself.

- Eat healthy foods and avoid junk foods. (Foods containing a lot of sugar, salt, or saturated fat). A healthy daily diet is usually:
  Five or six servings of vegetables and fruit
  Six servings of whole grain foods like bread, pasta, cereal, and rice
  Two servings of protein foods like beef, chicken, fish, cheese, or yogurt

Exercise, moving your body helps you to feel better and improves your self-esteem. Arrange time every day or as often as possible when you can get some exercise, preferably outdoors. You can get some exercise, preferably outdoors. You can do many different things. Taking a walk is the most common. You could run, ride a bicycle, play a sport, climb up and down stairs several times, put on a tape, or play the radio and dance to the music- anything that feels good to you. If you have a health problem that may restrict your ability to exercise, check with your doctor before beginning or changing your exercise habits.

- Do personal hygiene tasks that make you feel better about yourself- things like taking a regular shower or bath, washing and styling your hair, trimming your nails, brushing and flossing your teeth.

- Have a physical examination every year to make sure you are in good health.
- Plan fun activities for yourself. Learn new things every day.

Take time to do things you enjoy. You may be so busy, or feel so badly about yourself, that you spend little or no time doing things you enjoy—things like playing a musical instrument, doing a craft project, flying a kite, or going fishing. Make a list of things you enjoy doing. Then do something from that list every day. Add to the list anything new that you discover you enjoy doing.

Get something done that you have been putting off. Clean out the drawer. Wash that window. Write that letter. Pay that bill.

Do things that make use of your own special talents and abilities. For instance, if you are good with your hands. Then make things for yourself, family, and friends. If you like animals, consider having a pet or at least play with friends' pets.

Dress in clothes that make you feel good about yourself. If you have little money spend clothes, check out thrift stores in your area.

Give yourself rewards- you are a great person. Listen to a CD or tape.

Spend time with people who make you feel good about yourself- people who treat well. Avoid people who treat you badly.

Make your living space a place that honors the person you are. Whether you live in a single room, a small apartment, or a large home, make the space comfortable and attractive for you. If you share your living space with others, have some space that is just for you- a place where you can keep your things and know that they will not disturbed and that you can decorate any way you choose.

Display items that you find attractive or remind you of your achievements or of special times or people in your life. If cost is a factor, use your creativity to think of inexpensive or free ways that you can add the comfort and enjoyment of your space.

Make your mea ls a special time. Turn off the television, radio, and stereo. Set the table, even if you are eating alone. Light a candle or put some flowers or an attractive object in the center of the table. Arrange your food in an attractive way on your plate. If you eat with others, encourage discussion of pleasant topics. Avoid discussing difficult issues at meals.

Take advantage of opportunities to **learn something new or improve your skills.** Take a class or go to a seminar. Many adult education programs are free or very inexpensive. For those that are more costly, ask about a possible scholarship or fee reduction.

Begin doing those things that you know will make you feel better about yourself- like going on a diet, beginning an exercise program or keeping your living space clean.

Do something nice for another person. Smile at someone who looks sad. Say a few kind words to the check-out cahier. Help your spouse with unpleasant chore. Take a meal to a friend who is sick. Send a card to an acquaintance. Volunteer for a worthy organization.

Make it a point to treat yourself well every day. Before you go to bed each night, write about how you treated yourself well during the day.

You may be doing some of these things now. There will be others you need to work on. You will find that you will continue to learn new and better ways to take care of yourself.

You may be giving yourself negative messages about yourself. Many people do. These are messages that you learned when you were young. You learned from many different sources including other children, your teacher, family members, caregiving, even from the media, and from prejudice and stigma in our society.

Once you learned them, you may have repeated these negative messages over and over to yourself, especially when you were not feeling well or when you were having a hard time. You may have come to believe them. You may have even worsened the problem by making up some negative messages or thoughts of your own. These negative thoughts or messages make you feel bad about yourself and lower your self-esteem.

Some examples of common negative messages that people repeat over to themselves include: "I am a jerk", "I am a loser", "I never do anything right", "No one would ever like me", "I am a klutz." Most people believe these messages, no matter how untrue or unreal they are. They come up immediately in the right circumstance, for instance if you get a wrong answer you think "I am so stupid." They may include words like *should, ought, or must.* The messages tend to imagine the worst in everything, especially you, and they are hard to turn off or unlearn.

You may think these thoughts or give yourself these negative messages so often that you are hardly aware of them. Pay attention to them. Carry a small pad with you as you go about your daily routine for several days and jot down negative thoughts about yourself whenever you notice therm. Some people say they notice more negative thinking when tired, sick, or dealing with a lot of stress. As you become aware your negative thoughts, you may notice more of them.

It helps to take a closer look at your negative thought patterns to check out whether or not they are true. You may want a close friend or counselor to help you with this. When you are in a good mood and when you have a positive attitude about yourself, ask yourself the following questions about each negative thought you have noticed:

- Is this message really true?
- Would a person say this to another person? If not, why am I staying it myself?
- What do I get out of thinking this thought? If it makes me feel badly about myself, why not stop thinking it?

You could also ask someone else- someone who likes you and who you trust- if you should believe this though about yourself. Often just looking at a thought or situation in a new light helps.

The next step in this process is to develop positive statements you can say to yourself to replace these negative thoughts whenever you notice yourself thinking them. You cannot think two thoughts at the same time. When you are thinking a positive thought about yourself, you cannot be thinking a negative one. In developing these thoughts, use positive words like happy, peaceful, loving, enthusiastic, and warm.

Activities That Will Help You Feel Good About Yourself

Any of the following activities will help you feel better about your self-esteem over the long term. Read through them. Do those that seem most comfortable to you. You want to do some of the other activities at another time. You may find it helpful to repeat some of these activities again and again.

Making affirming lists

Making lists, rereading them often, and rewriting them from time to time will help you to feel better about yourself. If you have a journal, you can write your lists there. If you don't, any piece of paper will do.

Make a list of –

- At least five of your strengths , for example, persistence, courage, friendliness, creativity
- At least five things you admire about yourself, for example the way you have raised your children, your good relationship with your brother, or your spirituality
- The five greatest achievements in your life so far, like recovering from a serious illness, graduating from high school, or learning to use a computer
- At least 20 accomplishments- they can be as simple as learning to tie your shoes, to getting an advanced college degree
- 10 ways you can "treat" or reward yourself that don't include food and that don't cost anything, such as walking in woods, window-shopping, watching children playing on a playground, gazing at a baby's face or at a beautiful flower, or chatting with a friend
- 10 things you can do to make yourself laugh
- 10 things you can do to help someone else
- 10 things that you do that make you feel good about yourself

Reinforcing a positive self-image

To do this exercise you will need a piece of paper, a pencil or pen, and a timer or clock.

Set a timer for 10 minutes or note the time on your watch or clock. Write your name across the top of the paper. Then write everything positive and good you can think of about yourself. Include special attributes, talents, and achievements. You can use single words or sentences, whichever you prefer. You can write the same thing over and over if you want to emphasize them. Don't worry about spelling or grammar. Your ideas don't have to be organized. Write down whatever comes to mind. You are the only one who will see this paper. Avoid making any negative statements or using any negative words – only positive ones. When the 10 minutes are up, read the paper over to yourself. You may feel sad when you read it over because it is a new, different and positive way of thinking about yourself. Those feelings will diminish as you reread this paper. Read the paper over again several times. Put it in a convenient place- your pocket, purse, wallet, or the table beside your bed. Read it over to yourself at least several times a day to keep reminding yourself of how great you are. Find a private space and read it aloud. If you can, read it to a good friend or family member who is supportive.

Developing Positive Affirmations

Affirmations are positive statements that you can make about yourself that make you feel better about yourself. They describe ways you would like to feel about yourself all the time. They may not, however, describe how you feel about yourself right now. The following examples of affirmations will help you in making your own list of affirmations-

- I feel good about myself
- I take good care of myself. I eat right, get plenty of exercise, do things I enjoy, get good health care, and attend to my personal hygiene needs
- I spend my time with people who are nice to me and make me feel good about myself
- I am a good person
- I deserve to be alive
- Many people like me

Make a list of your own affirmations. Keep this list in a handy place, like your pocket or purse. You may want to make copies of your list so you can have them in several different places of easy access. Read the affirmations over and over to yourself- aloud whenever you can. Share them with others when you feel like it. Write them down from time to time. As you do this, the affirmations tend to gradually become true for you.

You gradually come to feel better and better about yourself. .

Your personal "celebratory scrapbook" and place to honor yourself.

Develop a scrapbooks that celebrates you and the wonderful person you are. Include pictures of yourself at different ages, writings you enjoy, mementos of things you have done and places you have been, cards you have received, etc. Or set up a place in your home that celebrates "you." It could be on a bureau, shelf, or table. Decorate the space with the objects in a special bag, box, or your purse and set them up in the space whenever you do this work. Take them out and look at them whenever you need to bolster your self-esteem.

Appreciation exercise.

At the top of a sheet of paper write "I like (your name) because: "Have friends, acquaintances, family members, etc., write an appreciative statement about you on it. When you read it, don't delay it or don't argue with what has been written, just accept it. Read this paper over and over. Keep it in a place where you will see it often.

Self-esteem calendar.

Get a calendar with large blank spaces for each day. Schedule into each day some small thing you would enjoy such as " go into a flower shop and smell the flowers," "call me sister," "draw a sketch", "buy a new CD, "tell my daughter I love her," "bake brownies," "lie in the sun for 20 minutes," " wear my favorite scent." Now make a commitment to check your "enjoy life "calendar every day and do whatever you have scheduled for yourself.

Assertiveness

What is Assertiveness?

We have all heard people say "You need to be more assertive!" But what exactly is assertiveness? Assertiveness is a communication style. It is being able to express your feelings, thoughts, beliefs, and opinions in an open manner that doesn't violate the rights of others. Other communication styles you may have heard of include being aggressive, which is a style that violates the rights of others, and being passive where we violate our own rights. You have probably also heard of passive-aggressive. This is where someone is essentially being aggressive but in a passive or indirect way. For example, someone may be angry but they don't act in an overtly aggressive way by yelling or hitting, instead they may sulk or slam a door.

Passive: Violates own rights. Others needs given priority.

Assertive: Respects both own needs and needs of others.

Aggressive: Violates rights of others. Own needs have priority.

Myths about Assertiveness

There are a number of myths about assertiveness. Some people use these as support for why they shouldn't try and be more assertive.

Myth 1: "Assertiveness is basically the same as being aggressive".

Debunking the myth: Some people who are aggressive think they are being assertive because they are stating what their needs are. It is true that both assertive and aggressive communication involves stating your needs; however there are very important differences between stating your needs assertively and stating them aggressively. There are differences in the words used, the tone taken, and the body language used. We will discuss these differences in more detail in the section on the verbal and non-verbal characteristics of each of the communication styles.

Myth 2: "If I am assertive I will get what I want".

Debunking the myth: Being assertive does not mean that you always get what you want. In fact being assertive is not a guarantee of any outcome at all. Being assertive is about expressing yourself in a way that respects both your needs and the needs of others. Sometimes this means you get what you want, sometimes you won't get what you want at all and sometimes you will come to a mutually satisfactory compromise.

Myth 3: "If I am assertive I have to be assertive in every situation"

Debunking the myth: Understanding how to be assertive provides you with the choice of when to be assertive. It does not mean you have to be assertive in every situation. You may come to the realization in certain situations that being assertive is not the most helpful way to behave. For example, if you are in a bar and someone begins to be very aggressive or violent, then being assertive may place you at risk as the other person is not being rational. In this case you may make the decision that a passive approach is the most beneficial. Learning to be assertive is about providing yourself with a choice!

The Effects of Being Unassertive

The main effect of not being assertive is that it can lead to low self-esteem. If we communicate in a passive manner we are not saying what we really feel or think. This means we can end up agreeing with and fulfilling other people's needs or wants rather than our own. This can result in a lack of purpose, and a feeling of not being in control of our own lives.

If we never express ourselves openly and conceal our thoughts and feelings this can make us feel tense, stressed, anxious or resentful. It can also lead to unhealthy and uncomfortable relationships. We will feel like the people closest to us don't really know us.

Lack of assertiveness is very common in social phobia. People with social phobia tend to think that other people are being judgmental and critical about them and will avoid social situations because of this.

If we constantly communicate in an aggressive manner we will eventually lose friends and people will lose respect for us. Again this can lead to low self-esteem. There is a large amount of research examining the negative impact of lacking assertiveness – that is, being either passive or aggressive. People who are more assertive tend to be less depressed and have better health outcomes. Less assertive people have a greater likelihood of substance abuse.

How do we Become Unassertive?

Assertiveness is a learned behavior and thinking style. We are all born assertive. Think of a baby. Babies cry when they want something, they express emotion freely. Then gradually they adapt their behavior to fit in with responses they receive from the environment, that is, responses they receive from family, peers, work mates, authority figures etc. For example, if your family or peer group dealt with conflict by yelling and arguing, then you may have learned to deal with conflict in that way. Or if your family taught you that you should always please others before yourself, then you may find it hard to be assertive about your needs. Or if your family or peer group believe that you shouldn't express negative emotion, and ignore or ridicule you if you do, then you will quickly learn not to express negative emotion.

Some questions that can be useful to ask yourself when you are thinking about how you may have learned to become unassertive are:

How did your family handle conflict?

_____

_____

_____

_____

_____

_____

What did they do when they disagreed with somebody or were upset with people?

_____

_____

_____

_____

_____

_____

_____

How did your parents teach you to deal with conflict?

_____

_____

_____

_____

_____

What were their messages?

_____

_____

_____

_____

_____

_____

_____

In what ways did you learn to get what you wanted without asking for it directly? (e.g., crying, yelling, making threats etc.)

_____

_____

_____

_____

_____

_____

Do you still use these ways to get what you want today?

_____

_____

_____

_____

_____

_____

As you can see from the examples above, there are often good and valid reasons why we become unassertive. As children and teenagers we learn to behave in a way that works for us at the time. If we were assertive to aggressive parents or friends it may have got us into trouble, so we learned to stay under the radar. Or we may have learned to be aggressive to survive. And it is likely that the family members and friends that we learned this from also learned their behavior from someone else.

It is important that you don't blame yourself or your family for your lack of assertiveness. It can be more helpful to think of it as a vicious cycle that you and your family have been caught in. Now you have decided to break the cycle and learn a new assertive way of thinking and behaving. This means that you will not pass on these unhelpful ways of behaving to your family and friends.

What stops us from being assertive?

A number of factors can stop us from being assertive:

Self-defeating beliefs: We might have unrealistic beliefs and negative self-statements about being assertive, our ability to be assertive, or the things that might happen if we are assertive. This is often a major cause of acting non-assertively. Examples of such beliefs are:

- It is uncaring, rude and selfish to say what you want.
- If I assert myself I will upset the other person and ruin our relationship
- It will be terribly embarrassing if I say what I think.

Skills deficit: It may be that we just don't have the verbal and nonverbal skills to be assertive. We may watch other people being assertive and admire their behavior but have no real idea how to be like that ourselves.

Anxiety and stress: It may be that we know how to be assertive but we get so anxious that we find we can't carry out the behavior. We may be so stressed that it becomes difficult to think and act clearly. We need to learn how to manage our anxiety and reduce the physical stress in our bodies.

Situation Evaluation: It may be that we can't really tell which behaviors to use in which situations. There are three main mistakes people can make with evaluating situations. We might mistake firm assertion for aggression; we might mistake non-assertion for politeness; or we might mistake non-assertion for being helpful.

Cultural and Generational Influences: There can also be strong cultural and generational influences on our behavior. For example, in some cultures assertiveness is not as valued as in Western society. If you are from one of these cultures it is important to weight up the pros and cons about being assertive in particular situations. You may find that the pros of living by your cultural values outweigh the pros of being assertive. Older generations may also find it difficult to be assertive. Men were once taught that it was weak to express their emotions and women were taught that it was aggressive to state their needs or opinions. Lifelong beliefs such as these can be difficult to change but they can change!

How assertive are you?

It can be difficult to know how assertive we are. In some situations we may feel very capable of being assertive but in other situations we may find ourselves not really expressing how we felt or thought, and feeling upset or frustrated with ourselves. This next exercise can help you determine how assertive you are and help you work out in which situations you would like to be more assertive. Down the left side we have a list of different situations that require assertiveness. Across the top are different groups of people. You work across cell by cell and rate each combination of situations and groups of people. For example, someone may find giving compliments to strangers relatively easy and rate themselves at 0 in this cell, but have a lot of difficulty giving compliments to authority figures such as their boss and so rate this cell at 4.

Exercise. Rating your assertiveness in different situations

Fill in each cell using a scale from 0 to 5. A rating of "0" means you can assert yourself with no problem. A rating of 5 means that you cannot assert yourself at all in this situation.

	Friends of the same gender	Friends of different gender	Authority Figures	Strangers	Work colleagues	Intimate relations or spouse	Shop assistants
Saying No							

Giving Compliments							
Expressing your opinion							
Asking for help							
Expressing anger							
Expressing Affection							
Stating your right and needs							
Giving criticism							
Being criticized							
Starting and keeping a conversation going							

Keep a copy of your responses to this exercise as you will use it when you create your own assertiveness plan. You will also be able to complete it again once you have finished this section of the book to see if you have improved your assertiveness.

How to Recognize Assertive Behavior

Recognizing the Difference between Passive, Assertive and Aggressive Communication Styles.

It is important that you learn how to recognize the verbal and non-verbal characteristics of the different communication styles. Once we know these we will be able to recognize passive, assertive or aggressive behavior in ourselves and others.

The first step to changing behavior is recognizing which bits we need to change. It may be that you are able to speak assertively, i.e. your verbal skills are assertive, but your nonverbal communication may be quite passive and contradicting your verbal communication. For example, if you say "I don't like it when you do that", which is an assertive statement, but you do it in a very quiet voice with no eye contact and shuffling your feet, then your nonverbal behavior will undermine your verbal and your message will probably not be taken seriously.

You will notice that each communication style has some payoffs or positive aspects and costs or negative aspects. It is important to acknowledge these as you may not have realized that there can be a cost to being assertive. For example, a cost of becoming assertive is that people around you may have been getting some benefit from your being unassertive. If they are typically aggressive and want things done their way, they may not want you to change. If you are aware of this possibility it will perhaps make it easier for you to change.

As you read the descriptions below take note of which behaviors you need to add your repertoire!

Characteristics of Passive Communication

Definition:

- Not expressing honest feelings, thoughts and beliefs. Therefore, allowing others to violate your rights. Can also mean expressing thoughts and feelings in an apologetic, self-effacing way – so that others easily disregard them.
- Violating your own rights.
- Also sometimes showing a subtle lack of respect for the other person's ability to take disappointments, shoulder some responsibility, or handle their own problems.

Verbal characteristics:

- long rambling sentences
- beat-around-the-bush
- hesitant, filled with pauses
- frequent throat clearing

- Apologize inappropriately in a soft unsteady voice • using phrases such as "if it wouldn't be too much trouble…"
- fill in words, e.g., "maybe" , "er", "um", "sort of"
- voice often dull and monotonous
- tone may be sing-song or whining • over-soft or over-warm • quiet often dropping away • frequent justifications, e.g., "I wouldn't normally say anything"
- Apologies, e.g., "I'm terribly sorry to bother you..."
- qualifiers, e.g., "Its only my opinion" or "I might be wrong" • self-dismissal, e.g., "It's not important" or "It doesn't really matter"
- Self-put-downs, e.g., "I'm useless...hopeless" or "You know me..."

Non-verbal characteristics:

- averting gaze
- looking down
- posture can be slouched
- wringing hands
- winking or laughing when expressing anger
- covering mouth with hand
- crossing arms for protection
- ghost smiles when expressing anger or being criticized
- raising eyebrows in anticipation
- jaw trembling
- lip biting

Thinking style:

- "I don't count"

- "My feelings, needs and thoughts are less important than yours"
- "People will think badly of me or not like me"
- "If I say no then I may upset someone, I will be responsible for upsetting them"

Payoff:

- Praised for being selfless, a good sport
- Rarely blamed if things go wrong because you haven't usually shown initiative
- Others will protect and look after you
- Avoid, postpone or hide conflict so in short term can lead to reduction of anxiety

Cost:

- Sometimes prone to build up of stress and anger that can explode in a really aggressive manner
- Others often make unreasonable demands of you
- Can get stuck in relationships that aren't healthy and find it very difficult to change
- Restrict self into other people's image of a lovable good person
- When repressing anger and frustration this diminishes other more positive feelings in you
- Loss of self-esteem

Aggressive Behavior

Definition:

- You stand up for your personal rights and express your thoughts, feelings and beliefs in a way which is usually inappropriate and always violates the rights of the other person.
- People often feel devastated by an encounter with an aggressive person
- Superiority is maintained by putting others down.
- When threatened you attack.

Verbal characteristics:

- Strident, sarcastic or condescending voice
- Fluent, few hesitations
- Often abrupt, clipped
- Often fast
- Emphasizing blaming words
- Firm voice
- Tone sarcastic, cold, harsh
- Voice can be strident, often shouting, rising at end
- Use of threats, e.g., "You'd better watch out" or "If you don't..."
- Put downs, e.g., "You've got to be kidding..." or "Don't be so stupid"
- Evaluative comments, emphasizing concepts such as: should", "bad", "ought"
- Sexual / racist remarks • Boastfulness, e.g., "I haven't got problems like yours"

- Opinions expressed as fact, e.g., "Nobody want to behave like that" or "That's a useless way to do it"
- Threatening questions, e.g., "Haven't you finished that yet?" or "Why on earth did you do it like that?"

Non-verbal characteristics:

- Intruding into the other person's space
- Staring the other person out
- Gestures such as pointing, fist clenching
- Striding around impatiently
- Leaning forward or over
- Crossing arms (unapproachable)
- Smiling may become sneering
- Scowling when angry
- Jaws set firm

Thinking style:

- "I'll get you before you have a chance of getting me"
- "I'm out for number one"
- "The world is a battle ground and I am out to win"

Payoffs:

- You get others to do your bidding
- Things tend to go your way
- You are less vulnerable
- You like the feeling of being in control
- Release of tension
- You feel powerful

Price:

- Your behavior will create enemies and resentment in those around you
- This can result in a sense of paranoia and fear
- If you are always trying to control others it can be difficult for you to relax
- Your relationships will tend to be based on negative emotions and are likely to be unstable
- Aggressive people tend to feel inferior deep down and try to compensate for that by putting others down
- Feelings of guilt and shame
- Decreasing self-confidence and self-esteem

Assertive Behavior

Definition:

- A way of communicating our feelings, thoughts, and beliefs in an open, honest manner without violating the rights of others.
- It is an alternative to being aggressive where we abuse other people's rights, and passive where we abuse our own rights.

Verbal characteristics:

- Firm, relaxed voice
- Fluent, few hesitations
- Steady even pace
- Tone is middle range, rich and warm
- Sincere and clear

- Not over-loud or quiet
- Voice appropriately loud for the situation
- "I" statements ("I like", "I want", "I don't like") that are brief and to the point
- Co-operative phrases, e.g., "What are your thoughts on this"
- Emphatic statements of interest, e.g., "I would like to"
- Distinction between fact and opinion, e.g., "My experience is different"
- Suggestions without "shoulds" or "ought's" e.g., "How about…" or "Would you like to…"
- Constructive criticism without blame, e.g., "I feel irritated when you interrupt me"
- Seeking others opinions, e.g., "How does this fit in with your ideas"
- Willingness to explore other solutions, e.g., "How can we get around this problem?"

Non-verbal characteristics:

- Receptive listening
- Direct eye contact without staring
- Erect, balanced, open body stance
- Open hand movements
- Smiling when pleased
- Frowning when angry
- Features steady
- Jaw relaxed

Thinking style:

- "I won't allow you to take advantage of me and I won't attack you for being who you are"

Payoffs:

- The more you stand up for yourself and act in a manner you respect, the higher your self esteem
- Your chances of getting what you want out of life improve greatly
- Expressing yourself directly at the time means that resentment doesn't build up
- If you are less driven by the needs of self-protection and less preoccupied with self-consciousness then you can see, hear and love others more easily

Price:

- Friends / family may have benefited from you being passive and may sabotage your new assertiveness
- You are reshaping beliefs and values you have held since childhood and this can be frightening
- There is no guarantee of outcome
- There is often pain involved in being assertive

How to Think More Assertively

Unassertive thinking

As mentioned, one of the factors that can make it difficult for us to be assertive is our thinking. We all hold beliefs about ourselves, other people and how the world works. Usually these beliefs came from our experience in the world and made sense to us at the time. However even though we have moved on from these experiences we may not have updated our thinking. For example, as a child we may have been taught by our family not to express sadness because if we did we would be ridiculed. In that situation it would have made sense for us to have the belief: "expressing sadness is bad and if I do people will make fun of me". As an adult however we may still have this belief even though we are no longer in the same situation. We continue to assume that the belief is true without checking it out. As a result we may never express our sadness which may result in us being stressed, depressed and not connected with ourselves and the world. Or alternatively our sadness may be expressed as anger towards ourselves or other people.

Below are listed a number of typical unassertive thoughts. See if any of them apply to you.

- I shouldn't say how I'm really feeling or thinking because I don't want to burden others with my problems.
- If I assert myself I will upset the other person and ruin our relationship
- It will be terribly embarrassing if I say what I think

- If someone says "no" to my request it is because they don't like or love me
- I shouldn't have to say what I need or how I feel: people close to me should already know
- It is uncaring, rude and selfish to say what you want
- I have no right to change my mind; neither has anyone else
- It will all work out in the end, and anyway it's not my fault
- People should keep their feelings to themselves
- If I express that I am feeling anxious people will think I am weak and ridicule me or take advantage of me.
- If I accept compliments from someone it will mean I am big headed.

Take a minute and see if you can identify any more unassertive beliefs that you have.

Our Assertive Rights

Many of the ideas now associated with assertiveness training were first proposed in Manuel J. Smith's book "When I say No I feel Guilty" published in 1975. This book outlined a ten point "bill of assertive rights". Assertive rights are the rights that we all have as human beings. Some of these rights are:

- You have the right to judge your own behavior, thoughts, and emotions, and to take the responsibility for their initiation and consequences upon yourself.
- You have the right to say "no".
- You have the right to offer no reasons or excuses for justifying your behavior.
- You have the right to judge if you are responsible for finding solutions to other people's problems.
- You have the right to change your mind.
- You have the right to disagree with someone's opinion.
- You have the right to make mistakes - and be responsible for them.
- You have the right to say, 'I don't know'.
- You have the right to be illogical in making decisions.
- You have the right to say, 'I don't understand'.
- You have the right to say, 'I don't care'.

An important part of these rights is that they come linked with responsibilities. You will notice the first point says that you have the right to your own thoughts, behavior and emotions, but that you must then take responsibility for the consequences of these thoughts and behaviors. Often people think they are behaving assertively, but they are ignoring the consequences of their actions and the rights of others. This would be more typical of an aggressive style of communication.

See if you can think of any other rights, particularly ones that balance out any unhelpful beliefs you identified in the last section.

_____

_____

_____

_____

_____

_____

_____

How to change your beliefs

Identifying your unhelpful beliefs is the first step towards changing them. In fact, for some people just realizing that they have been thinking this way can be enough to help them change, especially when they realize they have the right to change and think in a different way.

However, for most people just realizing they have been thinking in an unhelpful way isn't enough to change the thinking. One way of addressing unhelpful thoughts is to challenge them head on. This is also called disputation.

Challenging or disputation works on the principle that most of our thoughts and beliefs are learned opinions rather than facts. This means that they can be questioned rather than just accepted blindly, particularly if they are causing us distress.

To challenge or dispute your thoughts means that you examine the evidence for and against the thoughts. You evaluate them as if you were a detective or a lawyer. You are trying to get to the bottom of the truth of the thought.

There are two major strategies that can be used to help you challenge your thoughts. One is to use a Thought Diary. The other is to set up a Behavioral Experiment. We will take a look at each of these in turn.

Thought Diaries

It can be difficult to challenge your thoughts in your head as it is hard to remember all the information and it can get messy and confusing. The best way is to write it all down. To help you through this process we have a Thought Diary for Unassertive Thoughts. We have worked through an example to show you the questions that you will need to ask yourself in order to come up with a more balanced thought. Then we provide a blank one for you to work through with an example of your own.

The thought diary will ask you to identify the unassertive thought that you are having. In order to do this you first need to **identify the situation** you are in. In the following example the situation could be described as: "I asked my friend to go shopping and she said "no". In describing the situation think about what you would have seen if you had been filming the scene. It is important that you just stick to the facts and don't start making interpretations about what this may mean at this stage. For example, you wouldn't say "my friend was rude to me" as this is an assumption and an interpretation that we don't have any evidence for yet.

Next you need to **identify your emotions** in the situation that is, how you are feeling. Ask yourself:

What emotion(s) am I feeling?

How intense are they? (Rate the intensity from 0-100).

In the following example the person feels hurt and annoyed. The ratings are done individually for each emotion; they don't need to add up to 100.

You then **identify your behavior** and any physical symptoms that you felt. Ask yourself:

What did I do?

What did I feel in my body?

In the following example the person ignored a phone call from her friend and felt tense and sick whenever she thought about the situation.

Next you need to **identify your thoughts** in the situation. These thoughts can take the forms of assumptions, interpretations, beliefs, values and so on. Sometimes they could even take the form of images or pictures rather than words. Ask yourself:

What was I thinking?

What was running through my head?

In the example the person's thoughts were:

I said 'yes' to go shopping with her when I didn't want to.

So she should have said 'yes' to me

Saying 'No' is rude, uncaring and selfish.

Maybe she doesn't like me anymore.

You then need to **rate the strength of your beliefs** in these thoughts at the time. A rating of 0 means you didn't believe them at all and a rating of 100 means you believed them 100%. Once you have completed this first part of the Thought Diary you move onto the disputation. The questions you ask yourself in the disputation are:

Am I thinking in a passive, assertive or aggressive way?

Did I respond in a passive, assertive or aggressive way?

What is the evidence for this thought?

What is the evidence against this thought?

Am I ignoring my rights or the rights of my friends?

How else could I view the situation?

Are there any other interpretations of what happened?

The idea behind asking yourself these questions is to **come up with a more balanced and assertive way of thinking and behaving.** You ask yourself:

What would be a more assertive way of thinking and responding?

The final step is **to re-rate the intensity of the original emotion and strength of the belief.** If you have worked through the entire thought diary it is likely that you will experience a decrease in the intensity of the emotion and a decrease in the degree to which you believe your initial unhelpful thought. If you continue to practice this way of thinking you can find that you begin thinking and behaving in a more assertive manner.

Thought Diary: Part 1 Understanding your reaction.

Situation	I asked a friend to go shopping with me and she said "no."
What emotions was I feeling? How strong were these? Rate (0-100)	Hurt 70 Angry 80
What physical response did I notice in my body?	Tense, tight chest, clenched jaw. Felt sick when I thought about her.
What did I do?	Cried, then ignored the next phone call I had from her.
Was this a passive, assertive or aggressive way of behaving?	Passive-aggressive
What thoughts were running through my head?	I said 'yes' to go shopping with her when I didn't want to. So she should have said 'yes' to me. She is selfish to say "no." Maybe she doesn't like me anymore.
Which is the strongest thought?	She is selfish for saying "no."
How much do I believe this thought?	80
Are these passive, assertive or aggressive thoughts?	Passive because I thought I should do something I didn't want to do. Aggressive that I think she should do what I want her to.

Part 2: Disputing or challenging you unassertive thoughts

Is there evidence that my thought is true?	None
Is there evidence that my thought is not true?	She has done lots of things with me and for me over the course of our friendship.
Am I ignoring my rights or the rights of the other person? If so, what am I ignoring?	Yes, I ignored my rights by saying "yes" when I didn't want to go shopping. And I am ignoring her rights by acting as if she has to do what I want. The right I am ignoring is "everyone has the right to say "no"."
Are there any other ways of interrupting the situation?	She may be tired She may not want to go shopping She may have something else on I'm mind-reading what she is thinking I've said no to her sometimes and that didn't mean that I didn't like her.
What would be a more assertive way to think about this?	She has the right to say no and that doesn't mean she is selfish. Nor does it say anything about what she may or may not think of me.
What would be a more assertive way to behave?	I will suggest catching up another time doing something that we both like.
Rerate me original emotion: Rerate my belief in the original thought:	Hurt 20 Angry 10 Belief 10

Try using a Thought Diary for Unassertive Behavior next time you notice that you are feeling hurt, angry or upset after an interaction with someone. It may be that you have thought and /or reacted in an unassertive manner. Continue to use a

Thought Diary for these situations until it becomes second nature to you. You will then find that you can catch your unassertive thoughts before you act on them and dispute them in your head. This can take some time to happen, so for now continue to practice disputation in a Thought Diary. Now try a Thought Diary of your own.

Thought Diary: Part I Understanding your reaction.

Situation:	
What emotions was I feeling? How strong were these? Rate (0-100)	
What physical response did I notice in my body?	
What did I do?	
Was this a passive, assertive or aggressive way of behaving?	
What thoughts were running through my head?	
Which is the strongest thought?	
How much do I believe in this thought?	
Are these passive, assertive or aggressive thoughts?	

Part 2: Disrupting or challenging your unassertive thoughts

Is there any evidence that my thought is true?	
Is there any evidence that my thought is not true?	
Am I ignoring my rights or the rights of the other person? If so, what am I ignoring?	
Are there any other ways of interpreting the situation?	
What would be a more assertive way to think about this?	
What would be a more assertive way to behave?	
Rerate my original emotion: Rerate my belief in the original thought:	

Behavioral Experiments

Doing a Thought Diary can help us change our beliefs about a situation. This is especially true when we write then down and practice our new thoughts over and over again. Sometimes however it is hard for us to shift our beliefs when all we are doing is writing down our thoughts. We might see that it makes sense logically but feel inside that nothing has really changed. Thought Diaries may also be difficult to use when there is no real evidence for or against a particular situation. For example, we may have the belief that if we don't always do what someone else wants us to do then they won't like us anymore. We are unlikely to put ourselves in this situation to test this out so doing a Thought Diary on its own is unlikely to really convince us simply because we have no real evidence either way.

What may be more useful in this situation is to do a Behavioral Experiment. We are still trying to change our beliefs but whereas a Thought Diary helps us change beliefs by thinking differently about the belief, a Behavioral Experiment helps us change beliefs by actually giving us some evidence to support a new belief.

For example, someone may have the belief: "If I assert myself then I will upset the other person and ruin our relationship". This belief has meant that the person has always gone along with what others suggest even though it may be the complete opposite of what they really want to do. They believe it so much they have never considered trying to assert themselves. They have completed some Thought Diaries and realized that they don't really have any evidence to support their belief. However, neither do they have any evidence against it so they feel a bit stuck.

They decide that one way they can find out is to do an experiment where they actually test their prediction that the other person will be upset and the relationship will be ruined. This will be a challenge and can be quite anxiety provoking. When deciding to do an experiment it is important that you plan it carefully so that the results will be clear. Also you may need to start with an easier experiment and then build up to more difficult situations.

The following example is an experiment to test the belief: "If I assert myself then I will upset the other person and ruin our relationship".

The first step is to identify the prediction that you have about the situation and how you will know if it has happened. This is an important step, as if you don't make it clear how you will know it has happened then you can easily shift the goal posts after the experiment.

You also need to identify any unassertive or unhelpful behaviors that you would normally do so that you can make sure that you don't do these during the experiment.

Then you need to make some more helpful predictions about what may happen. These can come from having done a Thought Diary beforehand or you may be able to identify them without having done a Thought Diary.

You then set up the experiment. This involves being very clear about the steps you will take. Make it clear when, where and how you will do the experiment. This includes identifying some more helpful behaviors that you will do during the experiment.

You then do the experiment and evaluate the results. Ask yourself:

What happened?

Were your original predictions supported?

What did you learn from the experiment?

Example Behavioral Experiment

Step 1. Identify the prediction.

The situation	Telling my friend I don't want to go shopping with her.
My predication	She will be upset and angry and not want to my friend anymore
How much do I believe it will happen? (0-100%)	70%
How will I know it has happened?	She will hang up on me and not return my calls or ring me.

Step 2: Identify my unhelpful behaviors

What unhelpful behaviors would I normally engage in to cope (e.g. avoidance, escape, safety behaviors)	Make up excuses, pretend to be sick, avoid her until it is too late

Step 3: Identify a more realistic prediction

Remind myself of the more realistic prediction I have made (can be form a Thought Diary)	She has said no to me before and that was fine. She may be disappointed but if she is a good friend she won't be angry and our friendship will be fine.

Step 4: Carry out an experiment. Step 6: Evaluate the results

What actually happened?	She said it was fine and in fact suited her too. We made a time for a coffee next week.
How much did my original prediction come true? (0-100%)	0%
Which prediction was supported?	The more realistic one.
What was it like to behave differently?	Scary, difficult at first, got easier.
What did you learn from the experiment?	I tend to expect the worst and this has kept me

How to Behave More Assertively

Assertiveness Techniques

In this Section we introduce some general assertiveness techniques. These techniques can be used across a wide range of situations.

When you practice these techniques it can be useful to begin practicing them in a neutral situation. By this we mean one where your emotions aren't too strong. Then as you become more skilled you can begin using them in more difficult or emotional situations. Remember, as with any new skill you learn, the first time you try these techniques they may not go the way you planned. It is important you don't beat yourself up about this but look at what went wrong and how you might do it differently next time. And then have another go! Over time you will find that they get easier.

Warning! Remember the Nonverbal

With each of the techniques it is important to remember the nonverbal communication as well as the verbal. You may think you are being assertive because you are using a particular assertiveness technique; however it is possible to use all of these in an aggressive or a passive way if you are not careful with your nonverbal communication. To make sure you are using assertive nonverbal communication keep your voice calm, the volume normal, the pace even, keep good eye contact, and try and keep your physical tension low.

Basic Assertion

Basic assertion is when we make a statement that expresses clearly our needs, wants, beliefs, opinions or feelings. This type of assertion can be used every day to make our needs known. Typically basic assertion uses "I" statements. Examples of an "I" statement are:

• "I need to be away by 5 o'clock"
• "I feel pleased with the way the issue has been resolved"

You can also use basic assertion to give praise or compliments, information or facts, or when raising an issue with someone for the first time. For example: "I haven't thought about that before, I'd like time to think about your idea."

• "I thought your presentation was really good".
• "The cost will be $2,000"
• "I like it when you help me".

It is important to remember to be specific when making your statement. Decide what it is you want or feel, and say so specifically or directly. Avoid unnecessary padding and keep your statement simple and brief. This skill will help you to be clear about what exactly it is you want to communicate. Basic assertion also includes what some people refer to as the self-disclosure technique which essentially means disclosing your feelings with a simple statement. For example:

• "I feel nervous"
• "I feel guilty".
• "I feel angry"

The immediate effect of the self-disclosures to reduce your anxiety, enabling you to relax and take charge of yourself and your feelings. Using "I" statements to express your feelings in this way also shows you are taking responsibility for your own feelings.

Empathic Assertion

Empathy means that we try to understand another person's feelings, needs or wants. So this type of assertion contains an element of recognition of the other person's feelings, needs or wants, as well as a statement of your needs and wants. This type of assertion can be used when the other person is involved in a situation that may not fit with your needs, and you want to indicate that you are aware of and sensitive to their position.

Examples of Empathetic assertion:

- "I appreciate that you don't like the new procedure, however, until it's changed, I'd like you to keep working on it." "I know you're busy at the moment, John, but I'd like to make a request of you."
- "I recognize that it's difficult to be precise on costs, however, I need a rough estimate."

Empathetic assertion is useful in holding you back from over-reacting with aggression as it causes you to give yourself time to imagine the other person's position and therefore slow down your response.

It is possible to over-use certain phrases in empathic assertion and it can start to sound insincere. It can also be used to mask aggression. For example, if someone says "I appreciate your feelings, but..." then the empathic statement "I appreciate your feelings" is devalued by the word "but" and the phrase becomes aggression masked as assertion.

Consequence assertion

This is the strongest form of assertion and is seen as a last resort behavior. It is usually used in a situation where someone has not been considering the rights of others and you want to get their behavior to change without becoming aggressive yourself. In a work situation it may be used when standard procedures or guidelines are not being followed. When you use consequence assertion you inform the other person of the consequences for them of not changing their behavior. It can easily be seen as threatening and therefore aggressive. Only use this form of assertion when you have sanctions to apply, and only when you are prepared to apply them.

As this type of assertion can easily be seen as aggressive you need to be very careful of the non-verbal signals you use. Keep your voice calm and at an even pitch and volume, keep good eye contact, and try and keep your body and face relaxed.

Examples of Consequence assertion:

• "If you continue to withhold the information, I am left with no option, but to bring in the production director. I'd prefer not to."

• "I'm not prepared, John, to let any of my staff cooperate with yours on the project, unless you give them access to the same facilities that your people have."

• "If this occurs again, I'm left with no alternative, but to apply the formal disciplinary procedure. I'd prefer not to."

Discrepancy Assertion

Discrepancy assertion works by pointing out a discrepancy between what has previously been agreed and what is actually happening. This is useful for clarifying whether there is a misunderstanding or a contradiction, and when a person's behavior does not match their words.

Examples of Discrepancy assertion:

• "As I understand it, we agreed that Project A was top priority. Now you're asking me to give more time to Project B. I'd like to clarify which is now the priority."

• "Paul, on the one hand you are saying that you want to improve cooperation between our departments, but on the other hand you make statements about us that make it difficult for us to cooperate. I agree that we can improve the situation, so I'd like to talk about that."

Negative feelings assertion

Negative feelings assertion is used when you are experiencing very negative feelings towards another person - anger, resentment, hurt and so on. In a controlled and calm way you draw attention to the undesirable affect another person's behavior is having on you. This allows you to deal with the feelings without making an uncontrolled outburst, and alerts the other person to the effects of their actions on you.

There are four steps to negative feeling assertion:

Step	Example
1. Describe the other person's behavior Objectively. Be careful to do this without interpreting or judging.	*When you leave it this late to produce your report…*
2. Describe the impact of the person's behavior on you. Be specific and clear. Don't overgeneralize	*…it involved my working over the weekend…*
3. Describe your feelings	*…I feel annoyed about this…*
4. State how you would prefer the behavior to be in the future.	*…so in future I'd like to receive it by Friday lunch time*

Examples of negative feeling assertion:

"When you come home late, without telling me before, I worry that something is wrong and I feel angry. I would really appreciate it if you could ring and let me know u."

"When you continually interrupt me when I'm working on the balance sheets, it means I have to start all over again. I'm feeling irritated by this, so I would prefer you to wait until I have finished."

Broken Record

Children are experts at the broken record technique. This skill involves preparing what you are going to say and repeating it exactly as often as necessary, in a calm relaxed manner. This skill can apply in most situations. It is a good skill to use when you are dealing with clever articulate people as all you have to do is stick to your prepared lines. It helps keep you relaxed because you know what you are going to say and you can maintain a steady comment, avoiding irrelevant logic or argumentative bait. It is a particularly good technique good for saying no.

Example of the Broken Record technique:

Kate: Can I borrow $20 from you?

Dave: I can't lend you any money. I've run out.

Kate: I'll pay you back as soon as I can. I need it desperately. You are my friend aren't you? Dave: I can't lend you any money.

Kate: I would do the same for you. You won't miss $20.

Dave: I am your friend but I can't lend you any money. I've run out.

This broken record technique can be combined with the other assertiveness techniques you have just learned. Always begin with the mildest stance, getting more and more assertive as you see fit. Avoid jumping in first with the heaviest consequences stance; it will be a threat and aggressive behavior, NOT assertive behavior.

The following example of the broken record technique uses all levels of assertiveness beginning with basic assertion then moving through to empathic assertion and then consequence assertion.

Basic

• "I bought this clock here yesterday. The button for moving the hands isn't working properly so I'd like to exchange it please" At this point the assistant will either agree or:

• "The clock should have been checked before it left the shop"

Empathetic

• "I realize that would have made things easier, however, I would still like to replace it." At this point the assistant will either agree or:

• "I don't have the authority to exchange things" Response "I would still like it to be replaced."

• After a few exchanges the level could be raised to:

Consequence

• "I would like the item changed. If you are not prepared to do that I will take the matter up with your Head Office. I would prefer to resolve it now."

The one situation in which this technique can be a disadvantage is when you are making a request from someone who does not want to do what you are asking. When they continue to resist, your requests lose power every time you have to repeat them. If the requests are repeated too often it can backfire on the authority of your words. In these cases it is necessary to have some consequences on hand.

Practicing the Techniques

All of these techniques require practice. Start with basic assertion and practice this for a week or two before you begin trying the others. Pick one technique at a time and use it whenever appropriate. It can be helpful to keep a little log book or diary of the ways you have been able to use these assertive techniques. Then you can see how often you are using assertiveness and which techniques are the most useful ones for you. We have an example log sheet below. You can use this or make up one for yourself.

Practice Sheet for Assertiveness Techniques

Date/Time	Technique Used	Situation and how used	Things to remember for next time
Example: Tuesday 10 am	*Basic assertion*	*At work: Complimented Mary on her report*	*My voice was probably too soft and I didn't look at her much. Next time speak more loudly and make good eye contact*
Example: Wednesday 2Pm	*Discrepancy assertion*	*At work: My boss told me to do one thing then told me another 5 minute later*	*I think I got a bit angry and might have sounded annoyed. I need to be calmer*

Reducing Physical Tension

Physical Tension

When we are communicating in a passive or aggressive way we are often feeling anxious or angry and this can be reflected in our bodies. We can become tense in our shoulders, necks, jaw or through our entire body. Over time this tension can build up to the point where we can get headaches, backaches, stomach problems, in fact a whole range of physical problems. We also find it increasingly difficult to relax. To communicate assertively we must be able to control the arousal and tension that our bodies may feel when we are in difficult situations or situations in which we feel uncomfortable.

Identifying Physical Tension

The first step in reducing physical tension is to identify where you hold it in your body. Have a look at the following table. Put a check against each area that you feel tension in right now.

Body Area	Tension
Scalp	
Forehead	
Eyes	
Temples	
Jaw	
Neck	
Shoulders	
Chest	
Upper arms	
Lower arms	
Hands	
Stomach	
Lower back	
Buttocks	
Thighs	
Calves	
Feet	

See if you can notice any patterns in the areas of tension. Are you mostly tense in your stomach and lower back, in your arms and legs, or around your neck and shoulders? You may want to repeat this exercise when you are in a more stressful situation to see if you are tense in the same areas or different ones.

Reducing Physical Tension

Once people start to pay attention to their tension they are often surprised at how tense they really are. The good news is that there are a number of relaxation techniques that can be used to reduce physical tension. As with all the skills you are learning

in these Sections the more you practice them the more impact they will have for you.

There are a number of techniques you can use to reduce physical tension. Some of these are listed below:

- Exercise
- Meditation
- Massage
- Guided Visualization
- Progressive Muscle Relaxation
- Slow breathing
- Yoga
- Tai chi

See if you can think of some activities that you know reduce your levels of tension and list them below. These may be the techniques or activities listed above or they may be more personal activities that you know reduce your tension such as listening to music or soaking in a bath. While you are working through the rest of the Sections see if you can do one of these tension reducing activities and exercises daily!

_____

_____

_____

_____

_____

In the rest of this Section we will introduce you to some of the techniques that you may not have come across before.

Progressive Muscle Relaxation

Progressive muscle relaxation or PMR works through each of the muscle groups in progression. If we just try and relax muscles that have been tense for a while it can be difficult to get them to relax. Try it now. Try and just relax the muscles in your shoulders by telling yourself to relax. Most people find this very difficult to do. PMR works by first tensing and then relaxing the muscles. Tensing the muscle first teaches you how to take control of the muscle and recognize the tension. Try it now with your shoulders. Lift your shoulders up as high as you can and try to touch your ears with them. Hold that for 10 seconds. Now let them drop and feel the sensation of relaxation. This tensing and relaxing is followed for each of the major muscle groups.

Follow each of the steps below for the different muscle groups. As we move through each body part you can use the same pattern of tensing and relaxing. When tensing a body part hold the tension for about 10 seconds. Then let the tension go and wait for another 10 seconds before you tense again. You may notice that you tend to breathe in as you tense and breathe out as you relax. This is the natural rhythm of the body and it is easiest if you keep following this. Breathe in as you tense, and breathe out as you relax. You may want to make a recording talking yourself through each muscle group so you can follow it without having to keep referring to the handout.

First, get into a comfortable position in a chair. It is better to do these exercises sitting up to prevent you from falling asleep. To work through the whole exercise should take about 15 to 20 minutes.

Put both your feet flat on the floor and rest your hands gently on your legs. Allow your eyes to gently close. Become aware of the weight of your body, of your head, your shoulders, your arms, and your legs.

Now clench your right fist tightly, noticing the tension as you do. Clench it tighter and notice the tension in your fist, hand and forearm. Now let go of the fist and relax your hand. Notice the contrast with the tension. Repeat this with your right fist. Then repeat with your left fist. Then tense both fists together. Now tense your lower arm muscles by lowering your hand.

Bend it down at the wrist as though trying to touch the underside of your arm. Then relax the muscles by straightening the wrist again. Repeat. Now bend your elbows and tense your biceps. Tense them as hard as you can. Feel the tension. Then relax and straighten out your arms. Repeat.

Now move your attention to your shoulders. Tense your shoulders by lifting them up to try and touch your ears. Now relax by dropping them. Repeat. Now pull your shoulders forward while leaving your arms by your side. Hold and then relax by letting your shoulders go back to their normal position.

Now move your attention to your neck. If you have a sore neck or a neck injury, check with your doctor or physiotherapist before doing this exercise. Gently lean your head to the left until you feel the muscles tighten in the right side of your neck. Slowly roll your head forward around to the right and then slowly back to the left. This exercise should not cause any pain. If you feel pain you are stretching the muscles too tightly, and you need to be a little gentler. Repeat. Now move your attention to your head. Wrinkle your forehead as tightly as you can. It can help to lift you eyebrows. Hold this for 10 seconds and then relax. Now squint your eyes and hold that tension for 10 seconds. Relax, and then repeat. Now clench your jaw by biting your teeth together. Then unclench them and relax. When your jaw is relaxed your lips will be slightly parted. Really notice the difference between the tension and the relaxation. Repeat. Now press your tongue against the roof of your mouth. Then relax and let your tongue fall to the floor of your mouth. Repeat. Now press your lips together then purse them into an "O" shape. Relax your lips. Repeat. Make sure that the rest of your face is still relaxed.

Now move your attention to your chest. Breathe in and fill your lungs completely and tense your chest muscles. Hold and then let your breath go completely and your muscles relax. Make sure your lungs are empty before you take in the next breath. Repeat. Now move your attention to your stomach. Tighten your stomach and hold. Note the tension then relax. Now place your hand on your stomach. Breathe deeply into your stomach so that your hand is pushed out. Hold and then relax. Repeat. Now arch your back while keeping your head tilted forward. Feel the tension in your lower back. Hold then relax and sit up straight again. Repeat. Now tighten your buttocks by pulling them together. You should rise in the chair slightly. Hold and then relax. Repeat.

Now move your attention to your legs. Tense your thighs by pressing your heels into the floor as hard as you can. Hold and then relax. Repeat. Tense your calves by lifting your toes towards your shin. Hold and then relax. Repeat. Tense your feet by curling your toes into the floor. Hold and then relax. Repeat.

When you have finished it is a good idea to stay sitting for a few minutes to really appreciate the sensation of relaxation. Try not to stand up too quickly as you may tense up again.

Also your blood pressure drops when you relax, so if you stand up too quickly you may get dizzy.

Mini Relaxation 1

The more you practice the full PMR the more you will get to know the areas in your body that become tense. However, you won't always have 15 to 20 minutes to practice the whole exercise. In this case you can modify the exercise by just choosing the muscle groups that you know are tense and relaxing these.

Mini Relaxation 2

Alternatively you could try this mini-relaxation exercise:

1. Stand up.

2. Lips closed, jaw relaxed, breathe slow and low down in your stomach

3. Breathe in for 2 seconds and out for 3 seconds. Be aware of your breathing for the whole exercise and keep it slow and deep.

4. Cross one of your legs over the other leg, keeping your feet firmly planted on the ground. Try to place your feet even with each other.

5. Put both your hands behind your back and grasp your hands. Now twist your hands so that your palms are now facing the floor.

6. Keeping your hands together and your arms straight, gently raise your arms toward your head.

7. Notice the increase in tension in ALL of your different muscles. Hold all this for a count of 5.

8. Now uncross your legs and return your arms to your sides. Take two or three breaths to let go of all the tension.

9. Repeat steps '3' to '8' until you feel relaxed.

Slow Breathing Technique

Sit comfortably with your arms and legs uncrossed, your feet flat on the floor and your hands gently resting in your lap. You may find it easier to close your eyes while you are doing this exercise. Use your nose rather than your mouth to breath. Start by just observing your breath. Note the quality of your breath as you inhale and exhale. Now try to slowly lengthen each inhalation by drawing your breath down towards the abdominal area in a smooth and steady fashion. Have a brief pause before you observe the slow smooth and steady fashion in which your breath is released as you exhale. Now that you are paying attention to your breath, you can begin the counting rhythm of breathing in for three seconds and out for three seconds. This will produce a breathing rate of 10 breaths per minute. (A normal breathing rate is 10-14 breaths per minute.) Try to maintain this slow, even and controlled rhythm in your breathing by continuing to count in your head. Try not to speed up the count. Keep breathing for 10 to 15 minutes using this rhythm. When you have finished gently open your eyes and take your time before you rise from the chair. (If you suffer from panic attacks, slow breathing is particularly important to control over breathing. In fact the breathing retraining for panic slows the breath down even further than in this exercise.

Visualization

Visualization uses the power of our imagination to help reduce stress. There is a wide range of different types of visualizations. Many recordings are available if you want to try them. It is a matter of exploring until you find the one that suits and helps you. Visualization is practiced and studied in cancer and pain centers throughout the world. Visualization is effective in treating many stress-related illnesses including headaches, muscle spasms, chronic pain, and anxiety.

Sometimes the effects can be felt immediately and sometimes it takes several weeks of practice to feel any benefit.

Visualization involves imagining a scene or an image as completely as you can. Sometimes people use them to help set goals. For example, athletes can use them as part of their training. They visualize the race or event they are going to be in, in minute detail. They visualize themselves in the event, imagining all the sights, tastes, sounds and smells. They imagine the difficult parts of the race and how they will overcome them. They will feel the exhaustion and imagine overcoming this. You can use a more guided visualization for relaxation. A common version of this is to imagine yourself in one of your favorite places or a beautiful imaginary scene. Again, imagine it in as much detail as you can - the sights, the colors, the temperature, the sounds, the smell, and the feel of your body. It is a place where you feel completely safe and relaxed. Imagine yourself completely relaxing in this place. Here there are no problems to be solved, no work to do, just relaxing.

There are no real limits as to what you can use visualization for. However, there are some basic principles to follow. These are:

1. Loosen your clothing or wear comfortable clothing. Lie down in a quiet place and close your eyes gently.

2. Scan your body. Notice and tension and in which muscles. Relax those muscles as much as you can.

3. Begin creating mental sense impression. Involve all your senses: sight, hearing, touch, smell and taste. For example, imagine a beach. See the colors of the water, the sky, the sand. See any people around, what are they wearing, what do they look like? Smell the ocean, and the clean, fresh air. Feel the warmth of the sun on your body, feel the gentle breeze against your skin, and feel the sand under your toes. Hear the waves, the sounds of the birds, other people. Taste the salt in the air.

4. Use self-statements to aid your relaxation. Use the present tense and avoid negatives. For example, avoid saying: "I am not tense" which contains a negative. Try instead: "I am letting go of tension".

5. Visualize three times a day. Visualization is easiest in the morning and night while lying in bed. After you have practiced

for a while you will be able to visualize in most situations to help you reduce tension.

How to Say "No" Assertively

Saying "No"

Many people have great difficulty saying "No" to others. Even people who are quite assertive in other situations may find themselves saying "Yes" to things that they really don't want to do. Now saying "Yes" to something you don't really want to do can be appropriate in some situations. For example in a work situation if your boss asks you to do something and you don't really want to it wouldn't be appropriate to practice your assertiveness skills and say "No". You may get the sack. What we are talking about here is if you find yourself saying "Yes" in other situations. For example, if a friend asks you to do something which is a real inconvenience for you and you say "Yes", or if you find yourself volunteering for all sorts of jobs to the point that you are over-loaded.

The effects of not being able to say "No".

If you say "Yes" when you really mean "No", resentment and anger can build up towards the person you have said "Yes" to, even though they have done nothing wrong. You can also become increasingly frustrated and disappointed with yourself. And if you are taking on more that you can cope with, you can become over-worked and highly stressed. In the long term not being assertive in this way can decrease your self-esteem and lead to depression and anxiety.

At the other end of the spectrum some people are able to say "No" but do so in an aggressive manner without consideration or respect for the other person. This may result in people disliking you or being angry and resentful.

Neither of these situations is good assertive communication.

Unhelpful beliefs: Why is it hard to say "No"

As we saw in the beginning section we are all born assertive. Anyone who has spent any time around a toddler knows that they have no trouble saying "No!" However as we grow older we learn from our environment and our experience that it is not always appropriate to say "no". We can end up with a number of unhelpful beliefs about saying "no" that make it difficult for us to use this word. Some of these beliefs are listed below. See if any apply to you:

Unhelpful Beliefs about Saying "No"

- Saying "no" is rude and aggressive.
- Saying "no" is unkind, uncaring and selfish.
- Saying "no" will hurt and upset others and make them feel rejected.
- If I say "no" to somebody they won't like me anymore.
- Other's needs are more important than mine.
- I should always try and please others and be helpful.
- Saying "no" over little things is small minded and petty.

See if you can think of any others:

_____

_____

_____

_____

_____

_____

_____

**Changing your Thinking: More Helpful Beliefs about
Saying "No".**

The unhelpful thoughts above are not facts. They are just
thoughts or opinions that we have learned. Each of them can be
replaced by a more helpful thought or opinion about saying
"no". Below we have listed some of these:

• Other people have the right to ask and I have the right to
refuse.

• When you say "no" you are refusing a request, not rejecting a
person.

• When we say "yes" to one thing we are actually saying "no" to something else. We always have a choice and we are constantly making choices.

• People who have difficulty saying no usually overestimate the difficulty that the other person will have in accepting the refusal. We are not trusting that they can cope with hearing "no". By expressing our feelings openly and honestly, it actually liberates the other person to express their feelings. By saying "no" to somebody it allows them to say "no" to your requests while still being able to ask for further requests.

See if you can think of any others, try and come up with alternatives for your own unhelpful beliefs about saying "no".

_____

_____

_____

_____

_____

Remember that sometimes to come up with a new thought you will need to do a Thought Diary or a Behavioral Experiment. These techniques that you learned earlier can be applied to your beliefs about saying "no" as they can to any unassertive belief. You may not immediately believe these new beliefs or thoughts. This is normal. You have been thinking the old thoughts probably for a long time so it will take some time for these new thoughts to become as automatic as the old ones were. Keep practicing and you will get there.

Changing your behavior: How to Say "no".

So you have now worked through some of your unhelpful thoughts about saying "no" but you may still not be really sure how to go about it. There are some basic principles you can apply when you want to say "no". These are:

1. Be straightforward and honest but not rude so that you can make the point effectively.
2. As a rule keep it brief.
3. Tell the person if you are finding it difficult
4. Be polite – say something like "thank you for asking..."
5. Speak slowly with warmth otherwise "no" may sound abrupt.
6. Don't apologize and give elaborate reasons for saying "no". It is your right to say no if you don't want to do things.
7. Remember that it is better in the long run to be truthful than breed resentment and bitterness within yourself.
8. When saying "no" take responsibility for it. Don't blame or make excuses. Change "I can't" to "I don't want to".

Ways of saying "No"

There are also a number of ways you can say "no". Some of these are more appropriate in particular situations. Trevor Powell describes 6 ways of saying "No". These are described below:

1. The Direct 'no". When someone asks you to do something you don't want to do, just say 'no'. The aim is to say no without apologizing. The other person has the problem but you do not have to allow him or her to pass it on to you. This technique can be quite forceful and can be effective with salespeople.

2. The reflecting 'no". This technique involves acknowledging the content and feeling of the request, then adding your assertive refusal at the end. For example "I know you want to talk to me about organizing the annual department review, but I can't do lunch today". Or "I know you're looking forward to a walk this afternoon but I can't come".

3. The reasoned "no". In this technique you give a very brief and genuine reason for why you are saying "No". For example "I can't have lunch with you because I have a report that needs to be finished by tomorrow".

4. The raincheck "no". This is not a definite "no". It is a way of saying "no" to the request at the present moment but leaves room for saying "Yes" in the future. Only use it if you genuinely want to meet the request. For example "I can't have lunch with you today, but I could make it sometime next week".

5. The enquiring "no". As with the raincheck "no" this is not a definite "no". It is a way of opening up the request to see if there is another way it could be met. For example "Is there any other time you'd like to go?"

6. The broken record "no". This can be used in a wide range of situations. You just repeat the simple statement of refusal over and over again. No explanation, just repeat it. It is particularly good for persistent requests.

For example:

Dave: No, I can't have lunch with you.

Kate: Oh, please, it won't take long.

Dave: No, I can't have lunch with you.

Kate: Oh, go on, I'll pay.

Dave: No, I can't have lunch with you.

How to Deal Assertively with Criticism

Criticism

All of us have been criticized at some point in our lives. Being able to accept criticism assertively is one of the most important tasks we face on our journey to maturity. The word criticism comes from an Ancient Greek word describing a person who offers reasoned judgement or analysis, value judgement, interpretation or observation. So to accept criticism maturely we need to be able to accept feedback in the form of analysis, observation or interpretation from other people about our behavior.

Types of Criticism

Criticism can be either constructive or destructive. Constructive criticism is designed to provide genuine feedback in a helpful and non-threatening way in order that the person being criticized may learn and grow in some way. The feedback is typically valid, that is, it is a true criticism. For example, "I really liked the way you wrote your report; I think it could be even better if you focused more on improving your spelling".

Destructive criticism is criticism that is either not valid or true or criticism that if valid is delivered in an extremely unhelpful way. It is often given by someone without much thought or can be designed to embarrass or hurt. For example, "This report is atrocious, your spelling is appalling".

Why do we respond the way we do?

How we accept criticism is largely based on our experiences with criticism as a child. If we did not experience any criticism as a child then when we first experience it as an adult we may be devastated. If we received very constructive criticism as a child we may cope well with criticism as an adult. If we were criticized harshly and punitively then we may see criticism as hurtful and rejecting.

This latter case often occurs when our whole person was

criticized rather than just our behavior. For example, if we made a mistake as a child and were told "you are stupid", this implied that it was us as a whole person who was stupid. The criticism feels like a rejection and we can feel hopeless about how to change. On the other hand if we were told "that was a silly thing to do", then our behavior and us as a person, are seen as two separate things. It is the behavior that is stupid not us. Therefore, we have the power to change that behavior.

How Do You Respond to Criticism?

How do you respond to criticism? Some of the common non-assertive ways of responding to criticism are:

- Becoming confused
- Retaliating with anger and blame
- Becoming defensive
- Shutting down
- Acting silly
- Withdrawing
- Ignoring it and hurting inside
- Running away
- Internalizing anger and stewing over it

Take a minute and think of the last time you were criticized. Now jot down the situation and how you reacted.

The Situation:

_____

_____

_____

_____

How I reacted:

_____

_____

_____

_____

_____

Now read the following descriptions and see if you can identify which one best describes how you reacted.

Passive Responses to Criticism

If we are predominantly passive it can be difficult to respond well to criticism. We may just run and hide and feel hurt and confused. We may tend to just agree with any criticism whether it is valid or not. Then we reproach ourselves for it. For example, "Yes you're right am....., I'm useless, and I've got to stop". We can tend to see a criticism of our behavior as a rejection of ourselves. This type of response can lead to depression, anxiety and low self-esteem. We feel like the world is a critical place and we agree with all the criticisms!

Alternatively, we may laugh it off and criticize ourselves even more with the attitude "If I criticize myself more and make it a joke then no-one will know I am hurt". In the long run this has the same effect as agreeing openly with the criticism.

Aggressive Responses to Criticism

If we tend to respond aggressively then we will tend to hear criticism as a personal attack. Feeling attacked we will then become defensive and may go on the attack ourselves. For example, "How dare you, I'm not late. You're the one who is always late." This type of response can then lead to conflict and increased aggression, which in turn can lead to depression and low self-esteem.

Assertive Responses to Criticism

When we respond assertively to criticism we can identify the difference between constructive and destructive criticism and respond appropriately (see the skills below describing how to respond to criticism assertively). We can see that criticism about our behavior is not necessarily saying anything about us as a person. We don't get defensive, angry, blaming, hurt or run away. We stay calm and accept the criticism without negative emotions.

What Keeps us From Responding Assertively to Criticism? Unhelpful Beliefs about Criticism

As with other unassertive behaviors there is often some unhelpful thinking underlying the behavior. Some of these are listed below:

- If I am criticized it means I am stupid.
- They criticized me, they mustn't like me anymore.
- They are right, I did get it wrong, I can't do anything right. I'm a failure.
- I can't criticize them because then they won't like me. How dare they tell me I've done something wrong. They have no right.
- They're an idiot anyway. I'm not going to listen to them.
- If I criticize myself more and make it a joke then no-one will know I am hurt

Can you identify any other unhelpful thoughts that may stop you from responding to criticism assertively? List them below.

_____

_____

_____

_____

Responding Assertively to Criticism: More Helpful Thinking

Here are some more helpful and assertive thoughts to challenge any unhelpful thoughts you may have. Remember you can also use Thought Diaries and Behavioral Experiments help you come up with more helpful and assertive thoughts.

- If there is something wrong with what I've done it doesn't mean anything about me as a person. I need to separate the behavior from me.
- What can I learn from this criticism? Most criticism is probably based, at least in part, on some truths. Criticism may appear negative. But, through criticism we have the opportunity to learn and improve from their suggestions. Always ask yourself "What can I learn?"
- I have the right to let someone know if their behavior has hurt, irritated or upset me.

- Giving direct feedback can be loving and helpful. See if you can think of any other assertive thoughts about being criticized. If you identified your own unhelpful thoughts see if you can identify more helpful thoughts to challenge these.

_____

_____

_____

_____

_____

_____

_____

Responding Assertively to Criticism: Dealing with Constructive Criticism

We all need to be able to accept constructive criticism. Depending on the way the criticism is presented to you, you can respond in a number of different ways.

1. **Accept the criticism**
    If the criticism is valid then just accept it without expressing guilt or other negative emotions. Accept that

you are not perfect and that the only way we can learn is to make mistakes, see what we need to change and move on. Thank the person for the feedback if appropriate. See the criticism as a gift.

2. **Negative assertion.**
This technique involves not only accepting the criticism but openly agreeing with the criticism. This is used when a true criticism is made to you. The skill involves calmly agreeing with the criticism of your negative qualities, and not apologizing or letting yourself feel demolished. For example, someone may say: Criticism: "Your desk is very messy. You are very disorganized". Response: "Yes, it's true, I'm not very tidy". The key to using negative assertion is self-confidence and a belief that you have the ability to change yourself if you wish. By agreeing with and accepting criticism, if it is appropriate, you need not feel totally demolished. This type of response can also diffuse situations. If someone aggressive is making the criticism they may expect you to become defensive or aggressive back. By agreeing with them the tension in the situation is diffused. Another way of using negative assertion is to own up to your mistakes before they are pointed out. For example, if you arrive late say: "Hi, I'm late."

3. **Negative inquiry.**
Negative inquiry consists of requesting further, more specific criticism. If someone criticizes you but you are

not sure if the criticism is valid or constructive you ask for more details. For example:

Criticism: "You'll find that difficult won't you, because you are shy?"
Reply: "In what ways do you think I'm shy?"

If the criticism is constructive, that information can be used constructively and the general channel of communication will be improved. If the criticism is manipulative or destructive then the critic will be put on the spot.

Responding Assertively to Criticism: Dealing with Destructive Criticism

Unfortunately we are all going to encounter destructive criticism at some point in our lives. This can be more difficult to deal with than constructive criticism. If we practice the techniques below, we can become skilled at dealing with these difficult situations. As with all skills remember it will take practice and some time to feel confident using these skills. You will notice that some of the skills are the same as for dealing with constructive criticism.

1. **Disagree with criticism**
   The first technique for dealing with destructive criticism is simply to disagree with it. It is important that you remain calm and watch your non-verbal behaviors including tone of voice as you do this as

it is easy to become aggressive or passive when disagreeing. Keep your voice calm, your eye contact good. For example: Criticism: "You're always late". Response: "No, I'm not always late. I may be late occasionally, but I'm certainly not always late".

2. **Negative Enquiry.**
   As described above, if someone makes a comment you may not be sure if it is constructive or destructive criticism. We need to check what is meant. If the criticism is destructive then we can either disagree with it as above, or we can use one of the diffusion techniques described below.

3. **Fogging aka Clouding aka Diffusion.**
   The three names above all refer to the same techniques. The idea behind the techniques is to defuse a potentially aggressive or difficult situation. You can use this style when a criticism is neither constructive nor accurate. The tendency for most people when presented with destructive criticism is either to be passive and crumble or be aggressive and fight back. Neither of these are good solutions.

   Essentially what the techniques do is find some way of agreeing with a small part of what an antagonist is saying. By staying calm and refusing to be provoked or upset by the criticism you remove its destructive power.

There are 3 types of diffusion: you can
a) *agree in part,*
b) *agree in probability or*
c) *agree in principle.*

a) Agreeing in part.

In this technique you find just one accurate part of what the critic is saying and agree with that.

Example 1:

Criticism: *"You're not reliable. You forgot to pick up the kids, you let the bills pile up until we could lose the roof over our head, and I can't ever count on you to be there when I need you."*

Response: *"You're certainly right that I did forget to pick up the kids last week after their swimming lesson."*

Example 2:

Criticism: *"You haven't got a job, you're completely unproductive."*

Response: *"Yes, it's true, I don't have a job".*

b) Agreeing in probability.

With this technique you can still say something may be possible even though you really think the chances are likely to be a million to one. So you agree in probability.

Example:

Criticism: *"If you don't floss your teeth, you'll get gum disease and be sorry for the rest of your life."*

Response: *"You're right I may get gum disease."*

c) Agreeing in principle.

In this technique you acknowledge the person's logic without agreeing with what they say.

Example:

Criticism: *"That's the wrong tool for that job. A chisel like that will slip and mess up the wood. You ought to have a gouge instead."*

Response: *"You're right; if the chisel slips it will really mess up the wood".*

Additional tips to remember when being criticized:

1. **Respond to the words not the tone of the criticism.**
   It is important when you are being criticized to separate the suggestions in the criticism from the way that they are being spoken to you. Often when people are giving criticism they can come across as confrontational, even aggressive. This may mean that we dismiss what they are saying despite the fact that the criticism may be a useful one. We need to practice separating the

criticism from the style of criticism. Even if people speak in an angry manner, we should try to detach their emotion from the useful suggestions which lie underneath.

2. **Don't Respond Immediately**
   It is best to wait a little before responding. If we respond with feelings of anger or injured pride we will soon regret it. If we wait patiently it can enable us to reflect in a calmer way.

3. **When Feeling Criticized**

   1. Stop - Don't react until you are sure what is going on.
   2. Question – have you really been criticized? Are you mind-reading?
   3. Check if you need to by asking the other person. For example, you can say: "What did you mean by that?"
   4. Once you have worked out if it is really a criticism, decide if it is valid or not and respond using one of the techniques above.

Giving Constructive Criticism

So far we have talked about skills to deal with receiving criticism. There are also skills to learn when giving criticism so that the person is more receptive to what you are saying. You have a right to request a change in someone's behavior if it hurts, upsets or irritates you in some way. Remember that requesting change doesn't mean that the person will change. However, if you push your resentment down and don't express it, it could cause further problems with the relationship.

Giving direct feedback to others about their behavior can be both loving and helpful. This feedback can be negative or positive. It shows you value the other person and your relationship with them.

Try and follow the guidelines below when giving constructive criticism.

1. Time and place. Make sure you choose a good time and place. If you are giving constructive criticism about something that has led to you having a strong emotional reaction wait until you are away from the situation that is bothering you and have calmed down before criticizing. Don't wait until the next time the situation occurs to confront the behavior.

2. Describe the behavior you are criticizing rather than labelling the person. For example: "You made a mistake in the report" rather than: "What are you, an idiot?"

3. Describe your feelings (using "I" statements) without blaming the other person. For example: "I feel angry when..." rather than: "You make me angry".

4. Ask for a specific change. If you just make a complaint without giving alternative suggestions you don't give the person any help in knowing how to change the behavior. For example rather than saying: "I can't stand your loud music" you might say: "I find the loud music really disturbing could you please turn it down after 8.00pm?"

5. Specify both the positive consequences if the person does meet your request for change and negative consequences if they don't make the changes.

6. Be realistic in the changes you are suggesting and the consequences if they do not. Do not make empty threats. For example you wouldn't say: "I will kill you if you don't turn the music down".

7. Ask the other person how they feel about what you have just said. Being assertive is about having an equal interaction. Be careful this doesn't end us as an exchange of criticisms.

8. Try and end on a positive note. If appropriate add a positive statement of your feelings towards the other person.

How to deal with Disappointment Assertively

Being Disappointed

It would be impossible to get through life without being disappointed about something. Disappointment occurs when we have an expectation or desire about how we want something to turn out and it doesn't go the way we wanted.

How do you Cope with Disappointment?

There are a number of unassertive ways of responding to disappointment. These include:

- Sulking
- Anger at the thing / person that you see as cause of disappointment. This can include being angry at yourself.
- Depression
- Wanting revenge
- Giving up
- Self-criticism

Take a minute and think of the last time you were disappointed. See if you can remember how you reacted. Write this down.

Situation when disappointed:

_____

_____

_____

_____

What I did:

_____

_____

_____

_____

Now read the descriptions below and see if your behavior was passive, assertive or aggressive.

Passive Responses to Disappointment

If you respond passively to disappointment you are likely to give up what you were trying to achieve or become overly self-critical about why you didn't achieve it. You may feel sorry for yourself and sulk. If others have disappointed you, you may give up on them. All of these reactions can worsen your self-esteem and lead to depression.

Aggressive Responses to Disappointment

If you respond aggressively to disappointment you are likely to become angry about the situation or person that led to the disappointment. You may become increasingly resentful towards that situation or person and want to extract some revenge. Assertive Responses to Disappointment If you respond assertively you may still feel disappointment when things haven't gone the way you wanted them to. This is normal! However, you will not blame yourself or other people. Nor will you get stuck in negative emotions. You will take responsibility for your part in the disappointment and think through how you can move forward from here. You may need to make some changes; you may need to learn something from the disappointment. There may be nothing you can do differently. Either way you will be graceful in accepting the situation and move forward.

Unhelpful thoughts associated with disappointment

As with the other behaviors we have looked at there are a number of unhelpful thoughts associated with not dealing well with disappointment. Some of these are listed below.

• They should know I don't like it when they do that.

• The world is terrible, I can't bear this.

• That person is bad.

• I can't accept that person for being like that.

• I can't tolerate this.

Can you identify any other unhelpful thoughts that may stop you from responding to disappointment assertively? List them below.

_____

_____

_____

_____

_____

_____

Responding Assertively to Disappointment: More Helpful Thinking

Here are some more helpful and assertive thoughts to challenge any unhelpful thoughts you may have. Remember you can also use Thought Diaries and Behavioral Experiments to help you come up with more helpful and assertive thoughts.

- It is undesirable to be treated unfairly, but it is not awful.
- I can stand this hurt and frustration and I can do something about the situation.

- I accept how the other person is. They may have been rejecting one aspect of my behavior not me as a whole person.
- It is best to openly express my feelings; the consequences may not be as bad as I think.

See if you can think of any other assertive thoughts about being disappointed. If you identified your own unhelpful thoughts see if you can identify more helpful thoughts to challenge these.

_____

_____

_____

_____

_____

How to Give and Receive Compliments Assertively

Compliments

Being able to give and accept compliments is another assertiveness skill and one which is important in conversations and for building relationships and self-esteem. As with all the skills we have looked at in this series of Sections there is often some unhelpful thinking which stops us from being able to accept or give compliments. Or we may lack the skills needed to help us with this skill. This Section will help you identify and unhelpful thoughts you have about compliments and also show you the steps to take to improve the way in which you accept and give compliments.

Accepting Compliments

Some people find it extremely difficult to accept compliments. Understandably there are times when it may feel uncomfortable; however, being able to accept other people's positive comments about our appearance, our work or some other aspect of ourselves is an important assertiveness and social skill.

How do you Cope with Receiving Compliments?

There are a number of unassertive ways of responding to receiving compliments. These include:

- Ignoring the compliment and changing the topic.
- Disagreeing with the compliment or some part of the compliment. For example: "really, I don't like the color of the dress at all."
- Dismissing or deflecting the compliment. For example "oh, this old thing, it's nothing special."
- Being sarcastic. For example "Yeah right, it's just gorgeous isn't it?"
- Nervous laughing or smiling
- Self-criticism

Take a minute and think of the last time you were complimented. See if you can remember how you reacted. Write this down.

Situation when complimented:

_____

_____

_____

_____

_____

_____

_____

_____

What I did:

_____

_____

_____

_____

_____

_____

Do you think your response was passive, assertive or aggressive? Read the descriptions below and see if you were right.

Passive Responses to Being Complimented

If you respond passively to being complimented you are likely to either ignore the compliment completely, or deflect or minimize the praise. You may feel very nervous and awkward and don't know how to respond at all. This can result in the other person also feeling awkward. You may then leave the social situation feeling embarrassed and your self-esteem may suffer.

Aggressive Responses to Being Complimented

If you respond aggressively to being complimented you may become annoyed, angry or defensive, or disagree and respond sarcastically to the compliment. As with the passive response this may result in the other person feeling awkward.

Assertive Responses to Being Complimented

If you respond assertively you are able to accept the compliment in a positive way. The other person will not feel awkward and the interaction results in both of you feeling better about yourselves: you for accepting the compliment well and the other person for being able to provide some positive feedback. When we can learn how to embrace positive feedback and accept compliments graciously, we open up the door for more positive thoughts and interactions, and we can actually start to BELIEVE them.

Then, when we hear our old patterns of self-criticism, we can intentionally choose to believe the compliments we've been receiving instead.

Unhelpful thoughts associated with being complimented

As with the other behaviors we have looked at there are a number of unhelpful thoughts associated with not dealing well with compliments. Some of these are listed below.

- They don't really mean it. They are just trying to be nice.
- They are being smarmy.
- They must want something from me.
- If I accept a compliment it means I am being big-headed.
- If I accept a compliment they may think I am vain.
- It's too embarrassing to say something back.

Can you identify any other unhelpful thoughts that may stop you from responding to compliments assertively? List them below.

Responding Assertively to Compliments: More Helpful Thinking

Here are some more helpful and assertive thoughts to challenge any unhelpful thoughts you may have. Remember you can also

use Thought Diaries and Behavioral Experiments help you
come up with more helpful and assertive thoughts.

- The compliment may be genuine.
- Even if they are just trying to be nice that is still a
  positive thing and I can reply appropriately.
- If I don't accept the compliment I may make the other
  person feel awkward.
- Accepting the compliment may make the other person
  feel better too.
- Accepting a compliment gracefully doesn't mean I have
  to agree with it completely.
- If I start believing some compliments I may not feel so
  bad about myself.
- Accepting a compliment does not mean that I am going
  to become big-headed. If that were the case I would
  already be complimenting myself!
- People give compliments for a variety of reasons. Don't
  waste a lot of time wondering why someone gave you a
  compliment. Just appreciate the fact that someone took
  the time to say something nice to you!
- You are just as entitled to receive a compliment as
  anyone else.

See if you can think of any other assertive thoughts about
accepting compliments. If you have discovered some unhelpful
thoughts write down some more helpful thoughts to challenge
these.

_____

_____

_____

_____

_____

_____

_____

Steps to responding to Compliments Assertively

1. Look at the other person. Sit or stand up straight. If you
   shrink back or don't look at the person it may seem as if
   you don't like them or don't believe them.
2. Listen to what he or she is saying.
3. Smile when receiving the compliment. A compliment is
   intended to make you feel good. If you frown or look
   down or away the other person may be confused or
   uncomfortable.
4. Don't interrupt.

5. Say "Thanks," or something that shows you   appreciate what was said.
6. Remember to accept the compliment without trying to take the subject off yourself or feeling like you have to pay them back. This will make you feel more confident and let you grow to like yourself better.

Tips for Responding Assertively to Compliments

- As with all the skills you have been learning this one may require some practice. Try these steps in front of a mirror. Imagine someone says something nice, then say "Thank you. That means a lot to me."
- Don't change the topic without acknowledging the compliment.
- It's often good to use the compliment to further conversation. "Thanks! I found it in on eBay - it's amazing what you can get there." That way you've accepted the compliment and moved on to something about which you can both talk.

How to Give Compliments

It is also important to learn how to give compliments. Giving compliments is a way of showing that you have noticed and appreciated something about the person or the situation. People like being around others who are friendly and open. It also shows that you have the confidence to say what you really think, which as you remember is one of the cornerstones of being assertive. Give someone a compliment today!

Steps for Giving Compliments

- Think of the exact words you want to use before you give the compliment. It will make you feel more confident and you'll be less likely to fumble around for words.
- Be specific about the compliment. "That necklace looks really good on you" makes a bigger impact compared to "you look really good today". The more specific the better, it makes the person feel like you have really noticed them.
- Mean what you say. People can tell the difference between sincerity and phoniness.
- Don't overdo it. A couple of sentences will do. ("You did a good job at …" or "You really did well in ….")
- Smile and be enthusiastic when you give compliments. It makes the other person feel that you really mean it.
- Be appropriate: Consider the setting and your relationship with the person. Commenting on a colleague's new hair color is fine, but mentioning it to your boss could be stepping out of bounds.
- Ask a question with your compliment. If you want to use the compliment as a conversational starter, ask a question about the subject of your compliment; "that necklace looks really good on you. Where did you find it?"

Think about a recent example when you admired something about someone (e.g., their clothing, the work they handed in, a generous act they did) and when you did NOT compliment them. What could you have said to this person? Why didn't you give them a compliment? Spend a moment and write down some thoughts. And then think about what you could have said to them.

Putting it all Together

Steps to Improving Your Assertiveness

The steps are:

1. Identify the situations you want to work on. Think about how you normally deal with these situations. Do you normally deal with it in a passive or aggressive way? List these situations in order from easiest to hardest in an assertiveness hierarchy (see below).
2. Identify any unhelpful thinking associated with these situations.
3. Come up with a more assertive way of thinking about the situation. Use a Thought Diary if you need to.
4. Identify any unhelpful behavior you have been using when you have tried to do the task before. Remember to look at both verbal and non-verbal behavior.
5. Come up with a more helpful behavior.
6. Rehearse what you are going to say and do. It can be helpful sometimes to write down what you want to say.
7. Do the task you have identified.
8. Once you have done the task praise yourself for what went well and then work out what you might want to improve on next time.

9. Keep practicing until you feel comfortable being
    assertive in this situation.

Step 1. Creating an Assertiveness Hierarchy

In order to become more assertive you need to write down 10
situations in which you would like to be more assertive. This
can be at home, at work, with friends or out in public.

You will have got some ideas from the exercise "Rating your
assertiveness in different situations?" that you completed.. If
you didn't do this exercise, now would be a good time to have
a look at it. If you did complete it you may want to have
another look at it to remind yourself of your responses.

You may also have got some ideas from the Thought Diary
work you have been doing or some of the Sections that looked
at specific situations like saying "no", receiving and giving
criticism and dealing with disappointment.

If you are still struggling to identify situations to work on think
about the following situations. They may help you. How do
you respond when:

- The food you ordered is cold or overcooked?
- Someone is smoking in a non-smoking section?
- You want to ask a friend to return some money they
  borrowed from you?
- Everybody leaves the washing up to you?
- You are irritated by a habit in someone you love?

If you think you respond passively or aggressively in the above situations you may want to add these to your list.

Once you have written your list you need to work out the order of difficulty. To do this first give each situation a rating of how hard or difficult you think the task would be. Another way of thinking about it is to ask yourself how anxious would it make you. You give each situation a rating from 0-100. A rating of zero would mean the task wasn't difficult at all. A rating of 100 would mean it was the most difficult thing you could imagine doing. Using the ratings you can then work out which task would be the easiest and which would be the hardest. You can then give each task a rank going from the easiest to the hardest.

Below is an example hierarchy:

My Assertiveness Hierarchy

	Situation	Rating (0-100)	Rank
1.	Tell my mother-in-law that I don't want her to smoke in my house.	70	9
2.	Ring the loan agency and tell them I need more time to decide I want the loan or not.	50	8
3.	Tell the neighbor that their dog is keeping me awake at night.	40	6
4.	Tell my partner that I want a night to myself.	45	7
5.	Apologize to a work colleague for being irritable the other day.	30	3
6.	Ask the kids to do their chores.	20	1
7.	Ask my friend to return the book I lent her three months ago.	25	2
8.	Tell my boss I have too much work at the moment and can't take the new project she asked me to do.	80	10
9.	Ring my piano tuner and tell them that the piano is not tuned properly.	40	5
10.	Tell my dad how much I love him.	30	4

Once you have written your hierarchy you start with the easiest task on the list. In the case above it is asking the kids to do their chores.

Steps 2 and 3. Identify and Change any Unhelpful Thinking!

There is usually some unhelpful thinking underneath nonassertive behavior. So before you try the task see if you have some unassertive thinking that has been stopping you from doing the task.

In the example above the person identified an unassertive thought:

"If I keep telling the kids to do their chores they will get annoyed at me and might not like me or think I am a good mum"

They used a Thought Diary and came up with the more assertive thought:

"All kids get annoyed at their mum sometimes, it doesn't mean they don't like them. It is important for the kids to learn how to do chores. To be a good mum sometimes I will have to get the kids to do things they don't like. They may thank me for that later."

Once they had come up with this new thought they were able to do that task and move onto the next task.

Step 4 and 5. Identify and Change any Unhelpful Behavior

The person who wrote the hierarchy above recognized that when she asked the kids to do their chores she would usually feel guilty, apologies to the kids, and think she had to give the kids something to make them like her better. She would usually buy them some lollipops or fast food. She identified these as unhelpful behaviors. She worked out that a more helpful behavior would be to just ask them to do the chore without apologizing, and verbally praise them once they had done it rather than buy them something.

Step 6 to 9. Rehearse and Practice!

In this situation the person didn't feel the need to write anything down beforehand. However she did have to practice asking them to do their chores and not apologizing to them or buying them something for a couple of weeks before she started feeling more comfortable.

Your Turn!

Now that you have seen the steps to becoming more assertive have a go at writing your assertiveness hierarchy:

<u>My Assertiveness Hierarchy</u>

	Situation	Rating (0-100)	Rank
1.			
2.			
3.			
4.			
5.			
6.			
7.			
8.			
9.			
10.			

Assertiveness Worksheet

For each item on the hierarchy you can use the following
worksheet to guide you through the steps.

What is the situation I want to become more assertive in?

_____

_____

_____

_____

_____

What unhelpful beliefs are maintaining the unassertive
behavior?

_____

_____

_____

_____

_____

What are more assertive beliefs?

_____

_____

_____

_____

_____

What unassertive behaviors am I using?

_____

_____

_____

_____

What are more assertive behaviors I could use?

_____

_____

_____

Are you More Assertive?

Congratulations! You have now completed the section on assertiveness in the program "Assert Yourself". You can now redo the exercise from the beginning where you rated your assertiveness in different situations and see if you have become more assertive!

Exercise. Rating your assertiveness in different situations

Fill in each cell using a scale from 0 to 5.

A rating of 0 means you can assert yourself with no problem.

A rating of 5 means that you cannot assert yourself at all in this situation.

	Friends of the same gender	Friends of different gender	Authority figures	Strangers	Work colleagues	Intimate relations or spouse	Shop assistants
Saying No							
Giving Compliments							
Expressing your opinion							
Asking for help							
Expressing Anger							
Expressing Affection							
Stating your needs							
Giving Criticism							
Being Criticized							
Starting and keeping a conversation							

WHAT DID YOU LEARN FROM THIS CHAPTER?

Chapter 3

SPIRITUALITY AND EMPOWERMENT

This chapter is taken from my first book, Stepping on the Stones, A New Experience in Recovery. This book while intended for substance abuse and chemical dependency is also relevant in the psycho-educational process in relation to domestic violence and learned behaviors. For those who have read both books you will notice some changes to fit this subject.

The Second Stone

Stone Two is all about empowerment and learning how to again develop a personal relationship with your spiritual beliefs and/or rebirth of your faith so that you can restore a balance and sanity into your life.

What is balance? It is when all parts are equal, for example, when you can get angry without rage, or hungry without pigging out, tired and go to sleep, and hurt without escaping. It is when love is not co-dependency and when relationships are partnerships.

Here is my view on this:

I know that my being here today is no accident, and that somehow a higher power or in my concept, the creator, had a plan for me. I know that all the dangerous places, all the dysfunctional, dishonest and deceitful, dark places I have been, were all a part of where I am now. I know that I have had a power greater than myself with me in so many ways.

First of all, just the fact that with all the drugs that I have done, the abuse I survived, the abuser I became as a child, the lying, the fake identities and all the dangerous situations I have put myself in I am here writing this manual. I have always understood insanity as that it is where I thought I was, until I learned to understand more about the disease of addiction and how this disease affected everything in my world every day, all the time. And still does every day.

A power greater than myself started with just a white chair, music, walks, mountains and so many small and indefinable things, all the things that gave me a glimpse of hope. Maybe I could do this, was the beginning of the process of recovery and the beginning of the process of understanding this insane lifestyle could stop.

If you think of a moving train, to get off the train the train must come to a total stop. The danger of jumping off a moving train is endangers you and destroys you physically, mentally and spiritually. If the jump does not kill or wound you the sudden stop will.

Awareness can start with anything. It is power if it brings enlightenment; a chair that gives you a place to think and breathe or music that takes you to a place where you can think. Remember, it does not matter how long or how insane, with a belief in the power of understanding and spiritual principles you will restore yourself to the sanity you seek.

Something fabulous happened to me when I realized for the first time I was not crazy. That I was out of control and my thinking and perspectives were totally out of proportion and all my priorities were messed up.

If I slowed down, just allowed myself to release the need of control, if I believed that things would get better, if I just followed the suggestions of others who were where I was before me, I could find way back. When I look back it was all about change and that terrified me. The idea of being honest was a frightening new arena.

Even if I didn't know the difference between my needs and wants at the time, I did believe in the hope that that something was beginning to change. It all starts with respect, the respect to have self-esteem and self-worth. We all need to reconnect with our own personal quality and ability to live life on its own terms. There is no limit to the ability of our self-respect. This it will restore our lives back into to balance.

In our program a higher power represents anything at all that each of you believe is adequate such as nature, freedom from oppression, friendships, God, science, Buddha, or any religious interpretation. A higher power must be greater than you. It only needs to be loving and nurturing and always offer a feeling of goodness and something you can believe in. When you first try to define your higher power you may have to go back and look at all the things that you have experienced and cannot explain. *Examples: Birth of a child, overcoming a traumatic experience, getting your first job, your first kiss, or meeting your first true love.*

Name your own higher power and explain how it made you feel.

_____

_____

_____

_____

_____

_____

_____

_____

_____

_____

Where do you find peace of mind? *Examples: mountains, beaches, fields, lakes, sunny days, church, my mother's kitchen.*

Now let's look at the things that have come in the way of the above questions.

Insanity

Insanity is doing the same things and expecting different results.

How insanity never worked before and why did I think it would work this time? It's time to look back at your needs and wants and separate them. *Example: I never needed to get high. I wanted to get high.*

Name them here:

_____

_____

_____

_____

_____

_____

_____

Do I have balance in my life now when I look at everything overall?

_____

_____

_____

_____

_____

What are the areas of your life that you need to bring balance back into?

_____

_____

_____

_____

Where are your strong areas of self-growth and awareness?

_____

_____

_____

Let's talk about life experiences, a part of our growth that we overlook. We see the positive experiences as very limited and the negative experiences as overwhelming. We don't realize they both have had an equal part of bringing us to this wonderful place.

When did your dysfunctional lifestyle start feeling normal and what is this about?

_____

_____

_____

_____

_____

_____

_____

_____

_____

_____

_____

_____

If one does something long enough and becomes really comfortable with the feeling and the emotions of its pattern it becomes normal to them. What were some of your behaviors and emotions that became normality?

How do you handle change in patterns now?

Let's look at your patterns. What situations have you created as part of your unstable lifestyle? Work? Family? Economics? Home? Relationships? Others?

_____

_____

_____

_____

_____

_____

_____

_____

_____

_____

_____

_____

The following information is taken straight from the NA 12 step workbook:

<u>Insanity</u> is a loss of our perspective and sense of proportion. So we look at our problems as bigger, worse, more dangerous and less fixable than anyone else. We compare addictions, we misread information. Therefore, we are unable to consider others. We do not care about other people's feelings, needs and boundaries. We always see only ours. We are self-centered and we are always out of balance. We create drama all the time.

Now let's try a new exercise in creating. Write a small commercial about your life and see what the point would be. End it with a positive message even if the script is dark and hard to accept.

_____

_____

_____

_____

_____

_____

_____

What is the drama of my life? Describe your own soap opera.

_____

_____

_____

_____

_____

_____

_____

If you're the star in this drama describe your role and the character you play.

_____

_____

_____

_____

_____

How do you interpret information? Describe your patterns.

_____

_____

_____

_____

_____

_____

_____

What are you like when you feel people are not giving you the respect you deserve?

_____

_____

_____

_____

_____

Is part of the insanity, the hurts that are part of your past?

_____

_____

_____

_____

_____

_____

Why have you chosen to keep reinventing them and their negative consequences?

_____

_____

_____

_____

_____

Belief Systems

A belief system is the basis on what and how you believe in anything. *Example: religious belief is based on Bible interpretation, scientific belief is based on observation and reason.*

Myths are the personal beliefs, true or untrue, that we grow up with that form our judgment, opinions observations and way of life. *Example: Negative Myths - men don't cry, women are more sensitive, secrets are always kept in families. Negative belief systems are the base for prejudice, illegal activities etc. Positive myths - if you work hard you will always succeed.*

Is part of your insanity your belief system? Explain.

_____

_____

_____

_____

_____

_____

_____

If your belief system is other peoples' interpretation of facts such as; the parents' racism which is a learned behavior, patterns of drinking, neglected raising children, the need to get married if a partner becomes pregnant, religious doctrines, dispensary rules of the family and any others, describe them.

_____

_____

_____

_____

_____

_____

_____

_____

_____

_____

_____

_____

How are you defining your beliefs and making them work for you as a new open-minded, more understanding and recovering person?

_____

_____

_____

_____

_____

Many of us found that our understanding of insanity goes further than just every day patterns. We seem to be the black and blue generation. We make the same bad decisions over and over. We keep falling back into bad company even when we try to do it right, it does not work out. We then just say "screw it" and don't care about the consequences. We feel that our obsessive behavior will in the long run work out.

Describe this in your own words and how it all came about. Try to describe two incitements.

_____

_____

_____

_____

What was the end result?

_____

_____

_____

_____

_____

_____

Other information in which you think you need to write about on insanity:

_____

_____

_____

_____

_____

_____

_____

_____

"Coming to Believe"

What is "Coming to believe"? It's the wakeup call that says my way is not working so I need to try something else, and I am ready to embrace change. That's what it was for me; just being tired of the same old games, same results, same escapes, same payback, same day, and never understanding "just for today". I needed to look and overcome what was holding me in the insanity, which was my normal life. I needed to look at the fears I had of coming to believe and see what they were.

What keeps you from coming to believe there is a better way? Answer this question using the family myths you have been brought up with.

_____

_____

_____

_____

Are you afraid of change? Why?

_____

_____

_____

_____

What does coming to believe mean to you personally?

_____

_____

_____

_____

_____

_____

_____

Do you understand that this is a process and not an overnight miracle? Explain.

_____

_____

_____

_____

_____

Do you have the patience and understanding of this program, so far, to be able to wait, learn, begin the process, and allow the program to help with this transition?

_____

_____

_____

_____

What do you believe in that you cannot support with evidence or personal knowledge?

_____

_____

_____

Have you ever experienced an event that was amazing and should have never happened?

_____

_____

_____

Have you ever walked away from what should have or could have been life strengthening?

_____

_____

_____

_____

Have you ever allowed things to change your mind through knowledge, experience or just watching?

_____

_____

_____

_____

Are you coming to believe in yourself more every day?

_____

_____

_____

Anything else you want to write about?

_____

_____

_____

_____

_____

_____

A Second Look at a High Power

Each person has a story that is the base of your life experience. It is where you learn your behaviors, you change myths, you follow direction, you experiment with life and death, and you grow. These are the experiences that develop into what kind of power greater than ourselves that we believe in.

During my heavy drug years I believed that the only power greater than me was always negative and everything I did reflected that. Therefore, I could just keep blaming others and just keep getting high. I became a skilled liar, a skilled thief, a skilled manipulator. All of this I blamed on my karma and my destiny. Never understanding that my real destiny was being molded by this and my higher power was keeping me alive.

So that when the change finally happened and I was done, I could move on and achieve what I have: a recovery of 32 years, wonderful children who still have issues with me, great grandchildren and wonderful recovering people who come through my life, some with minimal success and some with fantastic achievements.

It is not about having a religious awakening, it's about realizing that I don't have the answers, and sometimes I don't even have the right questions. I just need to sit back and put down the defense and just stay clean that day. It's amazing what will be revealed to me when the time is right. I do not control anything as great as all the negative power. I know that positive power is mind blowing.

I have seen the wonders of the rain forest of South America, Peru and Ecuador more than once. I have lived in the wonderful Canadian Rockies, which I have considered my home for over 20 years and have always been blown away by the Northern Lights. I have heard every story including all the first nations' tales.

I have survived childhood sexual abuse. I have survived abusing my brother. I have survived being raped by a doctor while my mother waited in the lobby.

This was all made possible by me just turning it over and realizing it was too big for me to deal with. I worked to trust and knew it would be difficult. It took the responsibility from me to have the control. I never had to understand why the river was so beautiful I just had to enjoy it. I never had to understand the lights; I just had to watch them dance as both the negative and positive factors. All I had to do was learn from them how wonderful and how easy it made things.

What do you have a problem accepting?

_____

_____

_____

_____

_____

_____

_____

_____

_____

_____

_____

_____

_____

What do you still not want to accept from the following?
Childhood - Teen Years - Married or Adult Years

_____

_____

_____

_____

_____

_____

_____

_____

If you gave up the worry, how would things change for you?

_____

_____

_____

_____

_____

_____

By holding on to the guilt have you stopped the healing? Why?

_____

_____

_____

_____

_____

_____

If you turned over what is bothering you what do you think you could expect?

_____

_____

_____

_____

_____

_____

If you examine your expectations and keep them simple what can you expect?

_____

_____

_____

_____

_____

Name five areas in your life in which you need sanity now.

_____

_____

_____

_____

_____

Are you ready to turn your life around?

_____

_____

_____

Let's go even further into this question of a power greater than yourself and the restoring of sanity to your life. Let me set up a scenario about this wonderful oak table I found at a second hand store. It was clearly abused, layers of paint weathered and left in an outdoor shed.

However, living with a man who was once a logger I realized how wonderful the wood under all this crap must be and that this table was just like me. In order to restore it to its original beauty, steps would have to be taken day by day, one day at a time to restore it to the original wood.

My restoration was restoring myself to the sanity I deserved and needed to be healthy, as well as staying a recovering addict. So each day I worked on this table. I stripped the paints and I sanded the wood and did it again and again and again until I was at the base wood. It was so lovely but I knew I could not just leave it, as it was so vulnerable to the elements in its natural form.

I had to protect it by using natural oil so the table recovered and it would stay beautiful as long as recovery was kept up. So that was the deal about all the pain and the distortions, and the layers of neglect, and the drugs, and my lack of responsibility to all the people who loved me and depended on me. Then I was ready to be restored, which was the beginning of my road to recovery; giving back which is what I do, and remaining on my journey.

What are the things you consider your sanity?

_____

_____

_____

_____

_____

_____

_____

_____

Write down your restoration plan.

_____

_____

_____

_____

_____

_____

_____

_____

_____

How and why it will work.

_____

_____

_____

_____

_____

_____

What are the areas in which you still need lots of work, and have to begin the stripping down of the layers?

_____

_____

_____

_____

What area(s) of your life do you feel you are not ready to begin the process of restoration?

_____

_____

_____

Expectations

An expectation is looking forward to an event that is about to happen. Expectations need to be measurable based on the event. If one expects more than they are ready for or if the expectation is too high then a feeling of failure, guilt, or shame can be a negative result.

By keeping your expectations measurable to what you are ready for and what you need in the balance of your life you never set yourself up for disappointment. What if you have unrealistic expectations of restoring yourself to a whole person you need or want to be.

We set up barriers from the beginning, too high and too dense. We will not get angry, we will not have problems that we obsess over and we will now have balance in our lives. If we address all their expectations we will eliminate all turmoil. STOP! We are distorting sanity and fantasy.

Sanity means having realistic expectations. Such as understanding when we get angry we don't have to use over it. We can let go of things that are too big for us to handle, we can slow down and breathe again, we are going to look, listen, and learn.

Does this make sense to you? What are your thoughts?

_____

_____

_____

_____

_____

_____

_____

Can you separate expectations so you are not disappointed?

_____

_____

_____

_____

What are some expectations you need to revisit and scale down?

_____

_____

_____

_____

_____

_____

What areas do you need to challenge yourself more?

_____

_____

_____

_____

_____

What area(s) of your life have you been afraid to revisit but now think you're ready to write about and work through them either with your sponsor or fellow recovery friend?

_____

_____

_____

_____

_____

_____

My favorite part of the second stone is spiritual principles. Here is where the truth is exposed and the procrastination stops. Here is where each of us looks at our focus on open-mindedness, faith, trust issues, and humility. Open-minded people need to listen, to learn, to ask for help. We need to forget about what we have learned from others' negative influences and focus on our own interpretation, for many of us new territory.

- Faith is a very personal and self-gratifying part of this stone, only defined through one's own experiences, put simply, to believe in something.
- Trust is a major issue. It means to have confidence or faith in.

- <u>Humility</u> the removal and put down of our egos.

What are some of your spiritual principles pertaining to the following categories?

Environmental

_____

_____

_____

_____

_____

Relationships

_____

_____

_____

_____

Gender specific roles

_____

_____

_____

_____

_____

Children

_____

_____

_____

_____

_____

Family

_____

_____

_____

_____

Financial

_____

_____

_____

Trying new things

_____

_____

_____

Racial equality

_____

_____

_____

_____

Sexual equality

_____

_____

_____

_____

Word

_____

_____

_____

_____

Culture

_____

_____

_____

_____

Explain how you have changed from being closed minded to being open-minded.

Do you question your faith? How?

_____

_____

_____

_____

_____

_____

Do you feel comfortable with seeking a more personal
relationship with a god (of your understanding)?

_____

_____

_____

_____

_____

Do you want to explore the religious denomination you were
raised in? If not what are some of the other possibilities that
you might want to explore?

_____

_____

_____

_____

Make a list of the questions you have about faith and try to find the answers as you find an understanding of a God.

_____

_____

_____

_____

If you have a strong faith, explain why.

_____

_____

_____

_____

_____

_____

_____

_____

Write how and why your faith has grown.

_____

_____

_____

_____

_____

_____

Types of Denial

Denial of Fact

In this type of denial, someone avoids a fact by lying. Lying can take the form of an outright falsehood, leaving out certain details to tailor a story (omission), or by falsely agreeing to something. Someone who is in denial of fact is typically using lies to avoid truths that they think may be painful to themselves or others or detrimental to their character and/or reputation.

Denial of Responsibility

This type of denial involves avoiding responsibility by blaming, minimizing or justifying. Blaming is a direct statement shifting fault, and may overlap with denial of fact.

Minimizing is an attempt to make the effects or results of an action, seem less harmful than they may actually be. Justifying is when someone takes a choice and tries to make that choice look okay due to their idea of what is "right" in a situation. Someone using denial of responsibility is generally attempting to avoid potential harm or pain by moving the attention away from them.

Denial of Impact

Denial of impact involves a person's avoiding the knowledge of, or understanding the harms his or her behavior has caused to self or others. Doing this enables that person to avoid feeling remorse or guilt and it can prevent him/her from developing empathy for others. Denial of impact reduces or eliminates a feeling of pain or harm from poor decisions.

Denial of Awareness

This type of denial is best discussed by looking at the idea of being dependent upon being in a different state of mind in order to function or learn. People using this type of denial will avoid pain and harm by stating they were in a different state of awareness (such as alcohol or drug intoxication or on occasion mentally ill). This type of denial often goes hand in hand with denial of responsibility.

Denial of Cycle

Many who use this type of denial will say things such as, "it was a one-time thing" or "it won't happen again". Denial of cycle is where a person avoids looking at their decisions leading up to an event or does not consider the fact they have formed a pattern of decision making and repeat harmful behavior. They avoid pain and harm by using this type of denial and it is more of the effort needed to change the focus from a singular event to looking at past events. It can also be a way to blame or justify behavior.

Denial of Denial

This can be confusing for many people to identify with in themselves, but is a major barrier to changing harmful behaviors. Denial of denial involves thoughts, actions and behaviors which encourage ones confidence that nothing needs to be changed in their personal behavior. This type of denial goes hand in hand with all of the other forms of denial, but involves more self-delusion.

Now use all the above definitions of denial in a self-inventory starting with your youth and ending in the present whether it is adolescent years, adult years, or senior years.

_____

_____

_____

_____

Name the times you made up an excuse so that you could do what you intended to do from the beginning. Example: Starting a fight with a spouse so that you could use the stress of the argument as a reason to use drugs or drink. "You made me" or "Because of you" I did this or that.

_____

_____

_____

_____

_____

_____

Re-live two incidents in which you told yourself a falsehood so
that you could continue your behavior. This could include any
compulsive behavior such as: eating, shopping, sex, working,
drinking, drugging.

_____

_____

_____

_____

Problem Solving

When we are faced with a situation which requires a resolution
how do we figure it out? Do you quickly come to a decision?

_____

_____

_____

_____

_____

_____

Do you review all the facts and how do you do that?

_____

_____

_____

_____

How influenced are you by how others see a problem?

_____

_____

_____

_____

Do you weigh options?

_____

_____

_____

_____

Are you open to suggestions?

_____

_____

_____

_____

After all of the above are you willing to compromise if that is what is apparent?

_____

_____

_____

_____

Do you understand how to work through the pattern of making a decision?

_____

_____

_____

Chapter 4

A Conversation with Self

Patterns of negative and positive self-talk often begin in childhood. Children that have watched their parent's exhibit hostile behavior toward each other tend to have negative self-talk. Influence in the experience and the stress of lives however, is a tool that can help both the men and women who are struggling to be non-abusers to understand a little bit more about their behaviors

Some self-criticism is a good thing. It can be a reality check that spurs you to become a better person. There is a big difference between *I need to work out more* or *I have to work out more*. Excessive self-criticism tends to backfire because it leads us to focus on the so-called failures instead of the small ways to improve yourselves.

Putting down or continuously beating yourself up will only increase the lack of self-confidence and lack of the ability to change. The next time a negative thought starts to become overwhelming, it's time to take a few breaths and narrow it down to what the problem really is. An example of this is: You cannot eat the whole elephant, it is way too big. You need to take one bite at a time. That is the same as dealing with the overwhelming problems that have created the abusive behavior. If you think you're a constant screw up, you will behave like a constant screw up. If you think you have messed up or made a mistake, then you can fix that. Visualize what you think it takes to change overwhelming and stressful behavior into something that can be modified and worked on.

The power of positive thinking!

If you see things negatively all the time, in the same way as you have in the past, then nothing is going to change. But when you sit down, you focus, and you force yourself to look at every situation and come up with a positive plan. At this point, a positive behavior change can take place, such as: *"I'm overweight and I want to do something about it."* Well, if you dwell on being overweight you're probably going to be frustrated, and then do nothing. If you look at smaller things that you can do to get ready to be proactive than positive things can happen. Try to see yourself 10 pounds thinner and now 30 pounds. Can you visualize yourself eating healthy but not completely giving up everything you like?

Ask yourself if you are really such a bad person. If you think you are, try doing an inventory and seeing what it is about yourself that you can change immediately. What is about yourself that may take a little more time on? What is it about yourself that might need professional help?

We all have imperfections but understand holding yourself to a standard of complete perfection is a devastating feature no one can meet. Some successful CEOs of companies can tell you that their success is based on overcoming the mistakes that they made and finding a better way. Try to relax the standards in your life a bit and give everyone else in your life a chance to breathe. You just might find that you are not as angry as you once were!

Who is your best friend? Talk to yourself. Do you want someone like you to be your best friend? If the answer is no, identify what it is about yourself that would alienate you from being your friend.

_____

_____

_____

_____

_____

_____

_____

_____

Give yourself the right to change. Do not talk about it as you grow, just do it! Put your ego aside and find humility. This is part of what you feel and think and is going to help you grow.

Humility

Understanding humility was really hard for me as my ego always got in the way. I still wanted to be in control and a small piece of me still thought that if I gave up all control I was just a weak person.

Now let's look at ego:

Ego is the overtones of one's self importance. This is the part of the mind that is most conscious and meditates and takes in ones surroundings.

Where does your ego interfere?

_____

_____

_____

_____

_____

_____

Do you need a strong ego or do you need a balanced ego? Explain the difference.

_____

_____

_____

_____

Ego is "me me me". How do you relate to this?

_____

_____

_____

Can you identify a time when your ego got in the way of a decision?

_____

_____

_____

What is the state of your ego now?

_____

_____

_____

_____

Ego can also be referred to as pride. A lot of times we are too prideful to admit that we have a problem. The struggle with humility is putting your ego aside and listening and learning from others.

Are you able to stop and listen?

_____

_____

_____

_____

How hard is it for you to not always be right?

_____

_____

Do you ask your higher power for guidance?

_____

_____

_____

_____

Are you able to reach out for help from people you would have never asked help from before?

_____

_____

_____

_____

Have you sat down with a partner and honestly talked about your personal expectations?

_____

_____

_____

My Advice: Work a step program (my suggestion certainly would be my first book, Stepping on the Stones, A New Experience in Recovery). Even though this book was written for addiction it isn't about drugs or alcohol it is about compulsivity and behavior that you are/have experienced through your behavior of control and the need for power and control.

Chapter 5

Stone ONE

Domestic violence, also known as domestic or spousal abuse, occurs when an intimate family member or partner, ex-partner, brother, sister, father, mother or caretaker attempts to physically or psychologically dominate another person of the family. Domestic violence often refers to violence between spouses or spousal abuse, but can also include any co-inhabitant and especially non-married intimate partners, teens and same-sex couples.

The definition that comes from the Domestic Violence Act of 2005; this is a direct quote:

For the purposes of this Act, any conduct of the respondent shall constitute domestic violence if he/she,—

a) habitually assaults or makes the life of the aggrieved person miserable by cruelty of conduct even if such conduct does not amount to physical ill-treatment; or
b) forces the aggrieved person to lead an immoral life; or
c) otherwise injures or harms the aggrieved person.

Nothing shall amount to domestic violence if the pursuit of course of conduct by the respondent was reasonable for his own protection or for the protection of his or another's property.

Why do I think this is necessary? Because society has almost approved of the abuse, as long as it's not hitting, and that is unacceptable at any time. Violence can take the form of physical, emotional, mental etc.

How you communicate when you are feeling out of control?

_____

_____

_____

_____

What do you say to yourself to regain your self-control? Give three examples.

_____

_____

_____

_____

_____

_____

Give three examples of positive self-talk.

_____

_____

_____

_____

_____

_____

Give three examples of how positive self-talk can make you feel that you are accomplishing more than you have when in your negative mode.

_____

_____

_____

_____

_____

_____

Understanding Distress Intolerance

Introduction

We all experience emotions. Emotions are an important part of being human, and are essential to our survival. As humans we are designed to feel a whole range of emotions, some of which may be comfortable to us, and others may be uncomfortable.

Most people dislike feeling uncomfortable. There are many different ways that humans can feel uncomfortable…we can be hot, cold, tired, in pain, hungry, unwell, and the list could go on. The type of discomfort we will be talking about in these Sections is emotional discomfort, or what is often called distress. We may not like it, but experiencing uncomfortable emotions is a natural part of life.

However, there is a difference between disliking unpleasant emotions, but nevertheless accepting that they are an inevitable part of life and hence riding through them, versus experiencing unpleasant emotions as unbearable and needing to get rid of them. Some people tell us that they "can't face", "can't bear", "can't stand", or "can't tolerate" emotional distress. Being intolerant of experiencing emotional discomfort can actually breed a whole bunch of problems, as it interferes with living a fulfilling life, and can make worse any emotional discomfort we might be experiencing. If difficulty facing your feelings or tolerating distress sounds like you, then read on to learn ways to overcome this pattern.

What Is Distress Intolerance?

There are many different definitions of distress intolerance. What we mean by distress intolerance is a **perceived inability to fully experience unpleasant, aversive or uncomfortable emotions, and is accompanied by a desperate need to escape the uncomfortable emotions.** Difficulties tolerating distress are often linked to a fear of experiencing negative emotion. Often distress intolerance centers on high intensity emotional experiences, that is, when the emotion is 'hot', strong and powerful (e.g., intense despair after an argument with a loved one, or intense fear whilst giving a speech).

However, it could also occur for lower intensity emotions (e.g., nervousness about an upcoming medical examination, sadness when remembering a past relationship break-up). It is not the intensity of the emotion itself, but how much you fear it, how unpleasant it feels to you, how unbearable it seems, and how much you want to get away from it that determines if you are intolerant of distress.

There are varying types of negative emotions that could potentially be distressing for people. We thought it might be helpful to categories these emotions into the following 3 clusters:

The Sad

This group includes emotions that reflect sadness at varying degrees of intensity. This would include disappointment, hurt, despair, guilt, shame, sadness, depression, grief, misery, etc.

These emotions can be accompanied by either low physiological arousal (e.g., low energy, fatigue, heaviness) or heightened physiological arousal (e.g., intense crying, restlessness), thoughts of hopelessness, loss, regret and inadequacy, and the urge to hide away from life.

The Mad

This group includes emotions that reflect anger at varying degrees of intensity. This would include irritation, agitation, frustration, disgust, jealousy, anger, rage, hatred, etc. These emotions are usually accompanied by high physiological arousal (e.g., tension, increased heart rate, feeling sweaty or hot, etc.), thoughts of unfairness, injustice and wrong doing, and the urge to lash out in some way.

The Scared

This group includes emotions that reflect fear at varying degrees of intensity. This would include nervousness, anxiety, dread, fear, panic, terror, etc. These emotions are usually accompanied by high physiological arousal (e.g., increased heart rate, increased breathing, tension, sweating, shaking, butterflies in stomach, etc.), thoughts of threat, vulnerability and helplessness, and the urge to avoid or escape. For some people their distress intolerance might be very broad, in that they find all negative emotions distressing, for other people their distress intolerance might be very select to just one type of emotion (e.g., anxiety). How about you? What *Negative*

Emotions do you find difficult to deal with?

_____

_____

_____

_____

_____

_____

<u>Note</u>: Some people can be distressed by positive emotions, not just the negative ones. It is not uncommon for people to be concerned that positive emotions will make them lose control in some way. These Sections will only focus on intolerance related to negative emotions, but some of the strategies may be relevant if you have trouble experiencing positive emotions too.

It is important to realize that the term *distress* that we are using throughout these Sections, refers to emotions that are experienced as aversive, unpleasant, uncomfortable and upsetting. Now, the 3 clusters of negative emotion previously mentioned, are not necessarily in themselves distressing. For example, some people like the empowering feeling of being angry, and don't find it at all an upsetting emotion. Some people like watching horror movies because they enjoy the feeling of being scared. Some people don't mind feeling sad, because it gets their creative energy going when it comes to art, music or writing, or they may hold the attitude "it's good to have a cry every now and then". These examples show that **negative emotion in itself is not necessarily distressing,** and as you will see in the next Section, these emotions are normal and often helpful to us. **We only begin to feel distressed when we evaluate our emotional experience as a bad thing.**

The Paradox…

Now, it makes a lot of sense to try to get away from things that feel unpleasant. This strategy seems to work for other things that make us uncomfortable (e.g., heat, cold, pain, hunger, etc.). However, when we apply the same strategy to our emotions, it seems to backfire. This is the paradoxical nature of distress intolerance. That is, **the more we fear, struggle with, and try to avoid any form of distress, generally the worse that distress gets**. Our fear and avoidance of the distress actually magnifies the distress.

Imagine your emotional distress is a puddle of water blocking your path. If you can recognize that emotional distress is not something to be feared, nor something to run away from, then all you have is a puddle of water. If you just wait there it will eventually dry up enough to jump over it, or you could just splash through it and keep on going. However, if instead you fear your distress, struggle with it and try everything to escape from it, all you do is add more and more water to the puddle, and very soon you are faced with a deep pond that it impossible to jump over or splash through. The bigger the pond, the harder to find a way through it, and hence the longer you will feel stuck and unable to move forward.

Am I Distress Intolerant?

If you are still a bit unclear as to whether distress intolerance is a problem for you, take a look at the following statements. Put a check next to the statements you <u>strongly agree</u> with.

Feeling distressed or upset is unbearable to me	
When I feel distressed or upset, all I can think about is how bad I feel	
I can't handle feeling distressed or upset	
My feelings of distress are so intense that they completely take over	
There is nothing worse than feeling distressed or upset	
I don't tolerate being distressed or upset as well as most people	
My feelings of distress or being upset is not acceptable	
I'll do anything to avoid feeling distressed or upset	
Other people seem to be able to tolerate feeling distressed or upset better than I can	
Being distressed or upset is always a major ordeal for me	
I am ashamed of myself when I feel distressed or upset	
My feelings of distress or being upset scare me	
I'll do anything to stop feeling distressed or upset	
When I feel distressed or upset, I must do something about it immediately	
When I feel distressed or upset, I cannot help but concentrate on how bad the distress actually feels	

If you find yourself agreeing with a lot of the above statements, then this can be a sign of having difficulties with tolerating emotional distress.

To get an even better idea if distress intolerance is a problem in your life, keep a tally over the next week or so of any negative emotions you feel. Then make a rating of how intolerable (i.e., unbearable, unmanageable) these feelings were for you. Also note how you reacted to these emotions (i.e., did you frantically try to stop the feeling? Did you ride it out? Did you do things that seemed helpful or unhelpful to coping with the emotion?). You could use a notepad to keep track of these things, and it might look something like the example below. After having tuned in closely to how you tolerate negative emotions, you may then be in a better position to assess if distress intolerance is a problem for you.

Day/Time	Negative Emotion	Intolerable (0-5)	My reaction to the emotion
Monday 8 am	*Anxious*	*4*	*Stopped the anxiety by calling in sick to work. This was unhelpful given how many sick days I have had, and I will just have to face work tomorrow*
Monday 2pm	*Angry*	*3*	*Did some breathing, watched TV, the feeling passed*
Monday 8pm	*Sad*	*5*	*Drank, felt worse, hung-over*

Healthy Distress Tolerance

An important thing to consider when assessing your own level of distress tolerance, is that like many things in life, doing anything at the extreme can be unhelpful. Think of distress tolerance as a continuum where at one end people can be extremely intolerant of distress, and at the other end people can be extremely tolerant of distress. Sitting at either end of the spectrum isn't good for you.

 If you were always overly tolerant of experiencing all unpleasant emotions, then problems might result such as tolerating bad situations or bad people in your life. If you were tolerant in the extreme, you would never take action to change unhappy circumstances in your life that need to be changed. As you read through the rest of this Section, you will get a sense of all the negative consequences that occur on the other side of the spectrum when people are intolerant of distress. When working through these Sections we will be aiming for somewhere in the middle of the continuum, so that you learn to balance tolerating emotional discomfort when it does arise, with taking action to improve your emotional experiences.

 You might like to put a cross to mark where you think you are on this continuum at the moment.

How Does Distress Intolerance Develop?

It is likely a combination of biological and environmental factors that lead some people to be more intolerant of emotional distress than others.

There is some suggestion that biologically some people are more sensitive to negative emotions, experiencing negative emotions more easily, at a higher level of intensity, and for a longer duration than other people. This may mean that some people experience negative emotions as more painful, and hence have greater difficulty coping with the experience.

It is likely your experiences growing up through childhood, adolescence and through adult life, may shape how you deal with emotions. Some people may not have been shown ways to tolerate emotional discomfort appropriately, for example being punished for expressing normal emotions like crying when they were sad. Others may have only been shown unhelpful ways of dealing with their emotions, such as seeing a loved one use alcohol to deal with their own emotions.

Finally, if we have stumbled upon unhelpful ways to escape our emotions, these methods may have been reinforced by temporarily making us feel better. As such, we keep using unhelpful methods and don't have a reason to look for other more helpful ways of dealing with our distress.

Distress Intolerant Beliefs

Regardless of how a person's distress intolerance emerged, we take the view that this intolerance keeps having a hold over people's lives due to certain beliefs they have developed about experiencing negative emotions. These beliefs tend to center on the notion that negative emotion is bad in some way, unbearable, unacceptable, or will lead to disastrous consequences. These beliefs tend to make any negative

emotion that we may feel, become a highly distressing
emotional experience. Below are some of the common beliefs
that people with distress intolerance have when they start to
experience negative emotion:

- *I can't stand this*
- *It's unbearable*
- *I hate this feeling I must stop this feeling*
- *I must get rid of it*
- *Take it away*
- *I can't cope with this feeling*
- *I will lose control*
- *I'll go crazy*
- *This feeling will keep going on forever*
- *It is wrong to feel this way*
- *It's stupid and unacceptable*
- *It's weak It's bad It's dangerous*

Let's try to uncover your common **Distress Intolerant Beliefs**.
Firstly, do any of the statements above ring true for you? If so,
jot down the statements relevant to you. Secondly, ask yourself
the following questions:

What does it mean to me when I start to feel uncomfortable emotions? What do I think will happen if I let myself feel distressed? What must I do when I feel any emotional discomfort?

Distress Escape Methods

As mentioned earlier, a clear sign of distress intolerance is when someone takes desperate urgent measures to escape or get rid of uncomfortable emotions. This can be done in a number of different ways, and each way can lead to significant problems in a person's life.

Avoidance

One method is via avoidance, and avoidance can take many forms. Firstly, there is **situational avoidance.** This is when you avoid any situation, scenario, place, person, cue or activity that you know is likely to bring on distressing emotions. Examples of this might be avoiding a particular family member with whom you become angry, avoiding studying because you become frustrated, avoiding socializing or leaving the house because you become anxious, avoiding things that change your physical state because you feel nervous (e.g., sitting in a hot car, drinking caffeine), avoiding medical appointments or tests because you are frightened, or avoiding reminders of the past or certain topics of conversation because they sadden you.

A second method, is a more subtle form of avoidance known as **reassurance seeking or checking.** This is when you try to quickly allay your distressing emotions by <u>excessively</u> seeking reassurance from other people or engaging in some repetitive checking behavior. Checking or reassurance seeking temporarily brings you comfort and takes away your distress, but the relief is short lived and you have to keep doing these things the next time you feel distressed. Examples might include having to repetitively check things on your body (e.g., a physical sensation, symptom or feature) or in your environment (e.g., around the home), over-preparing for things (e.g., projects, work, social events), keeping things in excessive order, or overly questioning or consulting other people's opinions to calm you down (i.e., family, friends, medical or mental health professionals, internet research).

Finally, there is a third method called **distraction and
suppression** which involves trying to push away the distress,
rather than sitting with the emotion and feeling what needs to
be felt (i.e., telling yourself to "stop it" as soon as you feel any
distress, finding any mental or physical activity to distract
yourself from the slightest hint of emotion such as counting or
repeating positive statements, etc). The problem with
distraction and suppression is that you can't keep it up for long,
and the emotion ends up being like a beach ball you are trying
to hold under the water with your hands. You can only hold it
at bay for so long, it becomes exhausting, and eventually it
pops back up and hits you in the face!

Numbing & Withdrawing

Numbing and withdrawing capture things you do to tune out
from the distress. The most common ways of doing this would
be by using **alcohol** or **drugs** to escape emotional discomfort.
Binge eating is also a common method used to try to alleviate
distress. **Excessive sleep** can also be used in an unhelpful way
to zone out from and escape unpleasant emotions.

Harmful Releases

We have used the term 'harmful releases' to capture behaviors
we might engage in to release or vent our distress, that are also
directly physically damaging to ourselves. Rather than
allowing our emotions to run their natural course, we might
injure or harm ourselves as a way of stopping the emotional

discomfort. Such behaviors might include scratching, picking, biting, punching, and hair pulling, head banging, cutting or burning. The degree of harm we cause to ourselves could be minor or major, but the key is that doing harm to ourselves is being used to get rid of distressing emotions.

Please Note: **Whilst these Sections may be helpful to people who use drugs, alcohol or self-harm as a means of tolerating emotional distress, it is important to recognize that these are very serious problems in their own right that can cause a person significant harm. We strongly advise seeking help from a GP or mental health professional to address these concerns, rather than relying solely on these sections to overcome the problem.**

We have just outlined the most common ways people escape their distress. You may be able to think of other unhelpful methods. The important thing is to recognize your common **Distress Escape Methods**. Ask yourself, what do I do to get rid of unpleasant emotions? Take some time to jot these down now.

_____

_____

_____

_____

_____

The issue with each of these escape methods is that they only work in the short-term. In the short-term, as soon as you avoid or numb or release yourself, you experience instant relief from whatever distressing emotion you are trying to flee. In this way it may seem like a really good strategy, and that is probably why you have been using it, because there is some pay off. However, over the long-term it all falls apart because:

- The escape strategy itself is damaging and causes other problems in your life,
- Your negative emotions usually worsen because you feel you haven't coped well,
- By continually using your escape strategy, you never learn other more helpful ways of tolerating emotional distress, and
- By continually using your escape strategy you never have the opportunity to stay with the emotional distress and therefore challenge the beliefs you hold about not being able to tolerate negative emotions (maybe you can tolerate them, but you have just never given yourself the chance???)

Distress Intolerance Model

We have covered a lot of issues surrounding distress intolerance. Let's put together everything we have covered so far to help make sense of what is going on when you are having difficulties dealing with emotional distress.

Distress usually starts with some sort of trigger which can be big (e.g., a relationship break-up) or small (e.g., watching a distressing story on TV), internal (e.g., noticing a thought, image, memory, emotion, physical sensation, etc.) or external (e.g., a certain situation, event, person, place, cue, etc.). Think back to past times you haven't coped well with distress, what sorts of things were your **Triggers**?

_____

_____

_____

_____

_____

_____

_____

_____

_____

Whatever the trigger, we start to feel some sort of negative emotion. Now the emotion in and of itself is not necessarily distressing, unless we also hold distress intolerant beliefs which tell us the emotion is bad in some way and must be stopped. As a result of our beliefs, we start to experience the emotion as highly distressing and upsetting to us, and therefore engage in our unhelpful escape methods to stop it. In the short-term this takes the emotional pain away, but in the long-term makes everything much worse.

This chain of events captures what we mean by distress intolerance, and is mapped out in the model on the next page. Try filling in each box to make the model specific to you, so you can see your distress intolerance 'chain'. You will be able to fill in the **Triggers, Negative Emotion, Distress Intolerant Beliefs, and Distress Escape Methods** sections from what you have already written earlier in this section.

The Good News…

 The good news is that it doesn't have to be this way! No matter how your distress intolerance has come about, no matter what emotions you have trouble dealing with, and no matter how unhelpful your escape methods are, you can learn ways of tolerating distress.

 Distress tolerance is a good life skill for anyone to learn. Instead of fearing and fighting uncomfortable emotions and desperately trying to get rid of them, these sections we will teach you how to sit with and tolerate emotional distress, such that you learn the emotion will pass and that you can cope.

We will focus on things you can change in the here and now, particularly your escape methods and distress intolerant beliefs. When using self-help materials, some people might skip sections or complete things in a different order. The section in this information package have been designed to be completed in the order they appear. We recommend that you work through the sections in sequence, finishing each section before moving on to the next one in the series. We believe that by doing this, you will maximize the benefits you might receive from working through this information package. Emotional discomfort is impossible to get rid of, as it is an inevitable part of being human. So we all need to learn how to live with it, and not let our fear of distress restrict how we live our lives. You may have been telling yourself for some time now that you "can't stand it!" But stick with us to find out how you can face your feelings and learn to tolerate your distress.

Accepting Distress

Introduction

We assume you are still reading because you have worked out that distress intolerance is a problem in your life. Now that you know what distress intolerance is, the next step is to learn how to become more tolerant. You probably don't realize that over time you have learnt to tolerate lots of different things (e.g., people you don't like, or physical pain, or not getting your own way, or doing things you don't feel like doing, or bad drivers on the road, etc.), and so emotional distress will just be one more thing to add to the list. Learning how to tolerate distress when you have been in a pattern of constantly trying to escape it, may require practice, patience and persistence. This section will help you build your tolerance by learning strategies to help you accept emotional distress and face your feelings.

Seeing Emotions Differently

The first step to accepting distress is to start seeing your feelings and emotional experiences in a new light. Emotional discomfort is a very normal universal human experience. Negative emotions such as sadness, anger and fear are part of being human. These emotions are not just common, normal and OK, they are actually important and useful to us.

For example, fear is extremely helpful to our survival. Fear is helpful when it kicks in at appropriate times, like when there is a real threat to our safety (e.g., a gun pointed at us or a wild ferocious animal coming our way) or when the fear is proportional to the situation (e.g., nervousness before a big exam). At these times the fear we experience and all the physiological sensations that accompany that fear, help us to effectively deal with that situation. Heart pumping, breathing faster, feeling hot, sweaty, all these things are signs that the body has gone into 'fight or flight' mode. Being in this mode prepares us to either face the danger (e.g., study like hell) or escape the danger (e.g., run like hell from the gun or wild animal). In this way fear can be a very good thing. If we were really relaxed and didn't study or didn't try to get away from the gun or wild animal, we would have big problems.

Similarly, anger is a helpful emotion to have. Imagine if some wrong or injustice was being done towards ourselves or someone else, and we weren't phased at all by it. If we didn't experience anger then we would probably allow all sorts of bad treatment to come our way, or allow harm to be done to other people. Anger can spur us into action to try to change things for the better, for both ourselves and others.

Sadness is a tricky one. How on earth could sadness be helpful? Probably the easiest way to see how sadness is helpful is to think instead of what it would mean if we didn't feel sadness. We generally tend to feel sadness when we lose something important to us in some way (e.g., a person, job, possession, someone's attention or affection, etc.). If we didn't feel sadness when these things occurred, it would mean that nothing was important to us. It would mean we didn't appreciate or value the things we had, and we weren't interested in or connected to our lives or other people. So sadness inadvertently helps us to live a fulfilling life, because it means we care about the things in our life and don't want to lose them.

I guess the take home message to remember is that **negative emotions are important to our survival, rather than something to be feared and avoided at all costs.** Another way you might start to see your emotions differently is to recognize that your emotions are not permanent. Instead you might start to consider your emotions as changing experiences that are always fluctuating but eventually pass. When we feel distressed it can seem like the distress is going to go on and on forever, just getting worse and worse, until we emotionally combust. But we know this isn't how emotions work. Instead emotions act more like a wave, at times increasing and becoming more intense, but inevitably always reaching some plateau, subsiding and finally passing. Sometimes the emotion may rear up again, setting off another wave or smaller ripple. But the key is that emotions move and change, they are not permanent. This is particularly so when you don't fight against and try to block the emotion. Sometimes just being able to remind yourself that emotions pass like a wave, may allow you to better tolerate whatever upsetting feelings you are experiencing.

What Is Acceptance?

First, let's consider what the effect is of urgently needing to get rid of your distress? If you were following closely, you may now be realizing that it just ends up making your distress worse. The alternative to urgently trying to rid yourself of your distress, may well be adopting an attitude of willingly accepting the distress. A radical concept we know given the likely long history you have with pushing your distress away. If you are still a little concerned about this notion of accepting distress, another question to ask yourself is whether pushing your distress away has worked for you so far? It is likely that you are saying "of course it hasn't worked or I wouldn't be reading this Section!" So it might be time to try something quite different...like acceptance.

Accepting distress is not about having to like emotional discomfort, or being resigned to feeling miserable, or wallowing in negative emotions. Instead, accepting distress is about seeing the negative emotion for what it is, and changing how you pay attention to the emotion. Reacting in an accepting way towards your emotion, often changes the effect the emotion has on you.

This approach is often referred to as learning to watch your emotions "mindfully". Mindfulness is state of being where you are in the present moment, watching whatever you happen to be experiencing at that time, with an attitude of curiosity, and without judging or trying to change your experience. In this way our emotions are not some tumultuous chaotic vortex we are sucked into and from which we react impulsively. Instead we become the watcher of our emotions, noticing what is happening to us like a third person, observing and watching our distress with a sense of distance or detachment. As such we don't have to engage with, react to or stop our emotions. Instead we take the stance of just allowing, observing and making space for the emotion until it passes.

How To Accept Distress

There is no right or wrong when it comes to practicing accepting emotional distress, but below are some steps or guidelines that might help with the process. We stress that this is just a guide, and at the end of the day being able to watch and accept your emotions is something you will need to experience via trial and error practice, rather than something you can read about.

Watch or Observe

Foremost is adopting the stance of watching or observing your emotions, paying attention like a third person to whatever you are feeling in the present moment. Observing as the intensity might increase, hold its course, decrease or shift and evolve into a different feeling. Regardless of what the emotion is doing, you are not your emotions, you are the **watcher of your emotions** (Tolle, 2010).

Label or Describe

When being the watcher of your emotions you might find it helpful to label or describe to yourself the emotion you are experiencing. It is a little bit like being the commentator of your emotional experience. The self-talk that goes with this might sound something like "…there is fear, I can feel it in the fast beating of my heart", or "…there is sadness, I can feel it in the heaviness of my shoulders", or "…there is anger, I can feel it in the tightness of my jaw".

Curious and Non-judgmental

You'll notice that the language used to describe your experience has a sense of curiosity and nonjudgmental. The fear or sadness or anger that you feel is not deemed good or bad, or right or wrong, it is what it is.

Imagery

The use of imagery can often be helpful in allowing yourself to foster this detached observer perspective. Different images work for different people.

Some people like the image of an ocean wave* as we have already discussed. Previously you might have panicked in the wave, fiercely treading water and thrashing your arms against the wave, getting exhausted and feeling close to drowning. Instead when you are being mindful of your emotions you don't fight the wave, but instead allow the wave to carry you over its crest and down the other side, or you might choose to surf the wave allowing it to carry you into shore.

Others like to think of their distress as a **non-stop express train**,** in that it is impossible to stop the train, and it would be very dangerous to try to get on board while it is moving. Instead you just watch your emotions pass by like an express train until it is safely through the station.

Some people like to imagine their emotions as **clouds in the sky**** or **leaves on a stream***.** With either image you can't stop the emotions, but you can imagine each cloud or leaf as your emotions. As such, you can just watch your emotions floating by you in their own time, eventually passing out of sight.

Some people like to imagine themselves as an **empty room*** with a front and back door. Emotions enter through the front door and leave through the back, coming and going. Some emotions may take their time in the room, others may move quickly, and some may re-enter the room a number of times. But, they all eventually leave.

Or some like to think of their emotions like a **naughty child**** throwing a tantrum at the supermarket. There is no point trying to stop the child because the tantrum just gets worse, and it would be dangerous to abandon the child in the supermarket. Instead you might just keep a watchful eye over the child from a distance, until they exhaust themselves and settle of their own accord.

Maybe you can think of another image that works better for you. This may require some trial and error to discover what image you identify with. You also don't need to be someone who can imagine things in vivid detail. Most people have trouble doing this, and a more general 'felt' sense of the image is ok. The key is that if you can relate to your emotions like they are a wave or cloud or express train or whatever image works for you, then you are watching them for what they are, paying attention to them in a helpful way, and ultimately tolerating them rather than trying to rid yourself of them.

Present Moment

Once you feel you have fully watched and experienced the negative emotion, feeling it come to its natural conclusion, it might then be time to gently direct your attention to the present moment. This could be anything sensory, a particular task you are doing, a sound, taste, smell, sight or feeling of touch you may not have realized you were experiencing that you can now tune into. And if you can't think of anything to be present-focused on, there is one thing you can guarantee will always be present to practice on…your breath. Whatever you choose to anchor you to the present moment, become aware of its sensory intricacies and details, and allow yourself to fully experience it.

Dealing with Emotional Comebacks

Be aware that no matter how expert you are at doing all the previous steps just mentioned, it is normal for negative emotions to sometimes reappear. This does not mean that you have failed at being mindful of your emotions. The key is to be aware that the emotion has made a comeback, congratulate yourself for catching this rather than getting sucked in or swept up in the emotion, and repeat the steps as before. It doesn't matter how many times you have to catch and watch your emotions, because that in itself is the task…**catching and watching your emotions**. Sometimes people mistakenly think the goal is to be so completely absorbed in the present moment that they don't feel any emotions, and hence they get frustrated by any resurgence of emotion. When an emotion pops back it is just another wave, or express train, or cloud, or whatever it is that allows you to again be the watcher of your emotions.

And remember, if you do get frustrated by an emotion popping up again or bored when doing your mindfulness practice, just realize that these too are emotions that you can practice watching mindfully.

Practicing Acceptance

A good way to develop the skill of accepting distress is to start by being mindful of your emotions generally when you are not feeling distressed. This will give you some practice at the skill of watching your emotions under easier circumstances (i.e., when you are not distressed), so you might be better able to apply the skill under harder circumstances (i.e., when you are distressed). Over the page is a short script to guide you through the process of being mindful of your emotions at any time. You could start by practicing this new approach to your emotions daily when you are not distressed, and record your experiences on the Diary provided below. It may be helpful to record the mindfulness script onto tape, and then listen to the tape as part of your practice.

	Monday	Tuesday	Wednesday	Thursday	Friday	Saturday	Sunday
Time							
Duration							
Experiences							

Mindfulness of Emotions Script

 Position yourself comfortably in the chair…feet flat on the floor, arms placed comfortably, chair fully supporting your body... allow your eyes to close...begin by paying attention to your breathing, taking a few long breaths to get settled...

Now gently guide your attention to how you are feeling emotionally within yourself at this moment...note whatever feelings arise within you whether they be positive, neutral or negative...whether they be strong or weak in intensity...they are all just emotions...all just feelings to be felt. Whatever feelings arise, remind yourself that it is OK to allow yourself to feel it. Remember that you are not your emotions, you are the watcher of your emotions. Take some time just to observe your emotional experience, making no attempt to change how you are feeling...

You might label the emotion to yourself (i.e., "ah there is calmness/ happiness/ indifference/ surprise/ boredom/ frustration/ fear/ sadness, etc.")...You might describe where and how you feel the emotion in your body...take time to notice the physical signs that you are feeling the way you feel...

Watch as the emotion changes in intensity and nature. Bring whatever image to mind that helps you be the watcher of your emotions (e.g., seeing your emotion like an ocean wave, express train, cloud floating in the sky, leaf floating on a stream, an empty room, a naughty child, etc)...

You don't have to buy into your emotions and get swept up in them. You don't need to change your emotions, fight them or get rid of them. You are just here to watch, observe and experience what is going on right now. See if you can make some space for the emotion, seeing it as part of a broader landscape within you that contains lots of things like other feelings, thoughts, memories, body sensations, etc. Your emotions are just emotions…your feeling just feelings…nothing more and nothing less…

When you have fully experienced whatever emotion is there, and the experience has run its natural course, redirect your attention towards your breath…note each inhalation and each exhalation…bind your attention to the back and forth movement of the belly as you breathe in and out…note the sensations in your body as you draw breath in and then out again. Take some time now to allow your breath to be your anchor to the present moment…

If your mind wanders away from the breath to an emotion, or thought or sensation. That's ok, that's what minds do. Congratulate yourself for noticing, and give your mind the time to again observe and watch what you are experiencing… Once that observation has run its natural course, again gently bring your attention back to the breath as your anchor to the present…

Try to continue your mindfulness practice for the next 10 minutes or more…

When you feel ready, you can gradually open your eyes, bringing this mindfulness exercise to a close…

Practicing Acceptance When Distressed

Now that you are getting a good sense of how to be mindful of your emotions generally, another way to develop the skill of accepting distress is to plan specifically how you will extend this new attitude to dealing with the distressing emotions you most often struggle with. To help with this, you can devise your own step-by-step mindfulness plan of what to do when emotional distress arises for you. This is really about jotting down a few key words, phrases or images that will cue you into being mindful of your negative emotions at times when it is harder to do.

 Below is an example of the types of phrases that might be helpful. Take a look through the example script and then see if you can draft a script personalized to your needs on the next page. Your personalized script should be short and to the point, as you don't want to read through a mountain of stuff when you are distressed. You can draft your personalized script by either picking out the phrases from the example scripts that best suit you, or coming up with your own phrases. The aim is to find a few phrases that help get you in the mode of being the non-judgmental watcher of your distress.

Example Mindfulness of Distress Script

Recognize & Allow Emotion: Aha! I'm feeling… [angry/sad/scared]. It is OK, I can allow myself to have this feeling…I can make space for it…I don't have to be afraid of it or try to get rid of it.

Watch Emotion:

I can just watch this feeling and see what it does, I don't have to get caught up in it. Let's see, where do I notice the emotion in my body? This is just an emotion, just a feeling to be felt, nothing more and nothing less. I am not my emotions, I am the watcher of my emotions. The feeling is just like a…[ocean wave…I don't need to fight the wave frantically…I can just go with the wave, letting it bob me up and down, or riding it into shore]

Be Present:

I will turn my attention back to the task I am doing now …noticing what I can feel…hear... see… smell… taste… OR I will turn my attention towards my breath…the breath being my anchor to the present moment…noticing each in breathe and each out breath

Deal with Emotional Comebacks:

I feel the emotion returning…that's OK, that's what emotions do, they like to rear their head again. I will just go back to watching it again…it is just another [ocean wave]…

Personalized Mindfulness of Distress Script

Recognize & Allow Emotion:

Watch Emotion:

Be Present:

Deal with Emotional Comebacks:

Now you know how to watch your emotions generally, and have a script for how to adopt this attitude when distressing emotions arise, it is now time to get some practice with the emotions that distress you. There are 2 ways we can get this practice. One is putting what you have learnt into practice as best you can the next time distressing emotions spontaneously arise for you. The other method is to gradually seek out distressing emotions with the intention of practicing your new acceptance skills. The first option we will look at now, the second option we will look at in future sections.

The Next Time I Am Distressed...

This involves having a clear plan for the next time you feel distressed. You might make a commitment to yourself that the next time I feel distressed I will get out my personalized mindfulness script and try to watch my distress instead of engaging in my old escape methods (e.g., avoidance, numbing & withdrawing, harmful releases). If you think this will be a very difficult thing to do, you may decide to put a time limit on how long you will try to be mindful of your distressing emotions (e.g., "I will just do it for 5mins to start off with, at the end of those 5mins I will see if I can try it for another 5mins"). In this way you can gradually and gently start to 'expose' yourself to the distress you have been dreading. If you get to the end of your time limit and find you just can't go any longer being mindful of your distress, that is OK, you have made a start at accepting rather than avoiding your distress. If this is the case, try using skills from the next section (Improving Distress), rather than going back to your old escape methods.

Having made this plan to be mindful of your distress next time it arises, be aware if there is anything you will need to make your plan work. For example, a timer if you are setting a limit on how long you will practice being mindful of your distress. Also, consider the best place to keep your mindfulness script so it is easily accessible to you no matter where you are when you next feel distressed (e.g., on the fridge, stored in your mobile phone, on a piece of paper in your wallet). Take a moment to think about the logistics of making your plan work. Good luck!

<u>Please note</u>. If the distress you experience is extremely intense unbearable emotional pain, such that you are currently unable to apply the acceptance strategies outlined in this Section, then skip ahead to the next Section on tips for how to improve your distress. This is particularly relevant for people who engage in self-harm, or drug and alcohol use to manage their distress.

Improving Distress

Introduction

The previous Section focused on developing ways of accepting emotional distress. This Section takes a very different focus of learning how to improve your distress when you experience it.

To improve distress we focus more on your behaviors, looking at what to do and what not to do when you experience emotional distress. Depending on the type of escape methods you typically use (i.e., avoidance, numbing & withdrawing, or harmful releases), the strategies we will suggest for improving your distress will vary slightly. This Section will focus on helping you discover a variety of things you can try to improve your distress, so you can experiment and find out what works for you.

Balancing Acceptance & Improvement

Accepting and improving distress are quite different approaches, and maintaining a balance between acceptance and improvement is the key to building distress tolerance. It is unhelpful to be at either extreme (i.e., only accepting how you feel or only trying to improve how you feel). To tolerate distress you really need to learn how to do both. Our aim is to help you learn how to accept your negative emotions, and with that in mind, then work on improving your emotional experience. Imagine if you only tried to improve your distress without being able to accept it first, if this were the case then your efforts to find something to improve your negative feelings would be pretty frantic and desperate. If instead you could accept your distress, then your efforts to improve the distress would more likely be calm, considered and calculated.

We have purposely put Accepting Distress before Improving Distress in this series of sections, as we don't want "improving" to become just another strategy for avoiding your emotions. In summary, you need to feel the emotion first, accept it, ride through it, and then take action to improve it.

However having said that, if as you work through these sections the distress you experience is extremely intense and unbearable emotional pain, then you may not be able to apply the acceptance strategies outlined in the previous Section just yet. If this is the case, then it is ok to move straight to this Section and focus on improving your distress (particularly the Distress Improvement Activities). This is particularly relevant for people who engage in self-harm or drug and alcohol use to manage their distress. In these situations, temporary distractions may be necessary to help you get through the intense distress you might be experiencing, and avoid engaging in behaviors that are damaging to you.

Improving Distress

As we have seen, being distress intolerant can manifest is very different sorts of behaviors or escape methods. Some people avoid certain situations that make them distressed, engage in reassurance seeking or checking to alleviate their distress, or use distraction and suppression to stop their distress. Other people numb and withdraw via engaging in alcohol or drug use, binge eating or using sleep to escape their emotions. And other people may engage in harmful releases, hurting themselves in some physical way as a means of dealing with their distress. Although these behaviors are very different, and hence the strategies for improving distress can vary too, the common guiding principle for improving distress is to do the opposite of your escape urge, and find specific activities that improve your emotional state.

Please Note: As mentioned in a previous section, while these sections may be helpful to people who use drugs, alcohol or self-harm as a means of tolerating emotional distress, it is important to recognize that these are very serious problems in their own right that can cause a person significant harm. We strongly advise seeking help from a GP or mental health professional to address these concerns, rather than relying solely on these sections to overcome the problem

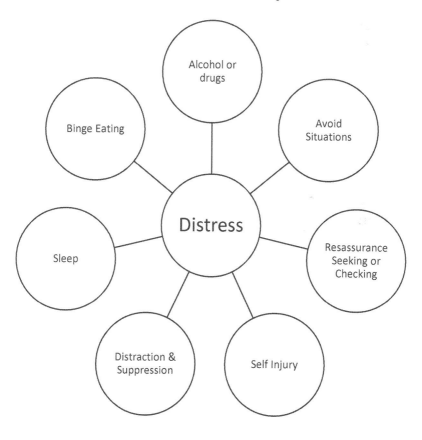

Opposite Action

Earlier, you identified your particular escape methods. Below is a table summarizing the opposite actions for each distress escape method we have covered. Look through the table and circle the opposite action box corresponding to your particular escape method(s). There is also a box at the bottom for if you engage in a particular escape method that we have not covered in these sections. If this applies to you, maybe you could try to think of what the opposite action would be.

Drop Escape Method	Do Opposite Action
Situational Avoidance	Don't avoid situations that distress you. Instead gradually **face** these situations **stay** in them, until you have ridden through the distress. Remember to reward your efforts when you are done, by doing things that are active or soothing.
Reassurance Seeking or Checking	Minimize or eliminate reassurance seeking or checking behaviors. Try to **cope independently** with the distress you feel, riding through, these feelings without resorting to checking things or seeking the reassurance of others. Remember to reward your efforts when you are done, by doing things that are **active or soothing**.
Distraction & Suppression	Don't push away the distressing feelings. Instead **allow and experience** these feelings. Remember to reward your efforts when you are done, by doing things that are **active or soothing.**
Alcohol or Drugs	Don't numb the distress by using alcohol or drugs. Instead allow and experience these feelings. Also do things that are **active or soothing,** rather than withdrawing from life.

Binge Eating	Don't numb the distress by binge eating. Instead **allow and experience** these feelings. Also do things that are **active or soothing**, rather than withdrawing from life.
Harmful Releases	Self-**soothe** and be **active** in the moment, rather than harming yourself.
Excessive Sleep	Don't numb the distress by using sleep. Instead **allow and experience** these feelings. Also do things that are **active and soothing** rather than withdrawing from life.

You will notice that most of the opposite actions initially require that you stay with, ride through, allow and experience the distress, rather than escaping it. As such, the acceptance strategies will be relevant in helping you do this. You will also notice that most of the opposite actions require engaging in some activity that is either about being active in the moment, or about soothing yourself in some way. The Distress Improvement Activities that follow this section will help you with ideas for activities that may help you achieve these aims.

Also notice that for the first 3 escape methods (i.e., situational avoidance, reassurance seeking or checking, distraction & suppression), distress improvement activities should be used as a reward after having faced and stayed with the distress until it naturally subsides of its own accord. For the remaining escape methods, engaging in distress improvement activities may be done sooner than this, as you do not necessarily have to wait until you feel the distress subside.

It is also worth mentioning that doing these opposite actions can be challenging, and so words of encouragement and compassion to ourselves may be important when we are finding it tough. It can be useful to think "what encouragement would I give to someone else feeling this way?", "what would I say to them and what tone would I use?" Some other examples of helpful self-talk might be things like... "I can stay with this feeling"; "it is good practice for me to get comfortable being uncomfortable"; "I can get through this"; "I can tolerate this"; "It will pass"; "this is good for me in the long run"; "I can focus on just getting through this moment"; "I can breathe with this feeling"; "this is helping me build my tolerance"...

Distress Improvement Activities

Finding small ways to participate and be active in the moment when distressed, or to self-soothe and self-nurture when you are feeling distressed, are important for improving your emotional experience. Activities that center on the concepts of activating and soothing we will call 'distress improvement activities', and a list of these is featured on the next page. The activities in the left-hand column are more about participating actively in the moment (i.e., being involved, active and absorbed in something that may improve your distress), whilst the activities on the right-hand side are more about soothing yourself (i.e., activities that make us feel a sense of warmth and being cared for and that help us get through things). You will notice there is a lot of overlap between activities that are about activation and activities that are about soothing, so don't get too caught up in which column you pick activities from. Also, some of the listed activating and soothing activities you may also find rewarding, and you can use them in this way if needed.

The idea is not that you have to use each activity on the list, but that some may appeal to you to try and others won't. Also, by having such a large list, it may help you to brainstorm other distress improvement activities that may work for you. Look at the list and underline any activities you may like to experiment with when you are feeling distressed, and feel free to add other activities that come to mind in the space provided. **Remember, the aim of these activities is not to take your distress away, but to make your distress more tolerable**.

Distress Improvement Activities	
Activate	**Soothe**
Exercise	Have a good meal
Walk	Have a nice snack
Jog	Favorite drink
Gym	Have a picnic
Weights	Light a candle
Exercise Class	Look at art
Boxing	Watch the stars
Cleaning	Go to a beautiful place
Washing	Soothing music
Dishes	Enjoy nature
Gardening	Singing
Cooking	Favorite perfume
Call a friend	Bubble Bath
Go out to lunch, dinner, a coffee	Shower
Shopping	Massage
Favorite movie	Pet dogs or cats
Favorite book	Brush Hair
Favorite music	Soak feet
Favorite TV show	Do nails
Magazines	Imagine a safe place
Games	Smile

Puzzles	Laugh
Volunteer somewhere	Count to ten
Give someone a present	Pray
Do something thoughtful	Take a break
Make something for someone	Breathe
_____	_____
_____	_____
_____	_____
_____	_____
_____	_____

The only way to get a sense of what distress improvement activities work well for you, is to start experimenting with those that sound promising, and then evaluate what impact they have on your distress. Below is a table to keep track of the findings from your experiments. The next time you feel distressed you might try one of the distress improvement activities you highlighted, recording the date you tried it, what the activity was and the outcome. By outcome we mean what actually happened when you tried it. Did it work well at improving your distress? Did it make no difference? Or did it make your distress worse? Based on the outcome you can then evaluate what you learnt from it, whether it is a worthwhile strategy to do again, or whether you need to redo it because you are still unsure if it is useful.

Date	Distress Improvement Activity	Outcome	Evaluation
10/05/2012	Warm Shower	Felt groggy after. Didn't feel great, but probably less angry than I was.	Not sure if this is the best activity to use. I could use it again, but I might try music next time.

Improving Distress Practice

Now that you have some general ideas of things not to do when you feel distressed (i.e., my usual distress escape methods), and things you can do to improve your distress (i.e., opposite actions and distress improvement activities), it is good to personalize and clarify these ideas for your own situation. Below gives two examples of what a personalized list might look like. The first example is of someone who numbs & withdraws by binge eating and sleeping, and also engages in harmful releases by scratching themselves. The second example is of someone who situationally avoids by not leaving the house, distracts themselves when they do venture out, and seeks reassurance from their family to deal with their distress. Following these examples is the opportunity to draft your personalized list of ideas. Use the examples below, the "opposite action" section(s) you circle, and what you learnt from your distress improvement experiments, to assist you with drafting your own ideas.

Example Improving Distress Ideas

What Not To Do	What to Do
Scratching myself when I feel distressed. *Binge eating when I feel distressed.* *Sleeping when I feel distressed.*	*Allow the distress rather than trying to get rid of it. Try active and soothing activities like... listening to my favorite song, taking a shower, reading a book, enjoy a nice cup of coffee.*

Personalized Improving Distress Ideas

What Not To Do	What To Do

Problem Solving

Once you have been able to tolerate rather than escape your negative emotions, and your distress has somewhat subsided, it may be worth asking yourself whether the distress you are experiencing is regarding a situation you can actually do something about? That is, is your distress regarding something you have some control over, and could take action with to improve how you are feeling?

If the answer is 'yes', then once the distress has subsided, you might be in a better position to problem solve regarding the situation that is distressing you. Problem solving involves working your way through the problem in a systematic, step-by-step, structured manner. This means identifying the problem that is distressing you, thinking through all the options for solving the problem, looking at the advantages and disadvantages of the options most preferable to you, picking one or more options to put into place, listing the steps required to put those options into action, and specifying a plan for when you will take each step. Finally, it requires taking action to put your plan in place, then evaluating the outcome, and reassessing if the problem has been solved or requires further action. As you can imagine, problem solving is difficult to do when you are in the thick of distress, but is a good thing to try once the distress is more manageable.

Below is an example of problem solving in action. If problem solving seems relevant to improving your distress, space is then provided for you to follow the same problem solving steps.

Step 1: Identify/Define Problem

Try to state the problem as clearly as possible. Be objective and specific about the behavior, situation, timing, and circumstances that make it a problem. Describe the problem in terms of what you can observe rather than subjective feelings.

Problem Definition

The gas and phone bills are due at the same time. I don't have enough money to cover both this month.

Step 2: Generate Possible Solutions/Options

List all the possible solutions. Be creative and forget about the quality of the solutions. If you allow yourself to be creative, you may come up with some options that you would not otherwise have thought of.

List All Possible Solutions

- Ring both companies – see if I can negotiate to pay it off gradually
- Priorities – I can live without the phone for a while, but not the gas, so I will pay the gas bill first
- Borrow money from family or friends to pay both bills
- Pay bills on my credit card – then pay that off later
- See a financial counsellor – they may be able to help me sort it out • Get a second job • Sell some of my possessions to pay the bills
- Don't pay the bills and move in with a friend instead now eliminate the less desirable or unreasonable alternatives only after as many possible solutions have been listed. Then, list the remaining options in order of preference.

Preferred Solutions/Options

1. Ring both companies – see if I can negotiate to pay it off gradually.
2. See a financial counsellor – they may be able to help me sort it out.
3. Priorities – I can live without the phone for a while, but not the gas, so I will pay the gas bill first.
4. Get a second job.

Step 3: Evaluate Alternatives

Evaluate the top 3 or 4 plans in terms of their advantages and disadvantages

	Advantages	**Disadvantages**
Potential Solution #1	*I may be able to keep both the phone and gas on.* *I will feel I have done something.*	*I will feel embarrassed having to ring the companies.* *I may not get what I want.* *I will still have to pay eventually.*
Potential Solution #2	*They are experienced and will know what to do.* *I'll have support.* *Someone to help me.* *Companies may listen to them.*	*I will need to do some research to find a free service- this will take some effort.*
Potential Solution #3	*The gas will stay on.* *I can still use the pay phone.* *I will survive.* *Problem will be reduced.*	*I won't have a phone on hand if I need it.* *I may have difficulties getting the phone reconnected in the future.*
Potential Solution #4	*More Money.*	*I will be too busy- no time for myself.* *This won't solve the immediate problem.*

Step 4: Decide On A Plan

 Decide on one, two or more of the plans. Specify who will take action, when the plan will be implemented and how the plan will be implemented.

Action Steps	Who	When
Contact gas and phone companies to negotiate options for paying the bills (pay off gradually or extended payment).	*Me*	*Monday Morning*
If that doesn't resolve the problem, contact center link to ask about financial aid counselling.	*Me*	*Monday Afternoon*
Visit financial counsellor for advice.	*Me*	*Tuesday*
If that doesn't resolve the problem, pay gas bill and use pay phone temporarily.	*Me*	*Wednesday*

Step 5: Implement Plan

Implement your plan as specified above.

Step 6: Evaluate the Outcome

Evaluate how effective the plan was. Decide whether the existing plan needs to be revised, or whether a new plan is needed to better address the problem. If you are not pleased with the outcome, return to Step 2 to select a new option or revise the existing plan, and repeat the remaining steps.

Problem Solving

Identify and Define Problem Area/Issue

Problem Definition

Generate Possible Solutions/Options

1. _____

2. _____

3. _____

4. _____

5. _____

Evaluate Alternatives

	Advantages	*Disadvantages*
Potential Solution #1		
Potential Solution #2		
Potential Solution # 3		
Potential Solution # 4		

Decide on a Plan

Action Steps	Who	When

Step 5: Implement Plan

Implement your plan as specified above.

Step 6: Evaluate the Outcome

- How effective was the plan?
- Does the existing plan need to be revised or would a new plan be needed to better address the problem?
- If you are not pleased with the outcome, return to Step 2 to select a new option or revise the existing plan, and repeat Steps 3 to 6.

Tolerating Distress

Introduction

By working your way through prior sections, we have introduced you to all the skills you need to start tolerating your distress. In this Section we will pull together all that you have learned in a Distress Tolerance Action Plan. It is then just a matter of lots and lots of practice, and we will give you some ideas on how to get the practice you need. As you will see, if you can apply your action plan regularly, then over time you can change the distress intolerant beliefs that are at the heart of your difficulties dealing with distress.

Distress Tolerance Action Plan

A good Distress Tolerance Action Plan requires 5 steps. Let's look at each in turn:

Triggers

For an action plan to be useful, you need to first have some awareness of the common things that trigger your distress. Being more aware of what ignites your distress, will give you a 'heads up' for when you might particularly need to be using your action plan. These triggers could be external, such as certain situations, events, people, cues in the environment, etc. Or these triggers could be internal, such as certain thoughts, memories, images, bodily sensations, etc. A good way to get in touch with your common triggers is to think of past examples of not being able to deal with distress. That is, past times you used your old escape methods (i.e., situational avoidance, reassurance seeking or checking, distraction and suppression, alcohol or drugs, binge eating, excessive sleep, harmful releases, etc.). See if you can work out what triggered off or led you to these behaviors in the first place. Below are some common triggers of distress, tick any that apply to you or note others that are specific to you that are not listed.

- o Relationship Problems
- o Hearing Bad News
- o Friendship Problems
- o Seeing Family
- o Family Problems
- o Seeing Friends
- o Partner Behavior
- o Arguments
- o Anniversaries
- o People Being Unfair
- o Socializing

- o Medical Appointments
- o Financial Problems
- o Work or Study Stress
- o Unemployment
- o Thinking about The Past
- o Body Symptoms
- o Thinking about the Future
- o Going Out In Public
- o Being Disorganized

Warning Signs

In addition to being aware of common triggers of your distress, it is also useful to be aware of the warning signs that tell you that you are having trouble dealing with your distress, and hence need to focus on using your action plan. Warning signs are the feelings, thoughts, physical sensations, and behavioral urges or actions that signal you are feeling overwhelming distress, and need to decide how best to handle this feeling. Like before, we have listed some common warning signs over the page. Underline any that apply to you or note others that are specific to you that are not listed.

Feelings	Thoughts	Physical Sensation	Urges or Actions
Disappointment	I can't cope	Low Energy	Pace
Hurt	This is hopeless	Fatigue	Can't Sit Still
Despair	This is unbearable	Heaviness	Lash Out
Guilt	This isn't going to	Crying	Yell
Shame	get better	Excessive	Throw Things
Sadness	I am losing control	Energy	Avoid
Depression	I can't deal with	Tension	Reassurance
Grief	this	Increased Heart	Seeking
Misery	I am a mess	Rate	Checking
Irritation		Fast	Distraction
Agitation		Breathing	Suppression
Frustration		Sweating	Alcohol or Drug
Disgust		Hot	Use
Jealousy		Shaking	Binge Eating
Anger		Stomach	
Rage		Problems	
Hatred		Chest Pressure	
Nervousness		Restlessness	
Anxiety		Fidget	
Dread			
Fear			
Panic			
Terror			
Other:	Other:	Other:	Other:

Commit To Dropping Escape Method & Doing Opposite Action

Once you acknowledge your distress, via being more aware of your triggers and warning signs, you are then in a better position to make a commitment to dropping your usual escape methods (i.e., situational avoidance, reassurance seeking or checking, distraction and suppression, alcohol or drugs, binge eating, excessive sleep, harmful releases, etc.). In an earlier section we saw how important it is to try to do the opposite of our escape methods. Our escape methods are usually automatic habits we quickly jump to when we feel distressed, hence the decision not to go down this path sometimes slips past us. By being more aware of triggers, warning signs and our distress, we can choose to take a different path of doing the opposite action.

The commitment you make might sound something like...

"I will try to tolerate this distress, rather than using my old habit of drinking to dull the pain"

> Or

"I will stay with this feeling, rather than avoiding situations that make me feel this way"

Making a commitment to drop your usual escape methods and do the opposite, could be something you do mentally, or say out loud to yourself, or write down, or tell someone else about. It is up to you. The main thing is making your actions a conscious choice, rather than an automatic habit.

Take time to write a statement that reflects the commitment you might like to make to dropping your usual escape method and instead doing the opposite action. You might gain inspiration from what you have already written in the What Not To Do and What To Do section.

_____

_____

_____

_____

_____

_____

Accepting Distress

Your Personalized Mindfulness of Distress Script is of most relevance here. The script you devised and have been practicing will help you to:

i)   recognize and allow the emotion;
ii)   watch the emotion by detaching from it, describing it and using imagery;
iii) be present focused on a task or your breath) deal with the inevitable emotional comebacks.

Improving Distress

List all the distress improvement activities (both active and soothing) that you have discovered work for you, the words of encouragement that can help you through the moment of distress, and aspects of problem solving that may be relevant when you do have some control over the situation distressing you.

Now we want to put all 5 steps together on a single page that becomes the most important page of all these sections. Try to keep this page somewhere easily accessible (you may even make multiple photocopies to put in various places). The idea is that when you are facing emotionally difficult times, you can look at this sheet to guide you through the new process of practicing distress tolerance, rather than giving in to old habits. As always, there is an example Distress Tolerance Action Plan on the next page, followed by a blank copy for you to complete using what you have already written in this Section. Put time and effort into your personalized Distress Tolerance Action Plan, refining it each time you use it, until you have a plan that works really well for you

Distress Tolerance Action Plan – example

My Triggers (external or internal)   *Any relationship, friendship or family problem. Arguments. Thinking negatively about myself, the past or the future.*
My Warning Signs (feelings, thoughts, physical sensations, urges or actions)   *Sadness, Hurt, Despair, Depression Thinking this is "hopeless", "unbearable", "unchangeable", "what's the point to anything" Low energy, heavy, tired, want to cry Isolate myself from everyone, urge to drink to dull pain*
My Commitment to Dropping Escape Method(s) & Doing the Opposite Action   I will stay with this feeling, rather than isolating myself and trying to escape with alcohol
Accepting My Distress (personalized mindfulness of distress script)   **Recognize & Allow Emotion:**   *Aha! I'm feeling sad. This is a normal emotion to have. I can allow myself to have this feeling…I don't have to be afraid of it or try to get rid of it.*   **Watch Emotion:**   *I can just watch this feeling…make space for it…see what it does…I don't have to get caught up in it. I notice the emotion in my stomach and shoulders. I notice my body feels lethargic and heavy. This is just an emotion, just a feeling to be felt, nothing more and nothing less. I am not my emotions, I am the watcher of my emotions. I can just observe the feeling like a cloud floating past in the sky – it will just hang around of its own accord until it drifts out of sight.*

Be Present:
*I will turn my attention back to the task I am doing now
...noticing what I can feel...hear... see... smell... taste...OR
to my breath – noting each in and out breath*

Deal with Emotional Comebacks:
*I feel the sadness returning...that's OK, that's what emotions
do, they like to rear their head again. I will just go back to
watching it again...it is just another cloud in the sky...*

<u>Note</u>: remember if the distress I experience is extremely intense
unbearable emotional pain, such that I am currently unable to apply
the acceptance strategies, then skip ahead to the next step of
'improving'. This is particularly relevant for people who engage in
self-harm, or drug and alcohol use to manage their distress, as it is
more important to avoid engaging in behaviors that are damaging to
myself.

Improving My Distress (active & soothing distress improvement
activities, words of self-encouragement, problem solving if relevant)
*Walk around block
Enjoy sunshine
Get out of house – beach, park, shops, friends
Singing Shower
 Clean the kitchen
Pat my dog
 Water the garden
Laugh out loud
Baking Plan and make a nice dinner
Call best friend*

*Encourage myself: "I can get through this", "This feeling
will pass". Is it a situation I can control? If yes then problem
solve: what's the problem, list all possible options for
solving, look at pros and cons, pick a solution(s), break into
steps, plan when to do each step, take action, revisit options
if needed.*

Note: remember that if I am dropping the following escape methods – situational avoidance, reassurance seeking or checking, distraction & suppression – then it is best to leave doing any distress improvement activities until after I have faced the distress and experienced it naturally subside. In this way the distress improvement activities become a reward for approaching rather than avoiding my distress.

My Distress Tolerance Action Plan

My Triggers (external or internal)

My Warning Signs (feelings, thoughts, physical sensations, urges or actions)

My Commitment to Dropping Escape Method(s) & Doing the Opposite Action

Accepting My Distress (personalized mindfulness of distress script)
Recognize & Allow Emotion:

Watch Emotion:

Be Present:

Deal with Emotional Comebacks:

He Said He Was Sorry   *Joanna Johnson, MSW, CAC, MAC, CCFC*

Note: remember if the distress I experience is extremely intense unbearable emotional pain, such that I am currently unable to apply the acceptance strategies, then skip ahead to the next step of 'improving'. This is particularly relevant for people who engage in self-harm, or drug and alcohol use to manage their distress, as it is more important to avoid engaging in behaviors that are damaging to myself.

Improving My Distress (active & soothing distress improvement activities, words of self-encouragement, problem solving if relevant)

Note: remember that if I am dropping the following escape methods – situational avoidance, reassurance seeking or checking, distraction & suppression – then it is best to leave doing any distress improvement activities until after I have faced the distress and experienced it naturally subside. In this way the distress improvement activities become a reward for approaching rather than avoiding my distress.

Distress Exposure

Aside from practicing your Distress Tolerance Action Plan the next time (and anytime) you happen to experience distress, another way to gain confidence that you can deal with your distress is to purposely seek it out. In other words, purposely expose yourself to emotional discomfort, and apply your action plan. Now, this approach may not be for everyone, but it is a good way of gaining practice and building confidence in your distress tolerance abilities, and reducing any fear of negative emotion you may have.

Distressing Situations I Could Approach

If you would like to give distress exposure a go, then the first step is to think of a variety of situations, places, people, activities, etc., that may bring on emotional distress for you. The key being that we are looking for situations that will allow you the opportunity to practice your Distress Tolerance Action Plan. Here are some examples of potentially distressing situations. Note those relevant to you, and add others you can think of.

Emotional movies, TV shows, music, books

Watching the News Looking at old photos/memorabilia

Visiting the cemetery

Thinking about the past or future

Emotional conversations with family or friends

Stating my opinion or raising an issue that might lead to an argument

Situations that make me anxious like public places, shops, socializing, public transport, etc. Activities that bring on physical sensations that make me anxious, like heavy exercise, sitting in a hot car, caffeine, breathing rapidly, spinning on the spot, etc.

Activities that make me angry like driving, standing in a queue, debating topics, etc.

Others:

_____

.
_____

Distress Exposure Stepladder

Now you can create a Distress Exposure Stepladder. This is a list of activities likely to be distressing for you, that you can now start doing gradually as a way of practicing your new distress tolerance skills. The first step is to work out your goal – that is, what would you like to be able to do, but can't because you fear feeling distressed. Each step can then be about working towards that goal.

Your steps could involve a variety of activities (like the stepladder example given over the page) or could involve just one activity. If it is just one activity that distresses you, then each step on your stepladder might involve increasing the amount of time you spend doing that activity, or changing who you do that activity with, or where you do that activity, or when you do it, etc. The main thing is trying to create manageable steps that go from easier activities to harder activities, and that each activity generates some distress which you can use to practice your Distress Tolerance Action Plan.

When planning your steps make a note of the distress rating (0-100) that you would give each step, that is, how much distress you think you will experience when doing each step.

This rating scale is a good way to check that you have your steps in order from easiest to hardest, that you are starting with a manageable first step, and that your steps are fairly evenly spaced without huge jumps in between each step.

My Distress Exposure Stepladder

GOAL:	DISTRESS (0-100)

STEP	DISTRESS
1		
2		
3		
4		
5		
6		
7		
8		

Distress Exposure Guidelines

Now that you know what the first step is, it is time to do it. But before you do, here are a few guidelines to keep in mind to ensure that your distress exposure is effective.

1. **Apply your Distress Tolerance Action Plan.** Don't forget to put the action plan you have worked so hard on, into practice each time you take a step on your stepladder. After all, distress exposure is your

2. Opportunity to practice distress tolerance, and fine-tune any teething problems.

3. **Stay in the situation.** As much as possible, try to stick with each activity by using your Distress Tolerance Action Plan, until you experience your distress subside. If you pull out too soon before you have experienced your distress drop, you will feel like the distress has gotten the better of you, and it may rock your confidence.

4. **Repetition, repetition**. With each step on your stepladder, repeat it until you no longer feel that activity is a problem for you, before moving on to the next step. This way your progress will be steady and solid.

5. **Reward your successes and learn from any negative experiences**. Building distress tolerance is a learning process. Purposely confronting your distress in order to put your Distress Tolerance Action Plan into practice is a big deal. So recognize this and reward yourself! However, when we are learning a new skill, we can't

6. expect things to always go smoothly. If things don't go
to plan, try to sit back and learn from it. How could you
do it differently next time? Do you need to refine
anything on your Distress Tolerance Action Plan? Do
you need to go back to an easier step on your stepladder
and do some more repetition, before tackling the harder
step again?

Distress Exposure Diary

You can use the following table to record your stepladder
progress. You can describe what you planned to do, and your
Distress ratings for how distressed you both expected to be and
how distressed you actually were. The last column asks you to
jot down any comments about the experience – were you able
to do the activity you planned? Were you able to put your

Distress Tolerance Action Plan into practice? If so, how did it
go? If you experienced a great deal of difficulty, you can note
down why you think this might have been the case, and how
you can approach it next time or rework your action plan.

Distress Exposure Step	Expected DISTRESS 0-100	Actual DISTRESS 0-100	Did you do it? Did you use your Distress Tolerance Action Plan? How did it go? OR Describe what made it difficult to complete the step and how you can prepare for next time.

Adjusting Distress Intolerant Beliefs

At the heart of distress intolerance are certain negative beliefs about what it means to experience negative emotions. These beliefs tend to center on the notion that negative emotion is either:

- bad in some way (e.g., "distress makes me weak", "it is wrong or bad to be emotional", "it's stupid", "it's unacceptable"), or
- unbearable ("I can't bear feeling distressed, I hate it, I can't stand it, I must get rid of it"), or
- will lead to disastrous consequences (e.g., "if I feel negative emotion, then I won't be able to cope/ I will

lose control/ I will go crazy/ I will be a mess/ I won't be able to function/ it will be dangerous").

Earlier you identified your Distress Intolerant Beliefs. Let's double check these beliefs by answering the following questions.

 If I experience emotional distress then...

What will happen?

_____

_____

_____

_____

What will it be like?

_____

_____

_____

_____

What will it mean about me?

_____

_____

_____

_____

What will I need to do?

_____

_____

_____

_____

See if you can summarize your answers above into one key Distress Intolerant Belief you strongly hold. Emotional distress is bad because…

_____

_____

_____

_____

_____

_____

It is important to realize that if you keep using your Distress Tolerance Action Plan, and keep facing your distress rather than trying to escape it, then over time your distress intolerant beliefs will weaken and erode. This is because by the very act of tolerating your distress, you will be gathering evidence and experiences that show you these beliefs are not true. This adjustment process does rely on time, and your persistence in practicing what you have learned throughout these Sections. However, let's see if we can help the process along a little by working through the worksheet. As always, we have provided a completed example, followed by a blank worksheet for you to work on. The worksheet will guide you through a series of questions that will challenge your distress intolerant beliefs, allowing you to start adjusting them and developing more distress tolerant beliefs. "What is a distress tolerant belief?" I hear you ask. This might sound something like…

Negative emotions are normal and nothing to be feared

Feeling distressed doesn't have to lead to disaster

Negative emotions pass if you don't fight or avoid them

I can stand uncomfortable emotions

Maintaining Your Gains

Congratulations! You have made it to the end of these Sections. You should feel proud of yourself for sticking with it. Now, at the end of the day the important thing is to keep going! Expect that changing how you deal with distress will take time, practice, persistence and patience. Expect that you will have good days and bad. Expect you will have days you feel like you are tolerating your distress really well, and days you feel like you have slipped back to being 'intolerant'. The old saying of "two steps forward, one step back" is very true. If you expect setbacks when you sign up for the journey of learning how to tolerate your distress, then when you face a bump in the road, you will be less likely to criticize your efforts and give up. As such, you will be better able to keep going with your Distress Tolerance Action Plan, to help you get back on track.

If you are struggling…don't give up! Revisit the earlier sections, take your time, and find someone who can support you through developing these new distress tolerance skills. If you are finding that you are continuing to use your old escape methods, particularly drug or alcohol use and self-harm, then we strongly advise seeking professional assistance.

Emotional Wellbeing

While these sections have focused on helping you learn skills to better tolerate emotional distress, we hope that they lead to much more than just 'tolerance' of emotional discomfort. These Sections are ultimately about building a sense of emotional wellbeing and resilience. This journey hasn't been about changing who you are as a person, but instead finding space and strength within yourself to face your feelings. Developing confidence that you can better cope with your emotions through applying the skills introduced in these Sections, will likely have flow on effects to feeling more content in your life and feeling a healthier human being all round. The take home message of these sections is that emotional discomfort is not the problem, it is how we react to our emotions that is the issue. If we can see emotional pain as a normal and inevitable human experience that we don't need to fear and avoid, but instead can ride through, then our distress no longer has power over us. Distress is just something to be tolerated, by balancing both accepting our distress with improving our distress. Remember, that your new distress tolerance skills and beliefs will be a 'work in progress' initially. But, if you keep at it consistently over time, you will soon be able to face your feelings with the new attitude…"I can stand it!"

Chapter 6

Stone TWO

Physical Abuse

Domestic violence can range from unwanted physical contact, to rape and murder. Indirect violence may include destruction of objects, throwing objects near the victim or harming pets. In addition to physical violence domestic violence can be any behaviors that increase fear and cause intimidation. Physical violence is the intentional use of physical force with the potential to cause injury, harm, disability or death. For example: pushing, shoving, biting, or restraining. Another example is the exploitation of children. Such as forcing children to watch or to take sides within a family.

Psychological abuse may also entail economic or social control such as controlling the victim's money or other resources, preventing a victim from seeing friends or preventing the victim from calling for help. Physical abuse isolates the person.

Sexual Abuse

The use of physical force to compel a person to engage in a sexual act against his or her will; whether or not the act is completed. The attempt to complete a sex act involving a person who is unable to understand the nature of the condition of the act, unable to decline participation and/or unable to communicate; such as people who are drugged or drunk.

Emotional Abuse

Emotional abuse is called psychological abuse or mental abuse. It is about humiliating the victim privately or publicly. This can be achieved by controlling what the victim can and cannot do without consent from the victim. They deliberately do something to make the victim feel embarrassed or diminished in front of friends and family such as attacking one's self-esteem until it is no longer visible. Learned helplessness becomes the only tool the victim has. This increases risk for suicide, eating disorders, drug abuse or self-mutilation.

Emotional abusing includes verbal threats, physical violence of victim or to self, with the intentions to induce again control and/or intimidation. Nonverbal threats may include gestures, facial expressions, and body posturing. Blackmail independency is keeping a person from happiness or denying the victim access

Economic Abuse

Economic abuse is when the abuser has complete control over the victim's money and other economic resources. It is also when the victim is no longer allowed to continue education or any social activities without permission.

Describe physical abuse and its effect on your partner, family, children and the community. List behaviors you believe would be classified as abuse you may have displayed.

_____

_____

_____

_____

_____

Describe emotional abuse and its effect on your partner, family, children and the community. List behaviors you believe would be classified as abuse you may have displayed.

_____

_____

_____

_____

_____

Describe sexual abuse and its effect on your partner, family, children and the community. List behaviors you believe would be classified as abuse you may have displayed.

_____

_____

_____

_____

_____

_____

Describe economic abuse and its effect on your partner, family, children and the community. List behaviors you believe would be classified as abuse you may have displayed.

_____

_____

_____

_____

Give examples of abuse you have witnessed. How did this effect you?

_____

_____

_____

_____

What have you learned from this lesson?

_____

_____

_____

_____

_____

_____

_____

Chapter 7

Stone THREE

An Overview of Domestic Violence

Domestic violence was once considered one of the most under-reported crimes and became more widely recognized during the 1980s and 90's.

Those who have been abused or attacked, may feel terribly afraid, shocked, angry, or just emotionally numb. Every person is different in all these feelings and emotions. They are natural and have been examined and discussed. They are displayed and experienced by one out of four Americans who experience abuse or attack and can lead to serious mental health problems; including post-traumatic stress disorder, depression, anxiety, alcohol and/or drug abuse, unacceptable sexual behavior, or even suicide. Sometimes a person tries using drugs, alcohol, smoking, or overeating to cope. This can lead to greater and more physical or emotional problems unless, at some point, the person comes to explore the fact that he/she is an abused person. The "normal", feelings of anxiety about their family's safety becomes overwhelming.

Learned helplessness, profound sadness and grief, anger and

abnormal reactions to fearful situations become part of everyday behavior. This creates the inability to acknowledge feelings so that one can recover from the abuse. This is one of the effects of this disaster or dramatic event that goes far beyond just the world of devastation. It is part of the way the victim lives and the abuser tries to keep it that way so they can stay in control.

Signs that Men and Women Need to Look for and Ask for Help:

- A need for stress management - part of the domestic violence management;
- Disorientation and confusion - difficulty communicating one's own thoughts about what is happening to them and their families and why they still feel that they love this person. (A perfect example of that is the movie "Sleeping with the Enemy");
- Limited attention span and difficulty concentrating - becomes the way that victims live and yet it also becomes something that is used against them by the abuser;
- Becoming easily frustrated and turning to aid such as food, sex, and alcohol or drugs;
- Overwhelming guilt and self-doubt that is created by the abuser with the continuous putdowns and attacks on self-esteem;
- Depression, sadness and/or the feeling of hopelessness - Mood swings and crying.

Physical signs - difficulty maintaining balance, headaches, stomach problems, tunnel vision, muffled hearing, difficulty sleeping, reluctance to leave home, fear of crowds, fear of strangers and the increase of alcohol and drug use.

First, the victim needs to talk to someone about their feelings. Anger, sorrow or anything they are experiencing. Emotions as difficult as this may be the first and only way to help them understand they are not alone, are being abused and that abuse is illegal. When the person finally realized that they can talk about what is happening to them, they take the first steps towards empowerment.

Men who batter need to understand that they can't hold themselves totally guilty of the pain and suffering that they have created to their families. At some point, they too have to look at their own victimizations. They need to hold themselves responsible for the disastrous events and frustrations that they have perpetrated on their partners, children, sisters, mothers and other family members.

Men need to take steps to promote their own physical and emotional healing by understanding the overwhelming problem of domestic violence. They can start this by beginning to take a healthy approach to life like eating right, adequate rest, exercise, relaxation, meditation, and honest communication about their need for control.

This small step of healing will begin when one learns to maintain a normal household of daily routines; including less demanding responsibilities for themselves and their families.

The feelings of being mentally drained or implicitly exhausted are normal and common both for the abuser and the abused. The loss of home, business income and unresolved emotional issues are problems that need to be addressed. Relationships may have to be redefined!

Focus on Emotional Abuse

Emotional Abuse is a way of hurting someone without necessarily being physical. It's when one person in a relationship tries to control the other person's feelings or thoughts in order to gain power over them.

I am evaluating my relationship with: _____

Some examples of emotional abuse (also called mental, verbal or psychological abuse) are listed below. Check any that you have done to this person, or that this person has done to you.

- Put-downs; calling names, telling them they're stupid or ugly, telling them they're not good enough or no one could ever love them
- Frequently cursing or yelling at the other person
- Threatening or intimidating – making the other person feel nervous or scared for themselves or someone they care about
- Frequently criticizing or correcting the other person – the way they look, talk, act, etc.
- Lying or cheating

- Playing mind games or making the other person think they're crazy
- Putting responsibility for your behavior on the other person
- Making fun of or putting down the other person's family, culture, religion, race or heritage
- Embarrassing or humiliating the other person, especially in front of other people
- Withholding affection as punishment – not giving them love if they don't do what you want them to do
- Controlling behavior – telling the other person what to do, what to wear, who to hang out with, etc.
- Making all the decisions in the relationship and ignoring the other persons feelings
- Guilt trips – trying to make the other person feel guilty when you don't get your way, especially by threatening to hurt yourself or commit suicide
- Keeping the other person from spending time with their friends or family members, or from work or other activities that are important to him/her
- Using the children to get the other person to do what you want
- Being extremely jealous, and using jealousy to justify controlling behavior
- Threatening to break up with the other person if you don't get your way
- Saying you don't love the other person just to get him/her to do what you want

- Accusing the other person of cheating on you as way of manipulating him/her to do what you want
- Keeping constant tabs on a person, expecting to know his/her every move

Here are some examples of emotional abuse I have experienced in my life (not necessarily from the person above):

Am I being emotionally abuse my partner?

Have I been emotionally abused in the past?

Am I being emotional abusive to my partner?

Have I been emotionally abusive in the past?

_____

_____

Focus on Physical Abuse

Physical abuse is any behavior that is meant to cause hurt to another person's body or to control another persona's physical freedom or movement. One person abuse another using his or her own physical strength, using an object or weapon, or using size or presence to intimidate or control the other.

I am evaluating my relationship with: _____

Some example of physical abuse are below.

Check any that you have done to this person or they have done to you.

- Pushing or shoving
- Grabbing
- Hitting, slapping or punching
- Pulling hair
- Kicking
- Choking

- Holding someone down or holding their arm so they can't walk away
- Throwing objects at another person
- Use of weapons to hurt or threaten someone
- Biting
- Pinching
- Spitting
- Arm Twisting
- Burning
- Carrying someone against their will
- Trapping someone in a room or car
- Abandoning someone in an unsafe place
- Chasing
- Standing in the doorway to block the other person from leaving
- Hiding car keys, shoes, clothes or money so the other person can't leave
- Standing in front of/behind car to prevent person from leaving
- Sabotaging car to prevent person from leaving
- Refusing to help someone when they're sick or injured
- Following or stalking

Here are some examples of physical abuse I have experienced in my life (not necessarily from the person above):

_____

_____

Am I being physically abused by my partner?

_____

_____

Have I been physically abused in the past?

_____

_____

Am I being physically abusive to my partner?

_____

_____

Have I been physically abusive in the past?

_____

_____

Focus on Sexual Abuse

Sexual abuse is any sexual behavior that is forced, coerced or manipulated. It includes sexual harassment. Sexual abuse overlaps with other types of abuse, because it can be physical (such as unwanted touching), verbal (such as calling someone sexual names) or emotional (such as using sexual behavior to humiliate someone.)

Some examples of sexual abuse are listed below.

Check any that you have ever done to someone or someone else has done to you.

- Threatening to break up with someone or spread rumors about them if they refuse sexual acts
- Threatening to hurt the other person or someone they care about if they refuse sexual acts
- Lying to or manipulating someone to get him/her to agree to sexual behavior
- Ripping or tearing at someone clothes
- Unwanted grabbing or touching of someone's rear end, breasts, or genital areas
- Forcing someone to take off his/her clothes
- Physically forcing someone into any kind of sexual behavior –even when they have agreed to one form of sex but not another
- Sex while one person is too drunk or high to make a sound decision about sex
- Taking pictures or videos of someone undressing or involved in sexual behavior without his/her consent
- Any sexual activity between an adult and child or a child and much younger child
- Rape with an object
- Sex that hurts

- Withholding sex as a way of manipulating someone into doing what you want
- Making partner dress in sexier way or less sexy way
- Sexual Harassment

Here are some forms of sexual abuse I have experienced:

_____

_____

Am I being sexually abused by my partner?

_____

_____

Have I been sexually abused in the past?

_____

_____

Am I being sexually abusive to my partner?

_____

_____

Have I been sexually abusive in the past?

WHAT DID YOU LEARN FROM THIS CHAPTER?

Chapter 8

Stone FOUR

You need to make a brave and invasive compilation of your morals and values.

Invasive means to search completely within you, leaving no stone unturned.

A **compilation** is just a list.

This is the time we need everyone to stop and look at all your work and decide if you are mentally and spiritually ready to move on.

You need to have a solid understanding of what domestic violence is. This is a good time to stop, look and listen to your spirit, heart and mind in that order and write down your thoughts.

_____

_____

_____

Please go back and review your work, as you are about to go further than you ever have. The principals of truth and revelation are now required. You are about to start the process of peeling away the old scales and exposing the truth in every light. We will be looking at the exact nature of our wrongs and how the use of power and control was not the beginning, but rather the middle or end of a progression of bad decisions and choices that started long before.

Freedom waits for you at the end of this stone but you have to be ready for it. In other words, the journey is about to take a lot of turns. You need to be able to mentally and emotionally take these turns and steep valleys. Whatever the force was, it is about to be opened and light is about to come into some really dark areas. Are you ready? Let's see.

What is your biggest fear about the fourth stone? What do you know about yourself that you are ready to expose and have not

_____

_____

_____

_____

_____

How can you benefit if participate in this stone and truly let go of the dark side of your secrets?

_____

_____

_____

_____

Brave and Invasive

"Brave and Invasive", what is this about?

This means go for it stop being afraid of the truth and allow the truth to set you free once and for all. Take the alternate risk and go ahead in spite of our fear and in spite of what we think others may think. Courage is about change and now we are about to change everything.

I want you to put this manual away for the day and do something you have never done before, be it whatever. If you have never ridden a Harley go and try one out. If you have never gone horseback riding, it's a good day to do so. If you have never cooked without a recipe, make one up. Color your hair, sing a song out loud, anything. Experience taking a chance. The only way to conquer fear is to face it. So now is the time.

What are your most hidden fears?

_____

_____

_____

_____

What can you do to face them?

_____

_____

_____

_____

What if you make a fool of yourself?

_____

_____

_____

_____

What if you fail?

_____

_____

_____

_____

What if you succeed?

_____

_____

_____

_____

What if you made a promise and you now need to break that promise?

_____

_____

_____

_____

This is where the rubber meets the road, if you have really learned to trust yourself, if you really have learned to turn things over and if you are ready to walk further on this journey than before it's time to go forward. If not, STOP here and go back to stones one, two, and three. Starting over will only give you more motivation and clear up more spider webs in your brain, heart, and spirit.

Talk about how you feel at this point.

_____

_____

_____

_____

_____

_____

_____

_____

_____

Do not go on alone. Have a sponsor, a mentor or a teacher now involved. The truth is being in charge of our own emotions can work against us if we do not take an inventory of our lives. You cannot allow the past to dictate your future.

What does this mean to you?

_____

_____

_____

_____

_____

_____

_____

_____

_____

_____

Improving Self-Esteem

Introduction

Everyone, at some point or another, is uncertain about themselves, lacks self-confidence, doubts their abilities, or thinks negatively of themselves. However, if you think that you might have problems with low self-esteem, or are not sure if you have this problem but want to find out, then this information package might be helpful to you. In this Section, we will discuss what low self-esteem is and what kind of impact low self-esteem might have on a person and their life.

What is Self-Esteem

Before we talk about what low self-esteem is, let's start with understanding the term "self-esteem." You might have heard and seen similar words like "self-image," "self-perception," and "self-concept." All these terms refer to the way we view and think about ourselves. As human beings, we have the ability to not only be aware of ourselves but also to place a value or a measure of worth to ourselves or aspects of ourselves. So, self-esteem usually refers to how we view and think about ourselves and the value that we place on ourselves as a person. Having the human capacity to judge and place value to something is where we might run into problems with self-esteem.

Before we go further, take a few minutes to write a short description of yourself.

_____

_____

_____

_____

How did you describe yourself? What words did you use? Is your description of yourself generally positive, balanced, or negative? What value did you place on yourself or aspects of yourself? Is that value positive, balanced, or negative?

What is Low Self-Esteem

Have you ever been dissatisfied or unhappy with yourself on the whole? Do you ever think that you are weak, stupid, and not good enough, flawed in some way, inferior to other people, useless, worthless, unattractive, ugly, unlovable, a loser, or a failure? Everyone uses these words on themselves at times, usually when they experience a challenging or stressful situation. However, if you often think about yourself in these terms, then you might have a problem with low self-esteem.

Low self-esteem is having a generally negative overall opinion of oneself, judging or evaluating oneself negatively, and placing a general negative value on oneself as a person.

Here are some examples of what people with low self-esteem might say about themselves:

"I get nervous talking to people I don't know at parties. I'm socially inept and I hate it!" "I couldn't understand a lot of what the instructor was saying today. I must be really stupid." "I'm overweight. I am so fat and ugly." "I'm unimportant." "I'm a loser." "I'm unlovable." "I'm not good enough."

In essence, people with low self-esteem usually have deep-seated, basic, negative beliefs about themselves and the kind of person they are. These beliefs are often taken as facts or truths about their identity. As a result, low self-esteem can have a negative impact on a person and their life.

Based on what has been described about low self-esteem, do you think you are experiencing this problem? Have you often had negative thoughts about yourself but had not included them in the previous description of yourself? Perhaps you might like to jot them down now.

_____

_____

_____

_____

_____

Impact of Low Self-Esteem

Low self-esteem can have an effect on various aspects of a person. A person with low self-esteem probably says a lot of negative things about themselves. They might criticize themselves, their actions, and abilities or joke about themselves in a very negative way. They might put themselves down, doubt themselves, or blame themselves when things go wrong. Often, they might not recognize their positive qualities. When compliments are given to them, they might brush such comments aside or say that "it was all luck" or "it wasn't that big a deal." Instead, they might focus on what they didn't do or the mistakes they made. People with low self-esteem might expect that things would not turn out well for them. They might often feel sad, depressed, anxious, guilty, ashamed, frustrated, and angry. They might have difficulty speaking up for themselves and their needs, avoid challenges and opportunities, or be overly aggressive in their interactions with others.

Low self-esteem can also have an impact on many aspects of a person's life. It can affect a person's performance at work or at school. They might consistently achieve less than they are able to because they believe they are less capable than others. They might avoid challenges for fear of not doing well. They might work extremely hard and push themselves to do more because they believe they need to make up for, or cover up, their lack of skill. People with low self-esteem might find it hard to believe any good results they get are due to their own abilities or positive qualities.

In their personal relationships, people with low self-esteem might become upset or distressed by any criticism or disapproval, bend over backwards to please others, be extremely shy or self-consciousness or even avoid or withdraw from intimacy or social contact. They might also be less likely to stand up for themselves or protect themselves from being bullied, criticized, or abused by their partners or family members.

People with low self-esteem might not engage in many leisure or recreational activities, as they might believe that they do not deserve any pleasure or fun. They might also avoid activities where they could be judged or evaluated in some way, such as competitive sports, dancing, art/craft classes or participating in any type of competition or exhibition.

Personal self-care might also be affected. People who do not value themselves might drink excessive amounts of alcohol or abuse drugs. They might not bother to dress neatly, wear clean clothes, style their hair or buy new clothes. On the other hand, they might try to hide any inadequacies by making sure that every detail of their appearance is attended to and not allow themselves to be seen by others unless they look absolutely perfect.

If you have problems with low self-esteem, take a few minutes to write down how having low self-esteem has affected your life.

_____

_____

_____

_____

The Problem of Low Self-Esteem

Low self-esteem can be part of a current problem. If you're experiencing clinical depression, low self-esteem can be a by-product of your depressed mood. Having a negative view of oneself is a symptom of depression. So is feeling very guilty and worthless almost all the time. Here are some other symptoms of depression:

- Feeling consistently sad, down, depressed, or empty
- Reduced pleasure in activities previously enjoyed or lack of interest in most things • Increased or reduced appetite
- Sleep difficulties (inability to sleep, sleeping more than usual, waking up in the middle of the night and unable to return to sleep)
- Feeling tired and without energy

- Being fidgeting and restless or slowed down compared to your usual speed of doing things (this is observed by others)
- Having difficulties concentrating or making decisions
- Having thoughts that you might be better off dead or thinking about hurting yourself

If you have experienced 5 of these symptoms, which include low mood or loss of pleasure or interest, and they are present on most days for the past 2 weeks or more, then it is possible that you are clinically depressed. We encourage you to seek help from your doctor or a mental health professional and get treatment. There are many effective treatments available for depression and the research has shown that when depression has been treated successfully, low self-esteem is no longer a problem.

Have you been depressed lately? Have you experienced any of those symptoms described above? If so, take note of those that have affected you most significantly.

_____

_____

_____

_____

Low self-esteem can be a result of other problems. Low self-esteem can sometimes be a result of current difficult and stressful life circumstances such as prolonged financial hardship, persistent illness, an accident that has caused some kind of impairment, chronic pain, relationship difficulties, or a problem situation that is difficult to solve. Sometimes when a problem is experienced over an extended period of time, one can become discouraged and demoralized. Self-confidence can be undermined and low self-esteem can develop. Experiencing other psychological problems such as panic attacks, chronic worrying, or social phobia can also chip away at a person's self-esteem.

What are your personal circumstances like at the moment? What sorts of difficulties might you be experiencing now? How long have these been going on for? Take a few minutes to jot these down.

_____

_____

_____

_____

_____

_____

Low self-esteem can be a problem in itself and be a risk factor for other problems. Sometimes low self-esteem can be a problem in and of itself because it puts the person at risk for experiencing other problems such as depression, having persistent suicidal thoughts, eating disorders, and social phobia. You may recognize that while things might be okay at the moment and you don't feel very depressed or anxious, or experience other difficulties, things might not have been that well in the past. If your mood often fluctuates depending on your circumstances or you have experienced depression in the past, and you recognize that you might have low self-esteem, then this could put you at risk of experiencing depression again. We call this a 'vulnerability factor.' Low self-esteem as a vulnerability factor is like something that is hiding in the background that could jump out and bite you when you least expect it.

Have you had problems with depression, anxiety, or any other mental health problems in the past? Do you think low self-esteem might put you at risk for any other problems in the future?

_____

_____

_____

_____

How Self Esteem Develops

Introduction

People with low self-esteem hold deep-seated, basic, negative beliefs about themselves and the kind of person they are. These beliefs are often taken as facts or truths about their identity. In this Section, we will explore how these beliefs about the self develop.

Facts & Opinions

Before we do that, let's discuss the difference between facts and truths, and opinions.

The dictionary definition of fact is "a piece of information presented as having objective reality." This means that a fact has evidence that says it is real – there is no doubt about it. An *opinion* is "a view, judgment, or appraisal formed in the mind about a particular matter." An *opinion* is how someone perceives something, and this view may be unique to them. Let's have a few examples to better illustrate the difference between facts and opinions.

"I have green eyes" is a fact. "I like blue eyes" is an *opinion.* Why? Because someone else might say, "I like hazel eyes." "I am a mother," "I have a car," "I live in Perth, Western Australia" are facts. These statements can be checked and verified. "Having heaps of money is really important," "Job satisfaction is about doing as little as I can get away with," "There is nothing wrong with combining drugs and alcohol," are *opinions*. Facts cannot be challenged, but opinions can be biased, inaccurate, mistaken, and unhelpful.

Our ideas of ourselves, the judgements that we make of, and the value we place on, ourselves as people are *opinions*, not facts. However, we often take these opinions as truth or facts and thus, believe in them very strongly. Therein lies the problem! So, where do these beliefs and opinions of ourselves come from? How did we develop these beliefs about ourselves?

Early Life Experiences

Beliefs about ourselves are learned as a result of the experiences we have had in our lives, especially our early life experiences. Often, the beliefs we have about ourselves are conclusions we arrive at based on what has happened in our lives. This means that at some point in time, it made sense to have those beliefs. Down the track, we'll explore whether or not such beliefs are helpful in the present, but first, let's discuss how we develop our beliefs about ourselves.

We learn things in different ways. We may learn from direct experiences, the media, observing what other people do, and listening to what people say. This will continue throughout our lives but beliefs about ourselves are often (though not always) developed earlier in life. This means that our experiences in our childhood, family of origin, the society we lived in, schools we went to, and with our peers have influenced our thoughts and beliefs about all sorts of things, including ourselves. If we have arrived at very negative thoughts and beliefs about ourselves, it is likely that we have encountered a variety of negative experiences that might have contributed to this. We will now talk about what some of these negative experiences might be.

Punishment, Neglect, or Abuse

How we were treated earlier in life affects the way we see ourselves and who we are. If children are mistreated, punished frequently in an extreme or unpredictable manner, neglected, abandoned, or abused, these experiences can leave some emotional and psychological scars. It is not surprising, then, that a person who has had these sorts of experiences in their earlier life can come to believe very negative things about themselves.

Difficulty in Meeting Parents' Standards

Experiencing less extreme punishment or constantly being criticized can also have a negative effect. If your parents, careers, and family members often focused on your weaknesses and mistakes and rarely acknowledged your positive qualities or successes (perhaps saying things such as "You could have done better," or "That's not good enough"), or if they frequently teased you, made fun of you, and put you down, you might also come to believe some negative things about yourself.

Not Fitting In at Home or at School

Some people may have experienced being the 'odd one out' at home or at school. They might have been less intelligent than their siblings at home or had different interests, talents or skills to others in the family (such as being artistic, musical, and sporty or love mathematics, science, arts). Although they might not have been criticized for their different interests or abilities, these might not have been acknowledged. At the same time, the activities or achievements of their siblings or peers might have been praised or celebrated. As such, they might come to believe thoughts such as "I'm weird," "I'm odd," or "I'm inferior."

Difficulty in Meeting Peer Group Standards

During late childhood and adolescence, our experiences with our peers and people around our age can also influence how we see ourselves. This is a time when physical appearance may be very important to the young person. Together with messages conveyed by the media, an overweight, plump, or 'well-built' young person who has not had many positive experiences with their peers can come to believe "I am fat and ugly," "I'm unattractive," or "I'm unlikeable." Young people who have had other problems with their appearance, such as problem skin, can also come away with negative beliefs about themselves if they have been teased or ridiculed for this by their peers.

Being on the receiving end of other people's stress or distress

Sometimes, when families experience stressful or distressing life events, parents may need to give their attention to dealing with the problems that have occurred. As such, parents may not be able to give much attention to their child or children. It is also possible that parents or careers in such circumstances become frustrated, angry, anxious, or depressed and respond negatively towards their children or become role models of unhelpful behavior.

Your Family's Place in Society

How we view ourselves is not only influenced by how we are treated as individuals but also how our family or group is viewed and treated by others in society. If your family or the group that you belonged to was seen to be different, less socially acceptable, or was on the receiving end of prejudice or hostility, these experiences can also influence how you see yourself.

An Absence of Positives

The absence of positive experiences in our lives can also affect our self-esteem. It might be that you did not receive enough attention, praise, encouragement, warmth, or affection. It could be that your basic needs were just adequately met but no more was given. Some parents or careers may have been emotionally distant, not physically affectionate, spending a lot of time working (perhaps to meet the needs of the family) or pursuing their own interests and had very little time with their children. These experiences might influence how people view themselves especially if they compare their experiences with their peers who might have had more positive experiences.

What early experiences did you have that might have contributed to the way you view, and feel about, yourself? Take a bit of time to jot down a brief description of those experiences.

_____

_____

_____

_____

_____

_____

Late Onset

Most of the time, the roots or beginnings of low self-esteem can be found in the experiences people have had in their childhood or adolescence. However, people with healthy self-esteem can also find their self-confidence being dented and chipped away at if they encounter negative experiences later in life. A person can come to develop low self-esteem if they have experiences such as being bullied or intimidated at work, being in an abusive relationship, experiencing prolonged financial hardship, continuous stressful life events, traumatic events, or life-altering illnesses or injuries.

Have you had any recent stressful life experiences that have negatively affected how you view yourself?

_____

_____

_____

_____

How the Past affects the Present: Negative Core Beliefs

We have explored and discussed how different sorts of experiences can influence and shape how we view, and feel about, ourselves. Often, these are experiences that have occurred earlier in our lives. So, if these experiences happened long ago, why is it that we still see ourselves in a negative light today? After all, haven't we had adult experiences that are quite different from the ones we had as children? Yet, we might still hear, in our minds, what our parents or other people had said to us years and years ago. We might hear ourselves saying things like "This is not good enough," "You could have done better," "You are so stupid."

Why we continue to experience low self-esteem today, even when our current circumstances are different from those of our past, is a result of our negative core beliefs. Negative core beliefs are the conclusions about ourselves we have arrived at when we were children or adolescents, likely as a result of the negative experiences we have had. For example, a child who was constantly punished and criticized may come to believe "I am worthless," or "I am bad." These thoughts are what we call negative core beliefs. To a child or young person, these beliefs seem to make sense during those experiences because they are probably unable to explore other explanations for what is happening to them. These negative core beliefs are thoughts that are usually deep seated, firmly held, and strongly ingrained in our minds. They are evaluations of ourselves and our worth or value as a person. These beliefs say, "This is the kind of person I am."

Here are some other examples of negative core beliefs:

"I am stupid."
"I'm not good enough."
"I'm not important."
"I'm unlovable."
"I'm fat and ugly."
"I'm unacceptable."
"I'm good for nothing."
"I am evil."

Protecting Ourselves: Rules & Assumptions

When we strongly believe these negative statements about ourselves, it is not surprising that we feel very bad about ourselves and experience strong negative emotions. While we were experiencing negative situations and coming to these negative conclusions about ourselves, the human survival instinct was also in operation. To ensure our survival and to keep on functioning, we begin to develop assumptions, rules, and guidelines for how we live our lives that help protect our self-esteem. They aim to guard and defend us from the truth of our negative core beliefs.

We might develop rules such as:

"I must be the best at everything."
"I must never make any mistakes."
"I must never show any emotion in public."
"I must always do the right thing."

We might also develop assumptions such as:

"If I ask for something I need, I will be put down."
"No matter what I do, it will never be good enough."
"If I can't control my food intake, I will never be able to control anything in my life."

Rules and assumptions can also be combined, for example:

"I must do everything I can to gain others' approval because if I am criticized in any way, it means I am not acceptable."
"I won't try anything unless I know that I can do it perfectly, because if I can't, it means I'm a total failure."
"I have to always be slim and dress well, or else I will never be accepted."

What sorts of rules and assumptions for living might you have to help you feel better about yourself? Take a few minutes to jot these down.

_____

_____

_____

_____

Rules & Assumptions Guide Behavior

The result of having these rules and assumptions is that they will guide your behavior. What you do on a day-to-day basis is largely determined by what rules for living you have. Makes sense, doesn't it? So, depending on your rules, you will try very hard to do everything perfectly, avoid getting too close to people, restrict your food intake and exercise vigorously to stay slim, do what it takes to please people, avoid doing anything too challenging, and avoid doing things you've never done before … and the list can go on.

Can you see how having such rules and assumptions for living might help you protect your self-esteem? What happens if one of your rules for living is "I must never make any mistakes?" The effect is that this rule will guide your behavior, making you become very careful about your work, checking your work many times so it is likely that you don't make many mistakes, if at all. This means that you are less likely to be criticized and so your self-esteem is protected.

Take a few minutes to jot down how your rules and assumptions might influence your behavior. What do you do to try to live up to your rules or standards and assumptions for living?

_____

_____

_____

_____

_____

What this means is that you can feel fairly good about yourself if you are able to meet these rules for living or live up to the standards you have set for yourself. For example, if you are able to always maintain your body shape and weight, you will feel okay about yourself. As long as you never make any mistakes, always gain your friends', colleagues', or bosses' approval, always get extremely good results at school or university, you can maintain an adequate level of self-esteem. However, there is a disadvantage to having these rules and assumptions. You can run yourself ragged by trying to live up to all the rules. Basically, you are putting yourself under a lot of pressure so that you manage your self-esteem and don't feel bad about yourself.

Actually, while things might seem to be going well on the surface, the negative core beliefs are still there. This is because the negative core beliefs have not been removed. In fact, they are still there because they have been protected by your rules and assumptions and your behavior. This is why these rules and assumptions and your behavior cannot really be considered to be helpful – because they serve to keep the negative core beliefs alive, as it were. At this point in time, if you have been able to live up to your rules, you may be feeling fine, but the low self-esteem lies dormant.

Model of Low Self-Esteem: How Low Self-Esteem Begins

As we go along, our discussions about how low self-esteem develops and what it keeps going will be put in the form of a diagram, which will tie everything together. We call all the concepts expressed in such a diagram a 'model'. We will begin with the concepts discussed in this Section and then add others in as we move on to the next Section. Here's the first part of the model of low self-esteem:

Negative Life → Negative Core Beliefs → Unhelpful Rules &
Experienced   about Yourself   ← Assumptions

ʌ   ʌ

Unhealthy Behavior

(Dormant Low Self-Esteem)

What this model depicts, is a snapshot of what has been discussed in this Section, Low self-esteem might begin with our having had negative life experiences, especially during childhood and adolescence. These negative experiences can influence how we see ourselves and we can come away with some negative conclusions about ourselves, which we call negative core beliefs. (The dotted arrow in the diagram signifies that negative life experiences do not automatically lead to negative core beliefs – it is just that they have some influence in their development). In order to protect our self-esteem and continue to function from day-to-day, we develop rules and assumptions for living. These rules guide us to behave in ways that end up not being very helpful because they serve to keep our negative core beliefs intact. While we are able to stick to these rules for living, we can feel okay about ourselves, but the low self-esteem remains dormant.

In the next Section, we will discuss what might cause low self-esteem to 'flare up' or be activated. We will also discuss a number of things that keep low self-esteem going.

How Low Self-Esteem Is Maintained

Introduction

Negative beliefs about ourselves can develop from past experiences. It is important to understand how and why we come to think about ourselves the way they do. To begin to tackle the problem of low self-esteem, it is also important to understand how negative beliefs about ourselves are maintained, that is, why these beliefs persist, long after the experiences that allowed them to develop have passed. In this Section, we will explore how negative beliefs about the self are maintained in the long-term.

How Negative Core Beliefs are Maintained from Day to Day

As you have seen, the negative beliefs we have about ourselves often have their roots in our early life experiences. Through various things that have happened to us and the way we interpret these events as a child or adolescent, we come to the conclusion that we are "stupid," "incompetent," "unlovable," "ugly," or some other negative judgement. That was then. However, now as adults, there are things we do on a day to-day basis that keep the negative beliefs we developed about ourselves in our early life, very much alive and well today. The way we make sense of information from the world around us, the things we do to live up to our unhelpful rules and assumptions, and particularly, our responses to certain day-to-day situations, all serve to keep our negative core beliefs going.

Information Processing

 The way we make sense of the things that happen around us (we call this "information processing"), plays a very big part in maintaining low self-esteem. There is so much happening in our environment at any one time – so much information – that to deal with or make sense of all of it is an impossible task. For this reason, our brain tends to choose what we pay attention to and how we think about and make sense of things. Often, what determines what we pay attention to and how we think about these things, are the beliefs we hold. We tend to pay attention to things we expect and interpret things in a way that is consistent with our expectations. As a result, we tend to remember only things that happen in our lives that are consistent with what we believe to be true. This process of attending to and interpreting things in a manner that is consistent (rather than inconsistent) with our beliefs, is something all human beings do and not just those with problems with low self-esteem.

Let's look at this further using an example not related to self-esteem. For example, you may have the belief, "My neighbors are noisy." Now, this belief may be based on your experience of the first night they moved into the house next door and had a loud party that kept you awake all hours of the night and early morning. However, your belief about your neighbors, which started from an initial experience, might still remain a few years later because:

- you only pay attention to your neighbors at times when they are noisy, not at times when they are quiet
- you interpret any noise you hear as coming from those particular neighbors, often without checking if this is the case. Therefore, whenever the topic of your neighbors comes to mind, you only remember the occasions that they have been noisy.

Therefore, your original belief, "My neighbors are noisy" holds strong.

Let's try another example, but this time related to low self-esteem. Let's say that your negative core belief is "I'm a failure." This is a conclusion you arrive at following certain experiences you had when you were younger, but how does this affect your information processing now? Holding the belief, "I'm a failure," means that you probably only focus on the times you make mistakes or don't do something well. You probably ignore any successes, or play them down (eg., "That was a fluke"). Also, it is unlikely that you acknowledge the times when you had done an acceptable job – those times are never given a second thought because to you they are "No big deal." Therefore, you only pay attention to negative incidents that confirm your belief that you are a "failure." You probably also have quite an extreme view of what success and failure is, with no middle ground. As such, words like "I did okay," rarely enter your vocabulary. You might easily jump to the extreme conclusion that you have failed at something, when realistically you might not have done too badly at all ("I didn't get an A on the assignment – I'm a complete failure!"). Therefore, you also tend to interpret the things that happen in your life as confirming your belief that you're a "failure" when there are likely to be other less harsh interpretations you could make.

The problem is that you seem to be always gathering evidence that supports your negative core belief, because you only ever pay attention to things and interpret things in a manner that confirms how you see yourself. In this way, your negative core beliefs are 'self-fulfilling.' Once they are in place, you will keep gathering information to keep them strong, and rarely gather information to challenge and expose them as biased and inaccurate opinions of yourself.

Unhelpful Rules & Assumptions Generate Unhelpful Behaviors

While the unhelpful rules and assumptions are designed to protect you from the truth of your negative core belief, these also play a part in keeping the core belief alive. Unhelpful rules and assumptions like, "I must do everything 100% perfectly, otherwise I will fail," or "If I get too close to other people, they will reject me" or "People won't like me if I express my true feelings and opinions," will tend to affect how you behave. You will run yourself ragged trying to do everything perfectly, or stay at a comfortable distance from others to avoid rejection, or not show anyone the true you in the hope that you will be liked. As long as you do these things, you will probably feel okay about yourself.

The problem is that these rules restrict your behavior in such a way that you don't get an opportunity to put your negative core beliefs to the test and see if they are true. You never intentionally do a mediocre job and see if dire consequences follow. You never get close to others to see if you really would be rejected. You never express your opinion and see if people still accept you. These rules make us behave in ways that are unhelpful to us. Essentially they stop us from putting ourselves 'out there' to see if the things we believe about ourselves are true or to see if the consequences we fear are true. In this way, the rules and assumptions we have limit our opportunities to have experiences that are inconsistent with our negative core beliefs. They restrict us from behaving in ways that allow us to have experiences that would challenge our beliefs and change them. Hence, the unhelpful behavior that is aimed at meeting our rules and avoiding our assumptions, also keep our negative beliefs about ourselves alive and well. In the previous Section, we mentioned that as long as we are able to live up to our rules and assumptions, we might not feel bad about ourselves, but the low self-esteem lies dormant.

At-Risk Situations

Life is full of all sorts of challenges every day. When these challenges relate to your negative core beliefs and unhelpful rules and assumptions, they become what we would call "At-Risk Situations" for low self-esteem. These are situations where your rules and assumptions are at risk of being broken or are broken outright (ex., you can't or will have great difficulty living up to your rules or avoiding your assumptions). Such at-risk situations are always going to arise because our rules and assumptions are unrealistic, extreme, and inflexible, and so because of the high and often impossible standards that have been set, these rules will always be susceptible to being broken.

What happens when we are faced with an at-risk situation? This is when the dormant low self-esteem becomes active. When you encounter an at-risk situation, your negative core belief about yourself is activated (i.e., it 'goes off' like an alarm, 'lights up' like a light bulb, is 'rekindled' like a burning flame) and influences how you think, behave, and feel in the situation. When a negative core belief is activated in an at-risk situation, you are likely to think that things will turn out badly or you become extremely critical of yourself. We call these two types of thoughts Biased Expectations and Negative Self-Evaluations, respectively. These types of thoughts will then influence how you behave. You might avoid doing certain things, try things out but quit when things get too difficult, take precautions to prevent a negative outcome, or withdraw from situations. These behaviors are unhelpful because they do not address the main issue or solve the problem. Instead, they lead to negative unhelpful feelings (such as anxiety, frustration, depression, or shame) and confirm the negative core belief. This also causes the negative core belief to remain activated and this time, the low self-esteem is no longer dormant – it is now acute low self-esteem.

Model of Low Self-Esteem: How Low Self-Esteem Is Maintained

Let's look at how these concepts fit together in our model and then we will further illustrate this with examples. In the previous Section, we presented the first part of the model. Here's the second part.

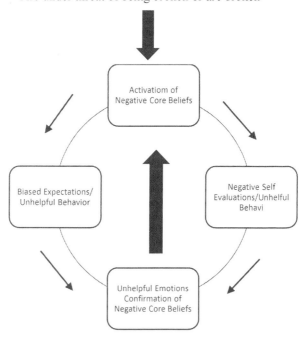

At-Risk Situations

Situations in which unhelpful rules & assumptions
Are under threat of being broken or are broken

(Acute Low Self- Esteem)

Here's an example. Let's say that your negative core belief is, "I am incompetent," and your unhelpful rule is, "I must do everything 100% perfectly, without mistakes, and without the help of others." As long as you follow your rule, you might feel okay about yourself, because your incompetence is quashed or hidden for the time being. However, let's say you encounter a new and challenging experience – you are starting a new and difficult course of study. You are now in a situation where you are probably unable do things 100% perfectly, without mistakes or without the help of others, because the situation you are in is new and challenging, and you lack experience in this area. You are now in an at-risk situation for low self-esteem, because your rule is either broken or looks likely to be broken. When this happens, your belief, "I am incompetent," is activated, and this belief is brought to the forefront of your mind and now affects how you respond in the situation.

Biased Expectations

If your rule is only threatened (i.e. it hasn't been broken yet, but looks likely to be broken at some point), your response might be to expect that things will turn out badly. We call this having biased expectations. This means that the way you think is consumed by predicting the worst and jumping to negative conclusions about how the situation will pan out, saying things such as, "I'm not going to be able to do this," "I will fail," "Others will criticize me," "I won't do a good job."

As a result of having these biased expectations, you might **behave** in certain ways. You might begin to avoid attending lectures or put assignments off until the last minute. You might become extremely cautious and over-prepared, such as staying up all hours of the night working on an assignment.

Alternatively, you might give the course a try but withdraw when an assignment seems too difficult. We call these three types of behaviors avoidance, taking safety precautions, and escaping. These thoughts and behaviors contribute to you **feeling** anxious, nervous, tense, afraid, uncertain, and doubtful. Your biased expectations, unhelpful behaviors, and anxiety may impair your performance, and confirm to yourself that you were right – "I am incompetent." Your negative core beliefs therefore remain unchanged and continue to be activated. By avoiding things or escaping from difficult situations, you never test out your biased expectations to see if they are accurate. Even if your biased expectations do not come true and things go well, by taking safety precautions, you might believe that everything is a "close call" this time, and that you might not be so lucky next time. Again, your negative core belief is not changed. So you can see that the way you think and behave in at-risk situations leads to unhelpful emotions and maintains your negative beliefs about yourself.

Negative Self-Evaluations

If your rule is actually broken, your response might be to engage in negative self-evaluations. This means that the way you **think** is consumed by self-blame and self-criticism. You become very harsh on yourself, beating yourself up about perceived mistakes or inadequacies saying things such as, "I should have done better," "If I can't even do this, I must be really dumb," "I knew I didn't have it in me," "It just shows that I'm really lousy."

Again, as a result you may behave in certain ways, such as isolating yourself, withdrawing, hibernating, not taking care of yourself, not doing much, being passive, not doing enjoyable things – all because you think you don't deserve positive things.

When you think and behave in this way, you will tend to feel depressed, sad, low, upset, dejected, and hopeless. Given that a sign of depression is negative self-talk, these feelings will also tend to keep your negative beliefs about yourself activated.

What then happens is that your negative self-evaluations, unhelpful behaviors, and depression all confirm to you that you were right – "I am incompetent," and keep this belief alive, well after the at-risk situation has passed. So again, you can see that the way you think, behave, and feel in at-risk situations, means your negative beliefs gather further support and become even more unwavering.

Model of Low Self-Esteem: The Full Model

Let's put what we know from earlier sections together and get it
clear in our minds how low self-esteem develops and is maintained.
Here is the full model.

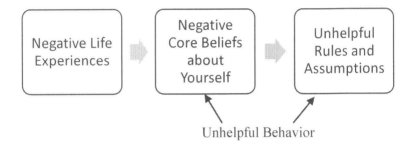

Unhelpful Behavior

(Dormant Low Self-Esteem)

At-Risk Situations
Situations in which unhelpful rules & assumptions
Are under threat of being broken or are broken

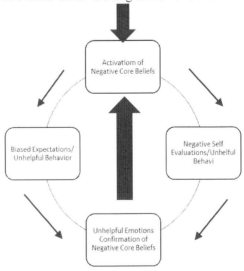

(Acute Low Self-Esteem)

This first part of the model shows that low self-esteem might begin with our having had negative experiences in our lives, which influence how we see and place worth on ourselves or aspects of ourselves. If we see ourselves in a poor light and place low worth on ourselves, it is likely that we have made some negative conclusions about ourselves, which are called negative core beliefs. In order to protect our self-esteem and continue to function from day-to-day, we develop rules and assumptions for living. These rules guide us to behave in ways that, in the end, are unhelpful because they serve to keep our negative core beliefs alive. While we are able to stick to these rules for living, we can feel okay about ourselves, but the low self-esteem remains dormant.

The second part of this model shows that at some point in our lives, we will encounter at-risk situations because it is extremely difficult to live up to our rules and assumptions, which are unrealistic and rigid. When these rules are at risk of being broken or have been broken, our negative core beliefs become activated and we engage in negative thinking. We expect that things will not work out (biased expectations) or criticize and blame ourselves (negative self-evaluations). We also engage in unhelpful behaviors and together with the unhelpful thinking, lead to negative unhelpful emotions and our negative core beliefs remaining activated. It is then that low self-esteem becomes acute.

The Good News

While it can be helpful to understand how the problems we have today might have developed from our past experiences, it might also be discouraging, because unfortunately we cannot change our past. However, what we have seen in this Section is that there are things we do on a day-to-day basis in the 'here-and-now' that maintain the negative core beliefs we have about ourselves, keeping them alive and active today.

This is good news, because given that these things happen on a daily basis, you can work on changing them. You can change the negative views you have developed about yourself. This means that things can be different and you can overcome low self-esteem. What is important now is that you commit yourself to making the effort in addressing your unhelpful thinking and unhelpful behavior from day to day. The rest of the Sections in this package will focus on the things that you can start doing to chip away at your low self-esteem. Before long, you will begin to see yourself in a better light and treat yourself more kindly.

The approach taken in this information package of identifying and changing unhelpful thinking and behavior to overcome low self-esteem comes from a type of treatment known as cognitive-behavioral therapy. This type of psychological treatment has been evaluated scientifically and shown to be effective in treating a number of psychological problems. Cognitive-behavioral therapy is aimed at changing your unhelpful thinking patterns and beliefs (the cognitive part), as well as any unhelpful style of behaving (the behavioral part).

This will bring about a change in how you see yourself and how you feel.

The Sections in the remainder of this information package will focus on how to deal with biased expectations and negative self-evaluations first. The Sections will then move to addressing unhelpful rules and assumptions, and finally negative core beliefs. You may ask why we do not start with negative core beliefs first, given that these are what determine how we think, feel, and behave from day to day. The reason we don't start with negative core beliefs is that these are a lot harder to shift than our thinking and behavior in daily situations. Examining our thinking and behavior in specific situations tends to be easier to do, so by starting here you can begin to get some immediate benefit for your efforts. Starting here can also have an effect of slowly chipping away at your negative core beliefs, and allows you to practice skills you will be applying to tackling your unhelpful rules and negative core beliefs later. So, we recommend that you work through this package in the order the Sections are presented (rather than skipping ahead), as this will bring the most benefit to you.

Biased Expectations

Introduction

Dormant low self-esteem becomes active and maintains itself until it becomes acute. When you encounter an at-risk situation, your negative core belief about yourself is activated and leads to two types of negative thoughts – biased expectations and negative self-evaluations. In this Section, we will examine biased expectations in more detail, and discuss ways of changing and overcoming them. By addressing your biased expectations in daily situations, you can prevent the negative beliefs you hold about yourself from being confirmed and re-activated. Ultimately, this will help you to chip away at your low self-esteem.

What Are Biased Expectations?

Biased expectations are negative thoughts that commonly occur when you encounter an 'At-Risk Situation' where it looks likely that your unhelpful rule or assumption will be broken and your negative core beliefs have been activated. When this happens, you will tend to make predictions about how things will turn out and these predictions often tend to be negative. You will tend to:

- Overestimate the likelihood that bad things will happen
- Exaggerate how bad things will be
- Underestimate your ability to deal with things if they don't go well, and
- Ignore other factors in the situation, which suggest that things will not be as bad as you are predicting.
- When you jump to such negative conclusions about the future, you will tend behave in particular ways – often engaging in unhelpful behaviors. You will tend to:
- Avoid the situation totally,
- Try the situation out but escape when things seem too difficult or the anxiety seems overwhelming,

- Be overly cautious and engage in safety behaviors. These are behaviors that you use to help you get through the situation. For example, you might take someone with you, over-prepare so that you can better face the situation, take medication to help you through, or place certain conditions on entering the situation (eg., turn up late/leave early).

At the end of the day, the unhelpful thoughts and behaviors contribute to you feeling incredibly anxious, nervous, uncertain, and unconfident about things – and this is confirmation that your negative core beliefs are true.

Here's an example of biased expectations in action. You can follow this example that is illustrated in the form of the model. Let's say that you have the negative core belief, "I am stupid." At present, your low self-esteem is dormant as you have developed the rule and assumption, "I must never let others see my true abilities, because if they do, they will know that I am stupid and not want to have anything to do with me." As long as you are able to live up to your rule, you might feel okay about yourself. However, the situation is about to change. A few of your friends invite you to join their team for a quiz night. You are now in an at-risk situation because you will have to show others your abilities at the quiz night. This means that your rule is likely to be broken.

At this point, you might have thought, "I'll be no good," "I'll let everyone down," or "Everyone will know how dumb I am," and are probably feeling anxious. It's also at this point that you could choose how to approach this situation. You could avoid the situation totally by declining your friends' invitation or you decide that you will accept the invitation. If you accept the invitation, you might then think about how you could make sure that people do not come to the conclusion that you are stupid. As such, you might prepare very hard for the quiz night by reading all of the week's newspapers, watching current affairs programs and documentaries on TV, and reading trivia books. You might also think about how you could leave the quiz night half way through if things are not turning out well. As discussed above, all these are unhelpful behaviors, and they maintain your negative emotions and confirm your negative core belief.

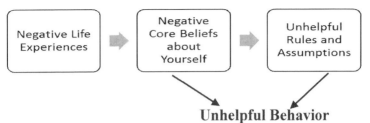

Unhelpful Behavior

Say yes to all requests made to me
Bend over backwards to please people
Observe people carefully to see if they are ever
Displeased with me

(Dormant Low Self- Esteem)

At-Risk Situation

Cancelled dinner with a friend because of work commitments

Activation of Negative Self-Evaluation
"I am Worthless"

Negative Self-Evaluation
" I am a useless and pathetic friend"
"I don't deserve to have friends"
" I shouldnt let people down"

Unhelpful Behaviour/s
Apologize profusely and put myself
down to my friend

(Acute Low- Self Esteem)

Continuing with the above example, your belief "I am stupid" gets confirmed in a number of ways. Firstly, it is confirmed by all the negative predictions you are making – all that 'negative self-talk.' Secondly, because you feel so anxious, you might use this as a sign that you are all the negative things you believe about yourself – "If I feel so anxious about this, I must be stupid." Thirdly, all your unhelpful behaviors mean that you are acting in a manner consistent with the idea that you are "stupid." So, if you act as if you are "stupid," you will continue to think and believe that you are "stupid." Finally, if things don't go the way you would like them to (eg, you get some of the questions wrong), you leave early. Because you do so, you don't give yourself a chance to answer a question correctly, or realize that getting a question wrong isn't such a bad thing, or just have fun regardless of the outcome. Alternatively, if things go okay and you answer a few questions correctly, you might ignore your efforts as "no big deal." If things go really well and you answer heaps of questions, you might attribute it to all your preparation or say, "The questions were really easy," but not acknowledge your own abilities.

What we have seen is an unhelpful way of responding to a daily situation, which helps keep your low self-esteem alive and well. So how could you respond differently, in a way inconsistent with low self-esteem? How could you have realistic expectations and engage in helpful behavior?

Challenging Biased Expectations

One way to address biased expectations is to challenge them 'head on.' In cognitive behavioral therapy, this is also called 'disputation.' Remember that our thoughts and expectations are often opinions we have picked up or learned, rather than facts. Therefore, they can be questioned, and should not be something we just blindly accept if they are causing us distress.

To challenge or dispute your biased expectations means that you dissect them, evaluate how accurate or likely they are, examine what evidence you base your expectations on, and look at any positive things you may be ignoring. In this way, you are like a detective or lawyer, trying to get to the facts of how realistic your expectations are, and putting things in perspective.

Challenging your biased expectations isn't something you should do in your head as this can get messy and confusing. The best way is to write it down. To help you through the process, we suggest using a Thought Diary for Biased Expectations. This helps you work through the challenging process step by step, on paper, making things clearer and more helpful for you.

On the next page is an example of how to complete a Thought Diary for Biased Expectations, and following that is a blank Thought Diary for you to practice on. The Thought Diaries guide you through how to get your biased expectations out on paper.

The Thought Diary will first ask you to **Identify Your Biased Expectations**. To help you do that, first ask yourself:

- What is the situation I am in?

Then:

- What am I expecting? • What am I predicting?
- What do I see happening in this situation?
- What conclusions am I making?

After you have written these down, you'll then need to ask yourself:

- How strongly do I believe this will happen? Rate the strength of your belief between 0
- and 100%
- What emotion(s) am I feeling?
- How intense are these emotions? Rate the intensity of your emotion(s) between 0 and 100%

Once you have completed the first section, you are ready to begin to Challenge Your Biased Expectations. Here are the questions asked in your Thought Diary to challenge these types of negative thoughts:

- What is the evidence for my expectations?
- What is the evidence against my expectations?
- How likely is it that what I am expecting will actually happen (Rate 0-100%)?
- What is the worst that could happen?
- What is the best that could happen?
- What is the most likely thing that will happen?
- How does it affect me when I expect the worst?

- If the worst did happen, what could I do to cope?
- How else could I view the situation?
- Are there any positives in me or the situation that I am ignoring?

The ultimate aim of doing this Thought Diary is for you to **Develop** more **Realistic Expectations**. Once you have explored the answers to the above 'challenging' questions in your Thought Diary, ask yourself:

- What would be a more realistic expectation?

The final step is then to:

- Re-rate how much I now believe the original biased expectation I was making,
- Re-rate the intensity of the emotions that I was originally feeling.

If you work through the entire Thought Diary for challenging your biased expectations, it is likely that you will experience a decrease in your belief in the negative predictions you were making and a decrease in the intensity of your emotions. Using a Thought Diary to develop realistic expectations will help quieten, rather than activate or confirm, your negative beliefs about yourself. This will help you approach situations with an open mind, try new things, and often be pleasantly surprised by what you find, instead of letting your negative opinion of yourself constantly interfere with how you live your life.

Try using a Thought Diary for Biased Expectations the next time you notice when you start feeling anxious, nervous and uncertain, or doubt yourself and your abilities. Stop yourself when you notice these sorts of feelings, and see if you can find any biased expectations that are contributing to the feeling. See if you notice any predictions you are making, negative conclusions you are jumping to, or bad outcomes you are envisaging. If you notice these biased expectations rearing their ugly head, use a Thought Diary to tackle them. Continue to use a Thought Diary to deal with these sorts of thoughts and feelings, until it becomes second nature. Then, you will find that you can easily catch the biased expectations in your head and challenge them in your head. This will take some time and a lot of practice, so for now, stick to writing it all down in your Thought Diary.

Thought Diary for Biased Expectations

Identify Your Biased Expectation

What is the at risk situation?	How much do I believe it will happen (0-100%)?
What am I expecting? What am I predicting? What do I see happening in this situation? What conclusions am I jumping to?	What emotions am I feeling?

Challenge Your Biased Expectations

What is the evidence <u>for</u> my expectations?	What is the evidence <u>against</u> my expectations?
How likely is it that What I am expecting will actually happen (0-100%)	
What is the worst that could happen?	What is the best that could happen?
What is most likely to happen?	How does it affect me if I expect the worst?
If the worst did happen, what could I do to cope?	
How else could I view the situation?	
Are there are any positives in me or the situation I am ignoring?	

Develop Realistic Expectations

What's a more realistic expectation?	
How much do I believe my original biased expectation now? (0-100%)	How intense are my emotions now? (0-100%)

Experimenting with Biased Expectations

By challenging your biased expectations as you did in the last section (using a Thought Diary), you can now be in a better position to approach situations with an open mind and with more realistic and balanced expectations. The next step of challenging biased expectations is to test them out to see how accurate they really are. This is like a scientist doing an experiment with your biased expectations, to test how true they are.

As with a Thought Diary, there are some steps you have to work through to properly experiment with your biased expectations. Below is an example of how to do this.

Step 1: Identify Your Biased Expectations

From the first section of your Thought Diary, you will already know what the at-risk situation is and what it is that you have predicted in this situation, and how much you believe it will happen. Also, write down specifically how you will know if your biased expectations have come true. Ask yourself: *What exactly would happen? What would an outsider see happening? What would you be doing? What would others be doing?*

The Situation: Friends invite me to be on their quiz team
My Biased Expectations: I'll be no good; I'll make them lose; I'll make a complete fool of myself; Everyone will see how dumb I am; The others will wish I wasn't on their team
How much do I believe it will happen (0-100%): 80%
How will I know it has happened: I won't know a single question. Everyone except me will know the answers. The others will make rude comments or glare at me

Step 2: Identify Your Unhelpful Behaviors

Next you need to identify what unhelpful behaviors you might be engaging in to cope with your negative predictions and anxiety (e.g., avoidance, escape, safety behaviors).

> *Over-preparing for the quiz (e.g., news, newspapers, trivia books), placing conditions on going (ex. planning to only answer if I am 100% sure), having an escape plan.*

Step 3: Remember Your Realistic Expectations

Next remind yourself of the new perspective that you developed from your Thought Diary, as you will also want to test your new realistic expectations against your old biased expectations.

> *I don't have to be really good, it's just a quiz night. They are my friends, they are just there to have fun and don't really care about winning or who answers what. It's likely that I will be able to answer some questions that are in my area of interest. How I do at a quiz night isn't a reflection of who I am as a person – everyone has their strengths and weaknesses.*

Step 4: Identify Your Helpful Behaviors

This involves noting what it is you will do differently to test out your new and old expectations, to see which is more accurate. This is really setting up the experiment and specifying what it is you will actually do. This will generally involve confronting rather than avoiding the situation, staying in the situation rather than escaping, and stopping safety behaviors to see how you go by yourself and without imposing conditions and restrictions on you entering the situation.

> *Ask my friends if they are doing anything to prepare for the quiz night. If they do any preparation, do only as much as they are doing. If they are not preparing at all, go to the quiz night, without preparing beforehand. Stay at the quiz night until the end, regardless of how I am going with answering the questions. Answer questions even if I am not totally certain. Purposely suggest an answer that I know is wrong.*

Step 5: Carry Out the Experiment

Follow through with what you set out to do in Step 4. Carry out the experiment, engaging in the more helpful behaviors you have identified, and see what happens.

Step 6: Evaluate the Results

The last step is to reflect on what actually happened and how this compares to what you were expecting in Step 1. What were the results of the experiment? What did you observe? How does this compare to your biased expectations? Which expectations did the results support (biased or realistic)? What was it like to carry the experiment out and act differently? What did you learn from the experience?

What actually happened? *I answered some questions that were in my areas of interest. I got some questions wrong, but so did others – no one saw it as a big deal. I had a good time. No one seemed to take it too seriously. They seemed to be pleased to have me on their team.*
How much did my biased expectations come true (0-100%)? 10%
Which expectations were supported by the experiment? *My more realistic expectations.*
What was it like to act differently? *It was hard at first. But not over preparing, purposely suggesting a wrong answer, and not planning how to escape showed me that I can do this, and that not knowing everything is not so bad.*
What did I learn? *This shows me that what I predict will happen in situations may be guided by my opinion of myself, and may not always be true. So I may need to make my expectations more realistic, act accordingly, and see what happens.*

If the results of your experiment do not support your biased expectations, which is often the case, that is great! It will be important to remember that the next time you find yourself making biased expectations. It will also be important to reflect and ask yourself "What does this mean for you as a person?"

However, should your biased expectations be supported, which may happen at times, it will be important to ask yourself some questions about this. Ask yourself: Were there are any other reasons for the result, aside from who you are as a person? *What else was happening at that time? Are there other ways of viewing what happened? What could you learn from the experience to improve or change things in the future?*

It is important to note that not everything we think is inaccurate, or has no grain of truth to it. However, often when we have problems with low self-esteem, we predict negative things about ourselves and our abilities **all the time**, and act accordingly. We never step back to question these predictions or test them out. This is a habit that is important to break. It is the automatic process of predicting the worst, because of our negative view of ourselves that we want to change. It is important to tackle this because if you can make more realistic predictions in your day-to-day life, you will think and act differently, in a manner inconsistent with someone with low self-esteem. Behaving in a manner that is inconsistent with your low opinion of yourself, is the path to overcoming this negative opinion. When you do this, you will start to gather new information about yourself, which will allow you to see yourself in a less harsh, more positive, and kinder light.

Now, it's time for you to do an experiment. Use the worksheet on the next page to help you plan an experiment to test out your biased expectations.

Experiment Record for Biased Expectations

Step 1: Identify Your Biased Expectations

The Situation:
My Biased Expectations:
How much do I believe it will happen (0-100%)?
How will I know it has happened?

Step 2: Identify Your Unhelpful Behaviors

Step 3: Remember Your Realistic Expectations

Step 4: Identify Your Helpful Behaviors & Set Up Your Experiment

Step 5: Carry Out the Experiment (from Step 4)

Step 6: Evaluate the Results

What actually happened?
How much did my biased expectations come true (0-100%)?
Which expectations were supported by the experiment?
What was it like to behave differently?
What did I learn from this experiment?

Negative Self-Evaluations

Introduction

Dormant low self-esteem becomes active and maintains itself until it becomes acute. When you encounter an at-risk situation, your negative core belief about yourself is activated and leads to two types of negative thoughts – biased expectations and negative self-evaluations.

By addressing your negative self-evaluations in daily situations, you can prevent the negative beliefs you hold about yourself from being confirmed and re-activated. Again, this will help you to chip away at your low self-esteem.

What Are Negative Self-Evaluations?

Negative self-evaluations are negative thoughts that commonly occur when you encounter an 'At-Risk Situation' where your unhelpful rule or assumption is broken and your negative core beliefs have been activated. When this happens you will tend to evaluate yourself in a negative way, becoming harsh and critical of who you are as a person. You will tend to:

- Tell yourself that you "should" have done this or "shouldn't" have done that, chastising yourself and beating yourself up, for not meeting the standards you have set for yourself
- Put negative and derogatory labels on yourself, calling yourself hurtful names like "pathetic," "useless," "idiot," and

- Make sweeping generalizations about yourself, based on a very specific event, saying things such as "I am always doing this," "I never learn," "Everything is ruined."
- When you are so critical of yourself, you will tend to tend behave in particular ways – often engaging in unhelpful behaviors. You will tend to:
- **Withdraw** or **isolate** yourself from family or friends,
- Try to **overcompensate** for things,
- **Neglect** things (opportunities, responsibilities, self-care), or
- Be **passive** rather than assertive with others.

At the end of the day, the unhelpful thoughts and behaviors contribute to you feeling depressed, low, sad, guilty – and this is confirmation that your negative core beliefs are true.

Here's an example of negative self-evaluations in action. Let's say that you have the negative core belief, "I am worthless." At present, your low self-esteem is dormant as you have developed the rule and assumption, "I must make everyone else happy to be accepted." As long as you are able to live up to your rule, you might feel okay about yourself. However, the situation is about to change. You have had to cancel dinner with a friend because of work commitments. You are now in an at-risk situation because you have disappointed someone. This means that your rule has been broken.

At this point, you might have thought, "I'm a useless and pathetic friend," "I don't deserve to have friends," or "I should not let other people down," and are probably feeling sad, depressed, and guilty. It's also at this point that you could choose how to behave in this situation. You could apologize profusely and put yourself down to your friend. You could try to make up for cancelling the dinner by offering to pay for the next outing or re-scheduling your dinner to a time that suits your friend but is inconvenient to you. This is overcompensation. Alternatively, you could withdraw from your friends for a while and avoid their calls and emails. All these are unhelpful behaviors, and they maintain your negative emotions and confirm your negative core belief.

Continuing with the example, your belief, "I am worthless," gets confirmed in a number of ways. Firstly, it is confirmed by all the negative self-evaluations you are making – all that 'negative self-talk.' If you keep telling yourself these negative things, you will continue to believe them. Secondly, feeling depressed can confirm your belief that you are "worthless," because a symptom of depression itself is thinking negatively about everything, including yourself. Thirdly, all your unhelpful behaviors (ex., acting in a passive and apologetic way, trying to overcompensate, or withdrawing) mean that you are acting in a manner consistent with the idea that you are "worthless." So, if you act as if you are "worthless," you will continue to think you are "worthless," and feel sad or depressed.

It is important to note that some people think that making negative self-evaluations is a good thing. Some people think that:

- Being critical and harsh on yourself keeps you grounded
- It stops you from getting too big for your boots
- It prevents you from becoming a 'tall poppy' that needs to be 'cut down'
- It spurs you on, motivating you to do better and better.

Some of these might be commonly held beliefs, but are they really true?

Is putting yourself down and criticizing yourself actually a good and healthy thing to do? If it is, then we would do it to our loved ones regularly. When something goes wrong and our loved ones are in distress, would we help them through by abusing them, calling them names, and telling them off? Is this what we do to the people we love?

Most people would probably not agree. Most people would say that they do the exact opposite – that when times are tough, they show compassion and kindness to the ones they love, comforting them and encouraging them. So if this is what you would do for other human beings, why is it that you don't do it for yourself?

Take a moment to think about this issue of whether being harsh and critical of yourself is a healthy or unhealthy thing to do? Perhaps write down the costs of making negative self-evaluations. Note the disadvantages of being so critical of yourself. Think about how talking to yourself in such a harsh manner affects you? Does it prevent you from doing certain things? Does it make you feel a certain way? Is it unfair to yourself in some way?

_____

_____

_____

_____

_____

_____

Hopefully you are coming to see that constantly making negative self-evaluations is not only generally unhelpful, it also helps keep your low self-esteem alive and well. So how could you respond differently, in a way that is inconsistent with low self-esteem?

Challenging Negative Self-Evaluations

As we did with biased expectations, one way to address your negative self-evaluations is to challenge them, and develop **balanced self-evaluations**. Remember that our thoughts and evaluations are often opinions we have, rather than facts. Therefore they are open to question, and should not be something we just blindly accept if they are causing us distress. Instead, you can dispute, dissect, examine, and assess them – like a detective or lawyer would, to see how realistic they are and put things in perspective.

 Again, challenging your negative self-evaluations isn't something you should do in your head as this can get messy and confusing. The best way is to write it down. To help you through the process, we suggest using a Thought Diary for Negative Self-Evaluations. This helps you work through the challenging process in a step-by-step way, on paper, making things clearer and more useful for you.

On the next page is an example of how to complete a Thought Diary for Negative Self-Evaluations, and following that is a blank Thought Diary for you to practice on. The Thought Diaries guide you through how to get your negative self-evaluations out on paper and challenge them.

The Thought Diary will first ask you to Identify Your Negative Self-Evaluations. To help you do that, first ask yourself:

- What is the situation I am in?

Then:

- What am I saying to myself?
- How am I evaluating myself?
- How am I putting myself down?
- How am I criticizing myself?

After you have written these down, you'll then need to ask yourself:

- How strongly do I believe these evaluations of myself? Rate the strength of my belief between 0 and 100%
- What emotion(s) am I feeling?
- How intense are these emotions? Rate the intensity of my emotion(s) between 0 and 100%
- What unhelpful behaviors did I engage in?

Once you have completed, you are ready to begin to **Challenge Your Negative Self Evaluations**. Here are the questions asked in your Thought Diary to challenge your negative self-evaluations:

- What is the evidence for my evaluations?
- What is the evidence against my evaluations?
- Are these opinions I have of myself or facts?
- How helpful is it for me to evaluate myself in this way?
- How else could I view the situation? What are other perspectives might there be?
- What advice would I give to a friend in this same situation? • Are there any positives in me or the situation that I am ignoring?

- What would be more helpful behavior I could carry out?

Note. If you have engaged in any unhelpful behaviors, ask yourself: How could I act differently? How could I behave in a manner that is inconsistent with my negative self-evaluations? For example, instead of withdrawing and isolating yourself, be active and a part of things around you; instead of overcompensating for things, just do what you think the average person might do in this situation; instead of neglecting things, make time for them; and instead of being passive, try to be more assertive.

The ultimate aim of doing this Thought Diary is for you to develop more **Balanced Self-Evaluations**. Once you have explored the answers to the above 'challenging' questions in your Thought Diary, ask yourself:

- What would be a more balanced self-evaluation to replace my negative self-evaluation?

The final step is then to:

- Re-rate how much I now believe the original negative self-evaluations I was making,
- Re-rate how intense I now feel the emotions that I was originally feeling.

If you work through the entire Thought Diary for challenging your negative self-evaluations, it is likely that you will experience a decrease in your belief in the evaluations you were making and a decrease in the intensity of your emotions. Using a Thought Diary to develop balanced self-evaluations will help quieten rather than activate or confirm your negative beliefs about yourself. This will help you approach situations with an open mind, rather than letting your negative opinion of yourself constantly interfere with how you live your life.

Try using a Thought Diary for negative self-evaluations the next time you notice yourself feeling down, sad, depressed, guilty or hopeless, and you have the sense that you are beating yourself up, being hard on yourself, telling yourself off, and criticizing yourself and your abilities. Stop yourself when you notice these sorts of feelings, and see if you can find the specific negative self-evaluations that are influencing your feelings. When you find these, use a Thought Diary to tackle them. Continue to use a Thought Diary to deal with these sorts of thoughts and feelings, until it becomes second nature. Then you will find that you can easily catch the negative self-evaluations in your head and challenge them in your head. This will take some time and a lot of practice, so for now, stick to writing it all down in your Thought Diary.

Thought Diary for Negative Self-Evaluations

Identify Your Negative Self-Evaluations

What is the at-risk situation?	How much do I believe these evaluation of myself (0-100%)?
What am I saying to myself? How am I evaluating myself? Putting myself down? Criticizing myself?	What emotion(s) am I feeling? (Rate the intensity 0-100%)
What unhelpful behaviors did I engage in?	

Challenge Your Negative Self Evaluation

What is the evidence for my evaluation? What is the evidence against my evaluation?
Are these options I have of myself or facts?
How helpful is it for me to evaluate myself in this way?
How else could I view the situation?
What advice would I give to a friend in the same situation?
What would be more helpful behavior I could carry out?

Balanced Self-Evaluations

A more balanced evaluation of myself is:	
How much do I believe my original negative self-evaluation now (0-100%)?	How intense are my emotions now (0-100%)?

As a preview, the next Section can be thought of as complementing the present Section. In the present Section, we have looked at how to quash your negative self-evaluations, allowing you to be less harsh and critical of yourself. The next Section also tackles this tendency to be very hard on yourself, but we will take a different route. Instead of trying to combat negative self-evaluations, we will look at how to promote balanced self-evaluations by paying attention to the positives aspects of yourself and treating yourself more kindly. Therefore, this and the next Section go hand in hand, working together to tackle our automatic tendencies to evaluate ourselves in a negative way.

Accepting Yourself

Introduction

Battling against some of the negative things you say to yourself is one path to overcoming low self-esteem. However, another path is to promote balanced evaluations of yourself. This means noticing and acknowledging the positive aspects of yourself, and behaving like someone who has positive qualities and is deserving of happiness and fun. In this Section, we will show you exactly how to go about doing these things to boost your self-esteem.

Focusing On the Positive You

Very quickly, jot down a few of your positive qualities in the space below, and then read on.

_____

_____

_____

_____

_____

_____

How easy was it for you to do that? Some people might struggle to bring things to mind. This is because, as we mentioned in earlier Sections, when you have low self-esteem, you have a tendency to only pay attention to negative things that confirm your negative view of yourself. You rarely pay attention to the positive things you do, your positive qualities, positive outcomes or positive comments from others. This will make the positive aspects of you very hard to get to at first, because you have not taken any notice of them. Other people might have less trouble recalling positive things about themselves, but instead might feel uncomfortable thinking about, talking about, or writing about the positive qualities they have. They might consider it as being conceited, arrogant, or stuck up to think about such things.

If either of these apply to you, you will need to approach this Section with an open mind. In this Section you will be asked to start noticing the positives in you that you often ignore and acknowledge these positives. Remember, most of the time all you pay attention to are your negative qualities and you feel comfortable dwelling on these negatives. Ask yourself how fair that is. By getting you to begin acknowledging your positives, you are really tipping the scales of self-evaluation back into balance. These scales have been pretty off balance (towards the side of negativity) for some time now.

Positive Qualities Record

So, where do we start? When we notice something and it's really important for us to remember it, what is it that we do to help us remember? We write things down, make a note of it, or make a list if there are many items. The same approach applies here. To start acknowledging your positives, you need to write them down.

What was your initial reaction to this suggestion of writing a list of your positive attributes? Did you feel any anxiety, shame, uneasiness, sadness, fear? Did you think "What could I possibly write?" "I have nothing worth writing down," "Me! Positive attributes? Ha!" You need to be careful here, and listen out for negative self-evaluations coming through, and the tendency you may have to discount or minimize anything positive about yourself. Remember that this is a nasty habit that may rear its head when you try to do this exercise. Should this happen, just acknowledge it and try to move on to the task at hand. If the negative self-evaluations simply won't release their grip on you that easily, then go back to the Thought Diary for Negative Self-Evaluations to help you out.

Now, start a 'Positive Qualities Record.' Make a list of the positive aspects of yourself, including all your good characteristics, strengths, talents, and achievements, and record them on the worksheet. You might want to record all of this in a special book or journal – one that is dedicated especially to this task of focusing on your positive qualities.

Here are some important tips for getting started:

When you are recording something in your Positive You Journal, make sure you **set aside a special time** to commit to the task and carry it out. Don't do it on the run, or while you are doing other things, or fit it in around other activities. Instead, give it the due attention and time it deserves.

Remember to **write them down** on the worksheet provided or in your special journal, rather than just making a mental note or writing something on the back of a napkin or scrap of paper. Write your positive qualities in your journal or worksheet so that you remember it and know exactly where to find it. In this way, the positive qualities won't get lost.

Write as many positive things about yourself as you can think of...there is **no limit**. Exhaust all avenues and brainstorm as many ideas as possible. If you run out of steam, take a break. Come back to it over the course of a few days, until you have a substantial list of your positives.

Get help if you feel comfortable to do so. Enlist the help of a trusted friend or family member – someone whom you know would be supportive of you doing this, rather than someone who may be a contributor to your self-esteem problems. Two heads are better than one and an outsider might have a different perspective of you, than you do of yourself. Who knows what nice things you might discover about yourself with their help.

 As already mentioned, **watch out** for negative self-evaluations or discounting your positives as "small" or "no big deal" or "not worth writing." You tend to remember detailed negative things about yourself, therefore we must do the same with the positives – it is only fair! Also remember, you don't have to do these positive things absolutely perfectly or 100% of the time – that is impossible. So be realistic about what you write down.

For example, if you tend to be 'hardworking,' but recall the one time you took a sick day after a big weekend, you might say to yourself "I can't write that down because I haven't done it 100%." If you take that attitude, you are not being fair and realistic with yourself.

Finally, don't just do this exercise for the sake of it, and then put it in the back of a drawer, never to be seen again. It is important that you **re-read** the things you write in your journal, reading them over and over with care and consideration. Reflect on what you have written at the end of the day, week, or month. Let all the positive qualities pile up and 'sink in.' this is really important so that you learn to take notice of these things and feel more comfortable acknowledging them, rather than just giving them lip-service.

Listing the positives:

Now, let's get you started writing down all your positive qualities. Use the worksheet to help you start writing down all the positive aspects of yourself. If you get stuck, the worksheet has some questions that can help you jog your memory. Ask yourself questions like:

What do I like about who I am?
What characteristics do I have that are positive?
What are some of my achievements?
What are some challenges I have overcome?
What are some skills or talents that I have?
What do others say they like about me?
What are some attributes I like in others that I also have in common with?

If someone shared my identical characteristics, what would I admire in them?
How might someone who cared about me describe me?
What do I think are bad qualities?
What bad qualities do I not have?

*Remember to include everything no matter how small, insignificant, modest, or unimportant they are!

After using these questions to identify your positive attributes, your list may look something like this (of course everyone's list will be different, as we are all different individuals with different positive qualities):

Considerate	Good Listener	Diligent
Good Cook	Reliable	Good Humored
Fun	Helpful	Health Conscious
Well-Travelled	Animal Lover	House Proud
Resourceful	Adventurous	Loved
A Good Friend	Avid Reader	Charitable
Movie Buff	Politically Conscious	Artistic
Creative	Active	Outdoors Person
Strong	Friendly	Responsible
Determined	Organized	Appreciative
Praise Others	Cultured	

'Positive You Journal'

Part 1: Remember Past Examples

Using the worksheet, recall specific examples of how you have demonstrated each of the positive attributes you have listed in the Positive Qualities Record. This way, you will make each attribute you have written not just meaningless words on a page. Instead, each attribute will become a real, specific, and detailed memory of something that actually happened. So for example:

Considerate

1. I took my friend some flowers and a book when they were sick.

2. I offered a listening ear to my colleague who was going through some difficult times.

3. I lent my brother some money when he was down on his luck.

Doing this will take some time, but is well worth the effort. Remembering the specific incidents that illustrate your positive qualities will allow the list to have an impact on your view of yourself, making it real.

Part 2: Noting Present Examples

Once you have spent time recalling past examples of your positive qualities, it is now time to turn to recognizing examples of your positive attributes on a daily basis. Use the worksheet to help you do this. This will be an ongoing exercise – something you do every day. Each day, set out to record three examples from your day, which illustrate certain positive qualities you have. Write exactly what you did and identify what positive attribute it shows in you. Here's an example:

Day/Date	Things I Did	Positive Attributes
	1. Mopped the floors	*House Proud*
Tue 5/7/05	*2. Finished project*	*Diligent*
	3. Played with kids	*Fun to be with*

Start with noticing three a day if that is comfortable (you can always start with fewer if need be), but try to build from there, increasing it to 4, or 5 or 6. By doing this, you will not only be acknowledging your positive qualities as things you did in the past, but also acknowledging them as things you are every day.

Positive Qualities Record

To help you make a list of your positive qualities, ask yourself the following questions:

- What do I like about who I am?
- What characteristics do I have that are positive?
- What are some of my achievements?
- What are some challenges I have overcome?
- What are some skills or talents that I have?
- What do others say they like about me?
- What are some attributes I like in others that I also have in common with?
- If someone shared my identical characteristics, what would I admire in them?
- How might someone who cared about me describe me?

- What do I think are bad qualities?
- What bad qualities do I not have?

*Remember to include everything no matter how small, insignificant, modest, or unimportant you think they are

1. _____
2. _____
3. _____
4. _____
5. _____
6. _____
7. _____
8. _____
9. _____
10. _____
11. _____
12. _____
13. _____
14. _____
15. _____
16. _____
17. _____
18. _____
19. _____

20. _____

21. _____

22. _____

23. _____

24. _____

25. _____

Positive You Journal

(Part 1: Past Examples)

For each positive quality that you have written in your Positive Qualities
Record, recall specific examples that illustrate that quality. Try to list as
examples as you can.

Positive Quality	**Specific Example**
_____	_____
_____	_____
_____	_____
_____	_____
_____	_____
_____	_____
_____	_____

Positive You Journal

(Part 2: Everyday Examples)

1. For each day of the week, think 3 examples of positive
   qualities that you have shown during the day
2. Write the day and date, what you had done during the day,
   and what positive qualities your actions demonstrate

Day/Date	What You Did During the Day	Positive Qualities Shown

Acting Like the Positive You

Another way of promoting a balanced view of yourself is by addressing your behaviors and how you treat yourself. When you think negatively about yourself, how do you tend to behave? Do you treat yourself as someone deserving of fun and recognition for your achievements? Or instead, do you neglect yourself and withdraw from life? If you have problems with low self-esteem, it is likely that you take the latter approach to life. This means that you probably engage in few activities that are pleasurable or do things that are just for you, and discount the things you accomplish from day to day. Taking such an approach keeps all those negative self-evaluations alive.

Experiencing enjoyment and a sense of accomplishment are an important part of everyday experience, which makes us feel good about ourselves and our lives. The problem for people with low self-esteem is that they often believe that they are undeserving. Therefore, enjoyment and achievement does not feature in their day, and this keeps them thinking negatively about who they are as a person. This is something we want to reverse, and get you treating yourself kindly and treating yourself to a fulfilling and satisfying life. Treating yourself well will help you start seeing yourself in a more balanced and accepting light.

Getting Started

The first step to changing the way you treat yourself is to first observe how your life is currently. Using the Weekly Activity

Schedule, start recording the activities you get up to during the week. Then, for each activity, rate the sense of pleasure and achievement (0-10) that you get from doing that activity. When doing this, it is important to remember that a sense of achievement does not only come from doing huge things (e.g., a promotion, an award, graduating), but achievement can come from the day-to-day things (e.g., cooking a nice meal, confronting a situation you had some anxiety about, doing some housework when feeling unmotivated, etc.).

By observing what you do during your week and rating your activities, you can see how much fun or sense of achievement you are having in your average week. If there is not much that is pleasant, fun, or enjoyable to you, this will be a sign that you need to increase your fun activities. By observing how your week is currently, you can also start recognizing your accomplishments and achievements, which you may have ignored or discounted previously, or tackle some tasks to give you a sense of achievement.

Making Changes

Once you have a good sense of what a typical week looks like for you, you can think about what you would like to change. Do you need more fun activities in your week? What activities would be enjoyable, pleasant, or relaxing? What would be something you can do just for you, to treat yourself kindly? On what days or at what times in particular could you do fun things for yourself? Are you avoiding or neglecting things in your life, so that there is little sense of achievement in your week? What could you start doing to rectify this? When could you do these things?

Once you have a sense of what needs changing, it is time to put the changes in place. In this book there is Fun Activities Catalogue. There are 183 activities listed in this catalogue. These are suggestions to help you think about what you might enjoy. You may be able to think of others. Choose two or three from the list to do in the coming week. Remember to also include one or two achievement-type tasks to your schedule as well. Use the worksheet to plan ahead which activity you will do, when you will do it (date), and then rate your sense of pleasure and achievement BEFORE and AFTER the activity. This will let you know if the activity has been helpful. You could also use the Weekly Activity Schedule from before to plan your fun and achievement activities for the week.

Starting Simple

 Even though there are a number of advantages to increasing your fun and achievement, it might not be easy to get started. Often, this is because you have rarely done things just for you, and you think negative thoughts such as "I don't deserve to do things for myself," "It's too hard," "I am not worth it," "I won't enjoy doing this," or "I'll probably fail at this too." These thoughts may stop you from getting started. Often the big mistake people make is trying to do too much too soon.

If you hadn't been doing any running for 6 months, would you try and run a marathon without doing any training? Of course not! You would go on a training program that starts out within your present capabilities, and then slowly build up your fitness and endurance. Similarly, when you are down on yourself, it is unreasonable to expect yourself to be able to jump out of bed and clean the house before going out to meet a friend for a late lunch. If you set your goals too high, you might end up not doing them, become disappointed in yourself, and feel worse than ever about who you are. Instead, plan to do things that are achievable at your current level of functioning. Start with small steps if necessary and slowly build yourself up to the large tasks that seem unmanageable right now. For example, don't try to tidy the whole house in one go – start with one room and just aim to tidy one particular area. If you're wanting to clean the kitchen, start with the dirty dishes. Then, aim to get the bench tops clean, before you move to the stove. Any task can be broken down into smaller steps until you find something achievable.

Sometimes it is easier to aim to do a task for a set period of time rather than trying to achieve a set amount. Exercise for 5 to 10 minutes rather than aim to do an hour's worth. Say you will spend 10 minutes weeding the garden rather than aiming to weed a certain area. In this way, it will be easier for you to achieve your goal. In the beginning, the important thing is not what you do or how much you do, but simply the fact that you are DOING. Remember that action is the first step, not motivation, and you'll soon find yourself feeling better about doing things for yourself or approaching challenging things.

Weekly Activity Schedule

Use this worksheet to record the activities you get up to during the week. Then, for each activity, rate the sense of pleasure and achievement (1-10) that you get from doing that activity. When you have done this, reflect on what you have recorded. What do you make of your activity schedule.

	Monday	Tuesday	Wednesday	Thursday	Friday	Saturday	Sunday
8-9 am							
9 to 10 am							
10 to 11 am							
11 to 12 pm							
12 to 1 pm							
1 to 2 pm							
2 to 3 pm							
3 to 4 pm							
4 to 5 pm							
5 to 6 pm							
6 to 7 pm							
7 to 8 pm							
8 to 9 pm							
9 to 10 pm							
11 to 12 pm							

Pleasurable Activities Catalogue

The following is a list of activities that might be pleasurable for you. Feel free to add your own pleasurable activities to the list.

1. Soaking in the bathtub
2. Planning my career
3. Collecting things (coins, shells, etc.)
4. Going for a holiday things
5. Recycling old items
6. Relaxing
7. Going on a date
8. Going to a movie
9. Jogging, walking
10. Listening to music
11. Thinking I have done a full day's work
12. Recalling past parties
13. Buying household gadgets
14. Lying in the sun
15. Planning a career change
16. Laughing
17. Thinking about my past trips
18. Listening to others
19. Reading magazines or newspapers
20. Hobbies (stamp collecting, model building, etc.)
21. Spending an evening with good friends
22. Planning a day's activities
23. Meeting new people
24. Remembering beautiful scenery
25. Saving money
26. Gambling
27. Going to the gym, doing aerobics
28. Eating
29. Thinking how it will be when I finish school
30. Getting out of debt/paying debts
31. Practicing karate, judo, yoga
32. Thinking about retirement
33. Repairing things around the house
34. Working on my car (bicycle)
35. Remembering the words and deeds of loving people
36. Wearing sexy clothes
37. Having quiet evenings
38. Taking care of my plants
39. Buying, selling stocks and shares
79. Making a gift for someone
80. Buying CDs, tapes, records
81. Watching boxing, wrestling
82. Planning parties
83. Cooking, baking
84. Going hiking, bush walking
85. Writing books (poems, articles)
86. Sewing
87. Buying clothes
88. Working
89. Going out to dinner
90. Discussing books
91. Sightseeing
92. Gardening
93. Going to the beauty salon
94. Early morning coffee and newspaper
95. Playing tennis
96. Kissing
97. Watching my children (play)
98. Thinking I have a lot more going for me than most people
99. Going to plays and concerts
100. Daydreaming
101. Planning to go to TAFE or university

102. Going for a drive
103. Listening to a stereo
104. Refinishing furniture
105. Watching videos or DVDs
106. Making lists of tasks
107. Going bike riding
108. Walks on the riverfront/foreshore
109. Buying gifts
110. Travelling to national parks
111. Completing a task
112. Thinking about my achievements
113. Going to a footy game (or rugby, soccer, basketball, etc.)
114. Eating gooey, fattening foods
115. Exchanging emails, chatting on the internet 116. Photography
117. Going fishing
118. Thinking about pleasant events
119. Staying on a diet
120. Star gazing
40. Going swimming
41. Doodling
42. Exercising
43. Collecting old things
44. Going to a party
45. Thinking about buying
46. Playing golf
47. Playing soccer
48. Flying kites
49. Having discussions
50. Having family get-
51. Riding a motorbike
52. Sex
53. Playing squash
54. Going camping
55. Singing around the house
56. Arranging flowers
57. Going to church, praying (practicing religion)
58. Losing weight
59. Going to the beach

60. Thinking I'm an OK person
61. A day with nothing to do
62. Having class reunions
63. Going ice skating, roller skating/blading
64. Going sailing
65. Travelling abroad, interstate or within the state
66. Sketching, painting
67. Doing something spontaneously
68. Doing embroidery, cross stitching
69. Sleeping
70. Driving
71. Entertaining
72. Going to clubs (garden, sewing, etc.) 73. Thinking about getting married
74. Going birdwatching
75. Singing with groups
76. Flirting
77. Playing musical instruments
78. Doing arts and crafts
121. Flying a plane
122. Reading fiction
123. Acting
124. Being alone
125. Writing diary/journal entries or letters
126. Cleaning
127. Reading non-fiction
128. Taking children places
129. Dancing
130. Going on a picnic
131. Thinking "I did that pretty well" after doing something
132. Meditating
133. Playing volleyball
134. Having lunch with a friend
135. Going to the hills
136. Thinking about having a family
137. Thoughts about happy moments in my childhood

138. Splurging
139. Playing cards
140. Having a political discussion
141. Solving riddles mentally
142. Playing cricket
143. Seeing and/or showing photos or slides
144. Knitting/crocheting/quilting
145. Doing crossword puzzles
146. Shooting pool/Playing billiards
147. Dressing up and looking nice
148. Reflecting on how I've improved
149. Buying things for myself
150. Talking on the phone
151. Going to museums, art galleries 152. Thinking religious thoughts
153. Surfing the internet
154. Lighting candles
155. Listening to the radio
156. Going crabbing or prawning
157. Having coffee at a cafe
158. Getting/giving a massage
159. Saying "I love you"
160. Thinking about my good qualities
161. Buying books
162. Having a spa, or sauna
163. Going skiing
164. Going canoeing or white-water rafting
165. Going bowling
166. Doing woodworking
167. Fantasizing about the future
168. Doing ballet, jazz/tap dancing

169. Debating
170. Playing computer games
171. Having an aquarium
172. Erotica (sex books, movies)
173. Going horseback riding
174. Going rock climbing
175. Thinking about becoming active in the community
176. Doing something new
177. Making jigsaw puzzles
178. Thinking I'm a person who can cope
179. Playing with my pets
180. Having a barbecue
181. Rearranging the furniture in my house
182. Buying new furniture
183. Going window shopping
Other Ideas:

_____
_____
_____
_____
_____
_____
_____
_____
_____
_____
_____
_____
_____
_____

Fun & Achievement Activities Schedule

Treat yourself to some fun and acknowledge your achievements. Experiencing enjoyment and a sense of accomplishment can help you to feel good about yourself and your life. Try it and see!

Identify a number of pleasurable and achievement-type activities that you might want to try. If you find it difficult to generate a list, see if you can get some ideas from the Pleasurable Activities Catalogue. Then, plan your activities and engage in them. Use the following rating scale to rate your sense of fun and achievement BEFORE and AFTER the activity.

0	1	2	3	4	5	6	7	8
Absolutely None	Minimal	Slight	Mild	Moderate	Much	Higher	Very High	Extreme

	Fun	Achievement
Before:		
After:		

Date:
Activity:

Fun   Achievement

Before:

After:

Date:
Activity:

Fun   Achievement

Before:

After:

Date:
Activity:

Adjusting Rules & Assumptions

Introduction

In previous sections, we discussed biased expectations and negative self-evaluations and introduced some strategies for you to work at challenging them. In the previous section, we discussed the importance of accepting yourself and explored strategies for identifying and acknowledging your positive qualities and experiences. We hope that you have found these strategies helpful in improving how you feel about, and see, yourself. Now that you have had some experience in working through these strategies, it is also important that we tackle some of the more difficult issues and work toward addressing negative core beliefs. In this section, we will discuss adjusting and changing the unhelpful rules and assumptions that restrict your behavior and keep your negative core beliefs alive.

Rules for Living

Here are some things to review and keep in mind, before we begin tackling our unhelpful rules.

Rules are learned. It is not often that unhelpful rules are formally taught. Rather these are developed through trial and error and observations you had made in your earlier life experiences. You may not consciously know that you have developed these rules but they consistently influence how you behave and live your life anyway. These rules often grew out of the conclusions you made about yourself as a result of your earlier life experiences. Therefore, these rules are also unique to you.

Rules can be culture-specific. The rules and assumptions for living that you have developed reflect the norms and culture of the family and the society or community in which you grew up. For example, you might have grown up in a family where boys are favored over girls and if you are female, you might have concluded that you are a second-class citizen. You might then have learned the rule, "Women must always be subservient to men," and continue to live according to this rule even if circumstances are different now.

Rules can be stubborn and resist change. Rules for living not only guide your behavior, they also influence how you perceive, interpret, and absorb information throughout your life. We talked about how there are many things happening, and there is a lot of information available, around us. Often we are not aware of all that is going on because our brains would be bombarded with too much information if we tried to make sense of everything. Therefore, we are equipped with an ability to sift out information and focus on only those things that are important to us. Unfortunately this could also work against us because we tend to only pay attention to, and make sense of, those things that are consistent with our beliefs and rules. So, if you have the negative core belief, "I am an unattractive person," and the rule "I must always be funny and witty or else no one will like me," you might only notice the person who doesn't laugh at your remarks and not the other three who were laughing heartily. You might also then interpret that as "People didn't laugh at my jokes, so they must not like me." This is why unhelpful rules for living and negative core beliefs can be resistant to change. However, now that you know this, you can learn to notice other things as well and to challenge any unhelpful interpretations so that you can have a more balanced view of yourself.

Rules for Living: What's Helpful, What's Not

Rules and assumptions for living guide our behavior and enable us to cope with our everyday lives. Rules for living are necessary for us to make sense of the world around us and to help us function on a day to-day basis. So, having rules, in itself, is not unhelpful. The question is what type of rules do we have? There are many rules for living that are helpful.

Helpful rules are realistic, flexible, and adaptable, and they enable us to function healthily and safely. For example, "People should not drive when they have had too much to drink (ie, have a blood alcohol level of more than .05)" is a helpful rule. These types of rules are realistic, that is, there is evidence to support them. There is evidence that the judgement of people who have more than a blood alcohol level of .05 can become impaired. They are less able to see clearly and concentrate on what they are doing. So, based on this evidence, keeping this rule can help ensure our survival! Helpful rules are also those that are flexible and adaptable. This means that they allow you to adapt your behavior to various situations. No one can be absolutely certain about everything in life nor does one have control over everything. That is why rules that have some 'give' in them are probably more helpful than those that are absolutistic. Consider the rule, "It would be great if we could all try our best and work as hard as we can for this project" compared with "We must always be the best at everything we do, at all costs." In the first rule, we are asked to work to the best of our abilities, given the circumstances, for a particular project. This means that the rule takes into consideration the times that for some reason, we are not able to match the standards that we reached previously. Perhaps we are ill or are experiencing a problematic situation in our personal lives. The rule is also flexible in that it applies to a particular situation (a project) as there are other times when we may choose not to work so hard at something (ex, gardening, cooking, or cleaning our house). We may decide that we want to work but also to take it a little easier.

Unhelpful rules are unrealistic, unreasonable, excessive, rigid, and unadaptable. Look at the second rule in the above paragraph. According to that rule, we have to achieve a particular standard ("best at everything") in every situation ("always") and not caring about what we might have to do or give up to achieve it ("at all costs"). If we believed strongly in this rule and made ourselves live up to it every day, what would happen? We will probably feel strong negative emotions when the rule is broken, which is quite likely. The reality is that we cannot be the best all the time. There are times when others might achieve better results. This rule also ensures that our self-esteem remains low because it is setting us up to fail.

Let's explore further how unhelpful rules keep low self-esteem going.

Unhelpful Rules & Low Self-Esteem

In essence, low self-esteem is viewing yourself and valuing your self-worth in a negative way. This is reflected in the negative core beliefs you might have about yourself, such as, "I am unlovable," or "I am not important." As discussed in, you might have come to these conclusions as a result of significant negative experiences early in life. To help you get by and manage from day to day, you might have developed rules and assumptions to help protect your self-esteem. Unfortunately, these rules and assumptions are usually unrealistic, unreasonable, rigid, and unadaptable. Let's say, for example, that you have the belief, "I am incompetent." You might have developed the rule and assumption "I must never ask for help, because if I do, people will laugh at me" or "I must never take on a task that seems too difficult for me because if I don't do well, people will think I'm a total idiot." If you are able to stick to, and carry out, these rules and assumptions, you might feel okay about yourself because then no one will know how bad you are at doing things. But what is the effect of having such rules?

Although these rules appear to help protect your self-esteem, they actually keep your negative core beliefs and your low self-esteem in place – they are 'locked in' as it were. Living up to such rules and assumptions means that your behavior is restricted in such a way that these rules and your negative core beliefs do not have the opportunity to be challenged. Let's continue with the previous example, with the rule and assumption, "I must never ask for help, because if I do, people will laugh at me." If you never ask for help, you will not be able to check out what people's responses are if you do. If you occasionally asked for help, you might find that some people were quite happy to lend a helping hand and did not laugh at you. In this way, your assumption that people would laugh at you if you asked for help would have been challenged. However, because of your reluctance in asking for help, you don't get a chance to debunk it. As such, your rule and assumption stays in place and your negative core belief also remains intact.

Not only do such unhelpful rules and assumptions keep low self-esteem in place, they also put a considerable amount of pressure on you. Note that the rule is "I must never ask for help." The words "must" and "never" are an indication of the inflexibility of the rule. The rule demands that you behave in a particular way all the time. It does not allow you to behave differently in, or adapt to, different environments and situations.

Identifying My Unhelpful Rules & Assumptions

Let's now begin to identify what unhelpful rules and assumptions you might have developed for yourself to live by. You might already have an idea of these now that you have learned to challenge your biased expectations and negative self-evaluations. When identifying your rules and assumptions, ask yourself:

What do I expect of myself when I am at work or school? What standards do I expect myself to meet?

What would I accept and not accept?
What do I expect of myself when I am socializing?
What do I expect of myself in my various roles – child, friend, partner, parent, staff member/supervisor?
What do I expect of myself regarding leisure or fun activities, and self-care?

Rules and assumptions for living can be in the form of statements such as:

"I must/should have to always…or else…."	Ex, "I must always be the best at everything." "I have to always keep it together and control my emotions."
"I must/should never…"	Ex, "I must never show any sign of weakness or back away from a challenge," "I should never ask for something that I need."
"If…, then…,"	Ex, "If I let people know the real me, they will think I'm a total loser."

The following are other sources from which you might be able to identify your rules and assumptions for living.

Thought Diaries. What you have recorded in your Thought Diaries are biased expectations and negative self-evaluations, which are also known as unhelpful thoughts. Often, there is another layer behind those unhelpful thoughts. For example, thoughts such as, "This report really sucks. I didn't have time to include colored charts. I should have done better," might reflect the rule, "I have to do everything perfectly." Usually, there are rules and assumptions for living that are already present that generate or "drive" the unhelpful thoughts. Can you recognize if there are any rules for living reflected in your unhelpful thoughts?

Themes. Another way of identifying the rules and assumptions that guide your behavior is to ask yourself if you notice any themes that might be common to the concerns you have or the issues that you are preoccupied with. You could ask yourself questions such as:

In what types of situations might I experience the most anxiety or self-doubt?
What aspects of myself am I most hard on?
What types of negative predictions do I make?
What behaviors in other people are linked with me feeling less confident about myself?

Negative Evaluations of Self & Others. Ask yourself:

In what types of situations do I put myself down?
What aspects of myself do I criticize most?
What does this say about what I expect of myself?
What might happen if I relax my standards?
What type of person do I think I might become?
What don't I allow myself to do?
What do I criticize in other people?
What expectations of them do I have?
What standards do I expect them to live up to?

Direct Messages/Family Sayings. Sometimes, your rules and assumptions for living might be direct messages given to you when you were a child or adolescent. Ask yourself:

What was I told about what I should and should not do?
What happened when I did not obey those rules?
What was I told then?
For what was I punished, criticized, and ridiculed?
What was said to me when I was not able to meet expectations?
How did people who were important to me respond when I was
naughty, made mistakes, or didn't do well at school?
What did I have to do to receive praise, affection, or warmth?

Some of those messages you received when you were much
younger could be in the form of particular sayings that some
families might have, or some sort of a "motto." For example,
adults in families might say, "The only person you can depend
on is yourself," "People who are nice to you always want
something in return," "Practice makes perfect," "If you can't
do something well, you might as well not try," or "If you don't
aim high, you will never be successful." Did your family have
any sayings or mottos that you remember or use today?

Now that you have read this section on identifying your rules
and assumptions for living, have you been able to identify or
recognize any that are operating right now in your life? What
are some of those rules and assumptions? Take a few minutes
to write them down.

Adjusting the Rules

By now, you might have come to recognize some unhelpful rules and assumptions for living that you might have developed when you were younger and have been trying to live according to them. Just as in the previous Sections, you can work at challenging your rules and assumptions for living in a step-by-step way using a worksheet. If you have worked through the previous Sections, you will probably find that changing the rules is not that difficult. It isn't easy, but it might not be that difficult either, given that you have already had some practice at challenging your biased expectations and negative self-evaluations. You will find a worksheet for you to work through. Before doing that, read through the following notes that will provide a guide for you.

1. Identify an unhelpful rule and/or assumption that you would like to challenge. If you have a number of rules and assumptions and are not sure which one to work on first, choose one that is related to an aspect of your life that you really want to change (eg, your social life or your relationship with your colleagues).

2. Have a think about how this rule and/or assumption for living has impacted your life. Ask yourself: What aspect of my life has this rule had an impact? Has it affected my relationships, work or studies, how I take care of myself or engage in social or leisure activities? How do I respond when things don't go well? How do I respond to challenging situations or new opportunities? How do I express my emotions? Am I able to ask for my needs to be met? Evaluating the effect of unhelpful rules and assumptions on your life is important because

you not only want to change and adjust these rules, you also want to change how they affect your life.

3. Ask yourself how do you know when this rule is in operation? How do you know when the rule is active in your life? How do you feel? What are the things you do and say (to yourself or others)?

4. Ask yourself, "Where did the rule come from?" The purpose of this question is to provide a context for your rule and assumption. It is to help you understand how this rule developed and what might have kept it going all this while. As we have discussed before, unhelpful rules and assumptions might have made sense at the time when you were experiencing a difficult situation and you adopted them so that you could cope and function from day to day. However, the main issue is whether or not this rule or assumption is still relevant today. Ask yourself, "Is this rule still necessary today? Is it useful?"

5. Next, ask yourself, "In what ways is this rule (and/or assumption) unreasonable?" Remember that we have discussed that unhelpful rules and assumptions are inflexible and rigid. Sometimes when you live according to such rules and assumptions, you don't recognize that the world around us does not behave that way in general. Also, these rules and assumptions were made when you were a child or young person. As an adult now, you don't have to live according to the rules you made as a child.

6. Although unhelpful rules and assumptions are not beneficial in the long term, there might be certain advantages in living according to these rules. It is probably why these rules and assumptions are still intact. Make a list of these advantages. Ask yourself, "What advantages do I gain from living according to this rule and/or assumption? What benefits have I obtained? How have these been helpful? What do they protect me from?"

7. What are the disadvantages of living according to this rule and assumption? You have identified the advantages but it is also important to evaluate whether or not the advantages are really genuine. Then ask yourself about how this rule/assumption might limit your opportunities, prevent you from experiencing fun and pleasure, downplay your achievements and successes, negatively impact on your relationships, or prevent you from achieving your life goals. Write these down on the worksheet and then compare them with the advantages you had written down. Do the disadvantages outweigh the advantages? If it is the other way round, then maybe you need not challenge this particular rule and assumption. If you decide that this rule and assumption is not helpful, then let's move on to the next important point.

8. Now, think carefully about what might be a more balanced rule – what would be more realistic, flexible, and helpful? Try and think about how you could maximize the advantages and minimize the disadvantages of the old rule. Think about the ability to

adapt this rule to different situations. Consider using less extreme terms such as "sometimes," "some people," "prefer," "would like," "it would be nice if," compared with "must," "should," "it would be terrible if…" For example, instead of the unhelpful rule, "I must do whatever it takes to stay slim, or else I will never have any friends," consider the alternative "I will try to maintain a healthy lifestyle and it would be nice if I could continue to be slim. However, it is unlikely that my friends only like me because I am slim." Balanced rules and assumptions might end up being longer than old ones. This is because they are more 'sophisticated' – you are making it more realistic, flexible, and adaptable. If you find it difficult to think of an alternative rule and/or assumption that is more balanced, don't worry. Just give it a try and put it in practice for a week or two. You can always revise your rule and adjust it as you become more familiar with the process of challenging and adjusting your unhelpful rules and assumptions.

9. The final step is to consider what you could do to put your new rule and assumption into practice. Why do you think it might be important to do this? Remember that your old rule and assumption had been in operation for some time now so it is important that you not only have a new rule but new behaviors so that the new rule can be 'house-broken' and settle into your balanced belief system.

This is an "Adjusting the Rules" worksheet, try working through a worksheet yourself.

Adjusting the Rules

Rule and/or assumption I would like to adjust
What impact has this rule or assumption had on my life
How do I Know this rule is in operation
Where did this rule or assumption come from?
In what ways is this rule or assumption unreasonable?
Advantages of this Rule Disadvantage of this Rule
What is an alternative rule or assumption that is more balanced and flexible?
What can I do to put this rule or assumption into practice on a daily basis?

Following Through

Now that you have worked through the worksheet, it might be a good idea to write down your new rule on a card that you can carry around with you and review every now and again. You could also write down the things you will aim to do to put this rule in practice.

Importantly, put the new rule into practice by carrying out those actions that you have planned. Although it might seem difficult to you now, it will get easier as you keep doing them. These behaviors are new to you so it's normal that they don't seem to be done naturally. With practice, will come progress!

Sometimes, the old rule might be activated again, so be prepared. This is because the old rule has been with you for a while and you have become quite used to it. But remember, circumstances have changed and the old rule is outdated. This is when challenging the old rule is important, as well as reviewing your flashcard, and practicing the new behaviors.

Developing Balanced Core Beliefs

Introduction

We have now come to the final step in tackling low self-esteem – changing the negative core beliefs you have about yourself. In earlier Sections, you learned how to tackle the negative unhelpful thoughts you might have in day-to-day situations, which sprout from your negative core beliefs. Earlier, you learned how to change the unhelpful rules and assumptions that have kept your negative core beliefs intact. All of these previous Sections have put you in a strong position to now directly tackle the negative core beliefs that are at the root of your low self-esteem. All the hard work you have done so far has been undermining your negative core beliefs, shaking the ground beneath them, and sowing the seed of doubt as to how accurate they are. So let's finish the job, and focus on adjusting those negative core beliefs – from negative and biased, to balanced and realistic.

Identifying Your Negative Core Belief

Remember, your negative core beliefs reflect the negative, broad, and generalized judgements you have made about yourself, based on some negative experiences you might have had during your earlier years. Based on the work you have done in the earlier Sections, you may already know what those beliefs are and you may have begun to question them. However, let's really focus on this now.

If you are not clear as to what your negative core beliefs are as yet, you need to first pin them down and identify them, before you can start changing them. Reflecting on the work you have already done will provide information and clues as to what your negative core beliefs are. To uncover those negative core beliefs, you will need to think about the implications of the specific clues and information you already have, that is, think about what they say about the overall view you have of yourself. Important questions to ask yourself throughout this 'identification' process are: What does this information mean about me as a person? What does this clue say about who I am? Asking yourself these questions will help you uncover your negative core beliefs from specific thoughts and experiences you have already identified.

Below are the various clues and information you can use to identify your negative core beliefs. Go through each of them, and see if you can discover the specific negative core beliefs that ring true for you.

Negative Life Experiences

The negative life experiences that you identified as contributing to the development of your low self-esteem could provide clues as to what your negative core beliefs are. Reflect on these experiences and ask yourself the following questions. Jot down any ideas about the negative core beliefs that come to mind. Did these experiences lead me to think there was something wrong with me in some way? If so, what was wrong?

_____

_____

_____

_____

_____

Do I remember specific situations that accompany the negative thoughts or feelings I have about myself? What do my memories of these situations say about me as a person?

_____

_____

_____

_____

_____

Can I link a specific person I know to the way I feel about myself? Has that person used certain words to describe me? What does their treatment of me say about me as a person?

_____

_____

_____

_____

_____

_____

Biased Expectations

The biased expectations that you identified could provide some ideas as to what your negative core beliefs are. Reflect on the key concerns you identified in your Thought Diaries for biased expectations, and ask yourself the following questions. Jot down any ideas about the negative core beliefs that come to mind.

If my biased expectations were to come true, what would that mean about me as a person?

_____

_____

_____

_____

If I didn't avoid or escape or use my safety behaviors, what would I be worried about revealing to other people about who I am?

_____

_____

_____

_____

Negative Self-Evaluations

The negative self-evaluations you uncovered will also provide clues regarding your negative core beliefs. Think about the sorts of criticisms you made of yourself in your Thought Diaries for negative self-evaluations, and ask yourself the following questions. Jot down any ideas about the negative core beliefs that come to mind.

What do my negative self-evaluations say about me as a person?

_____

_____

_____

_____

What are the common themes, labels, words, or names I use to describe myself? What do they mean about me?

_____

_____

_____

_____

Do my negative self-evaluations remind me of criticisms I have received from others when I was young? What do those criticisms tell me about myself?

_____

_____

_____

_____

What things make me critical of myself? What do these things say about who I am?

_____

_____

_____

_____

Difficulties Promoting Balanced Self-Evaluations

The difficulties you may have had with focusing on the positive you (by writing down your positive qualities) and acting like the positive you (by doing pleasant activities that are just for yourself) may give you some ideas regarding your negative core beliefs. Reflect on any troubles you had with thinking about yourself kindly and treating yourself kindly, and ask yourself the following questions. Jot down any ideas about the negative core beliefs that come to mind.

What made it difficult to think about myself kindly or treat myself kindly?

_____

_____

_____

_____

What was I telling myself when I tried to do these things?

_____

_____

_____

_____

What do my reactions to thinking/treating myself well tell me about how I see myself?

_____

_____

_____

_____

Perceived Outcomes Of Not Fulfilling The Rules

In a prior section, you clearly identified your unhelpful rules and assumptions. You can also use these to uncover your negative core beliefs. Think about what you fear will happen if your rules are broken. Sometimes your rule will incorporate the negative core belief (ex., "If I don't do things perfectly, I am incompetent," "If people see the real me, then they will know I am inferior," "If I disappoint someone, then I am a bad person."). Ask yourself the following question and jot down any ideas about the negative core beliefs that come to mind.

 If my rule was broken, then what would that mean about me?

_____

_____

_____

_____

Using all of the above clues and asking yourself what these things tell you about how you see yourself will help you to uncover your negative core beliefs. Once you think you have a clear idea as to what they are, write them down in the space below.

Adjusting Your Negative Core Beliefs

1. Choose One Negative Core Belief

If you have identified a number of negative core beliefs, choose only ONE to begin working on. You could choose the one that is of greatest concern to work on now or one that is related to any biased expectations, negative self-evaluations, or unhelpful rules and assumptions that you have previously worked on. Write that negative core belief in the top box of the 'Adjusting Core Beliefs Worksheet'. Also note how much you believe the negative core belief at now, when it's most convincing, and when it's least convincing. Note how the negative core belief makes you feel. Throughout this Section, you will need to keep referring to this worksheet and completing the relevant sections as we go. This will ensure that as you work through your negative core belief and tackle it, you have a clear record of this process to refer to at any time in the future.

Once you have worked through the process of adjusting this first negative core belief, you will then be able to apply it to other negative core beliefs you might want to change.

2. Develop a Balanced Core Belief

Now it's time to develop an alternative core belief to replace your old negative one. When developing a new core belief, you want to aim for something that is more positive, balanced, and realistic. Think of something that is a more accurate reflection of yourself. It is important that the work you do on your negative core beliefs is not just about squashing the belief that you have been carrying around, but also about promoting a new balanced view of yourself. So it is not so much about saying what you are not (ex., "I am not stupid"), but more about saying what you are (ex., "I am capable in many ways").

From the work you have done in previous Sections, you may already have some idea of what a more balanced core belief might be. It might be the opposite of your old belief (ex., "I am incompetent" ¤ "I am competent"), a more moderate view of yourself (ex., "I am a failure" ¤ "I am great at many things, average at other things, and weaker in some areas like anyone else"), or something else (ex., "I am no good" ¤ "I am a worthwhile person"). The important thing is that the new belief is more balanced, weighing up all the information (not just the negative) available, and including both your strengths and weaknesses. When developing a new core belief, ensure that your worth as a person is not being determined by only your faults or weaknesses. Also make sure that you are not painting an overly positive view of yourself (ex., "I am perfect in every way"), as this will be unrealistic, and it is unlikely that you will believe it. Remember not to discount any new alternative core beliefs on the basis that you don't fulfil these 100% (ex., "I can't put down that I am competent because sometimes I get things wrong."). No one is capable of such feats of perfection, so instead, accept that you are your new view of yourself – not perfect, but "good enough."

Now that you have an idea of your new balanced core belief, write it in the 'Adjusting Negative Core Beliefs' worksheet'. Also note how much you believe this new core belief at various times (now, when it is most convincing, and when it is least convincing) and how it makes you feel when you reflect on it. In these early stages, you might not believe it a whole lot. That is to be expected, given that you have carried the other negative view of yourself around with you for some time. To help you be more open to the new balanced view of yourself, let's work through the process further.

3. Examining the Evidence for Old Beliefs

To start to chip away at your old negative core belief, we first need to examine the evidence you base this belief on. What evidence do you have for this negative view of yourself? What experiences do you use to justify this negative core belief? To try to uncover what you base your belief on, ask yourself the following questions:

- Are there current problems I am having that I base this belief on? (ex., problems with depression or anxiety, relationship problems, etc.)

- Am I condemning myself because I need help and can't manage alone? (ex., turning to friends, family or mental health professionals for assistance)
- Am I condemning myself based on past mistakes I have made? (ex., failing school, trouble with the law, infidelity in past relationships, etc.)
- Am I condemning myself based on specific weaknesses of mine? (ex., not being academically minded, not being good at sport, etc.)
- Am I condemning myself based on my physical characteristics or my personality attributes? (ex., my body size, my attractiveness or my shyness, my untidiness)
- Do I base my view of myself on how I compare to other people? (ex., whether I am better than them in certain tasks, achievements, appearance, etc.)
- Do I use how other people treat or have treated me as a basis for how I view myself? (ex., abuse, neglect, mistreatment)
- Do I use the behavior of other people as a basis for how I view myself? (ex., my child's poor behavior)
- Have I lost something that is important to my self-worth? (ex., job loss, relationship break-up)

Once you have a clear idea of some of the evidence you use to justify the negative view you have of yourself, write the evidence down in the column marked "Evidence For" your Old Negative Core Belief, on the worksheet. When you have identified the evidence for your negative core belief, it is time to assess how credible and accurate the evidence is. This is like being a lawyer who questions how good or trustworthy the evidence is, whether or not it stands up under scrutiny. This is where you also ask yourself: Are there alternative ways of understanding this evidence? Are there other explanations you have not considered? Are there other ways of interpreting or making sense of the evidence, other than condemning who you are as a person? Try to uncover other ways of understanding the evidence by asking yourself the following questions:

- Are there other explanations for the current problems I am having, other than personal shortcomings? (ex., "I have not been meeting my commitments – not because I am lazy – but because procrastination and neglect are symptoms of depression")
- Are there benefits in getting help from other people? How do I view people that ask me for help? (ex., "I guess two heads are better than one, and I don't think badly of people who ask me for help, sometimes it takes a stronger person to admit they need help")
- Is it reasonable to base my self-esteem on my past mistakes? (ex., "Everyone makes mistakes. It is unfair to beat myself up over things I can't change")
- Is it reasonable to base my self-esteem on my specific weaknesses? (ex., "Just because I am not good at something, does not make me useless as a whole person. Everyone has their strengths and weaknesses")
- Is it reasonable to base my self-esteem on my appearance or on certain personality attributes I have? (ex., "I don't' judge others by how they look, so why do it to myself"; "Just because I am shy, doesn't mean I am a freak, it is just who I am, everyone is different in that way")
- Is it fair to compare myself to others, and base my self-esteem on whether I am better than they are? (ex., "Just because someone is better than me at this doesn't make them a better person. There will always be people I am better than at certain things and others who are better than me at certain things")

- What are other reasons for the way people treat or have treated me, other than personal shortcomings? (ex., "The way they treated me was probably due to the type of person they are and problems they have, rather than who I am")
- Can I be 100% responsible for other people's behavior? (ex., "As much as I try to do my best, I don't have absolute control over my child's behavior. There are other factors involved, it is not all my fault")

Once you have identified some other ways of understanding the evidence for your old negative core belief, list these new perspectives in the column marked "Alternatives Ways of Looking at the Evidence" on the worksheet. Now that you have completed this section of the worksheet, what did you make of what you had written? Hopefully this exercise will show you that the evidence you base the old negative view of yourself on is not totally accurate and probably unfair in many ways. Did you find this difficult to do? It can be in the beginning, because you have always accepted your negative core beliefs and the evidence for them. However, with practice, and putting on a different perspective (like putting on a different pair of spectacles), you'll soon find that you can do this exercise with ease.

4. Supporting New Beliefs

You have spent time gaining a new perspective on the evidence you have used in the past to support your old negative view of yourself. Now let's turn to supporting the new balanced view of yourself that you have developed. To support your new core beliefs, to take them on board, let them sink in, and make them believable, you need to do two things. Firstly, you need to gather evidence that is consistent with this new view of yourself, paying attention to evidence from the past/present and looking out for appropriate evidence in the future. Secondly, you need to act on, and experiment with, this new view of yourself. This means that you need to test it out, try it on for size, and act in ways that are consistent with the new you.

Evidence

In previous sections, we have discussed how when you have a core belief about yourself, you will tend to only pay attention to things that confirm your belief. Therefore, to enhance the new balanced view of yourself, you will need to start paying attention to evidence from the past and present that confirms this new view. You also need to be ready to pay attention to evidence that arises in the future that confirms this new view. On the 'Adjusting Negative Core Beliefs' worksheet, fill in past or present examples or experiences you have had that are consistent with your new balanced core belief. When doing this, pay attention to things that have happened that support this kinder view of yourself. Once you have done this, fill in the types of evidence likely to arise in the future, which will confirm your new balanced view. This will act as a reminder of what to be on the lookout for, to help you strengthen this kinder view of yourself.

Experiments

The last part of adjusting your negative core beliefs involves behaving as if the new balanced view of yourself is true. At the moment it doesn't sound very good, does it? But of course, it is true! It's just that you might not quite believe it as yet. Do you agree? This is because you have been carrying around the negative core beliefs for a while. However, you are beginning to loosen their hold on you. Let's loosen it further by changing how you behave and live your life! Ask yourself how someone who believed this kinder view of themselves might act or behave from day to day? How you can test out this new perspective you have of yourself? What things could you do to obtain more evidence for your new balanced core belief? What new experiences might further support this new perspective you are developing?

In general, to create new opportunities for more experiences that will support your new core belief will involve:

- Approaching rather than avoiding things
- Sticking with challenges rather than escaping
- Stopping safety behaviors and approaching things without taking precautions
- Treating yourself well
- Doing pleasant things for yourself
- Taking note of achievements and positive qualities
- Being active and engaged in life
- Being assertive

At a more specific level, think about exactly what you could do to 'test-drive' this new view of yourself. Exactly what new behaviors will you need to try out? How will you be behaving differently to before? Once you have some specific ideas about how to experiment with this new core belief, write these down in the "New Behavior/Experiments" section of the 'Adjusting Negative Core Beliefs' worksheet.

5. Evaluating Your Beliefs

Now that you have been through the step-by-step process for adjusting your negative core beliefs, it is important to reflect on what impact this process has had on you. You can do this by re-rating how much you now believe your old negative core belief and compare it to how much you now believe your new balanced core belief. Complete these ratings at the bottom of the worksheet.

An Ongoing Process

It is important to remember that changing your core belief about yourself is a difficult task that might take some time and practice. It will involve revisiting the steps in this Section a number of times, reflecting on what you have written, and perhaps adding more things. It will involve continually re-training your attention in everyday life so that you take note of all the future evidence that will arise to further support your new belief. It will involve behaving differently and using experiments to help accumulate more experiences and evidence for your new belief. It is an ongoing process. Remember, you have carried this old belief around for many years, so it will take some time to adjust it and embrace your new belief. However, you will find that if you continue to apply these strategies over time, your conviction in your old negative core beliefs will decrease and your conviction in your new balanced core beliefs will rise.

An Ongoing Process It is important to remember that changing your core belief about yourself is a difficult task that might take some time and practice. It will involve revisiting the steps in this Section a number of times, reflecting on what you have written, and perhaps adding more things. It will involve continually re-training your attention in everyday life so that you take note of all the future evidence that will arise to further support your new belief. It will involve behaving differently and using experiments to help accumulate more experiences and evidence for your new belief. It is an ongoing process. Remember, you have carried this old belief around for many years, so it will take some time to adjust it and embrace your new belief. However, you will find that if you continue to apply these strategies over time, your conviction in your old negative core beliefs will decrease and your conviction in your new balanced core beliefs will rise.

Healthy Self -Esteem

Introduction

Congratulations on making it to the end of this information package! We're glad you stayed on with us. If you haven't read all the Sections, it might be good to go back to the ones you missed. In this Section, you will find a summary of all the important concepts and strategies introduced to you in the previous Sections and a discussion on how to continue to improve on what you have learned and maintain your gains.

Putting It All Together

Just as we provided a model to help you understand how low self-esteem developed and what kept it going, we will leave you with a model of healthy self-esteem. This model brings all the important concepts and strategies you have learned together.

This model begins with an at-risk situation and the activation of old negative core beliefs. Having healthy self-esteem doesn't mean that you will never encounter an at-risk situation again. It also doesn't mean that you will never again think of yourself in a negative light. Everyone might think of themselves in a negative way or get down on themselves at times. The important thing to remember is not to do it too often. Healthy self-esteem is about thinking about ourselves and our worth in a BALANCED way. It is absolutely okay and appropriate that we recognize our weaknesses. What we need to do is accept that we all have weaknesses, and make a decision about whether or not we want to improve on them. We also need to recognize, acknowledge, and celebrate our strengths and successes. Also, don't forget any skills and abilities that might be neutral. Remember, it's all about being balanced!

The reason we might still encounter at-risk situations is that we cannot change our past experiences. We discussed that some of these experiences, especially if they are negative, can influence how we see ourselves and the rules and assumptions that we have developed. So, it is because we cannot go back and change those experiences that they might have a lingering effect on our self-esteem. The important thing to remember is that the effect of your past experiences on how you see yourself can be worn down the more you practice those strategies in the previous Sections.

So, the model of healthy self-esteem begins with an at-risk situation and the activation of old negative core beliefs. However, by this time, you will be able to tackle any biased expectations or negative self-evaluations by using Thought Diaries to challenge them. You will also have learned to identify and celebrate your positive qualities and recognize new achievements. It is also important that you engage in helpful behaviors, which means that you are dropping any avoidance, escaping, use of safety measures, approaching new situations with an open mind, engaging in life and doing pleasant activities, treating yourself kindly, and not withdrawing. If you then add to these, the adjusting of your old negative core beliefs and unhelpful rules and assumptions, and put these new rules and assumptions into practice…the possible consequences of all these actions are numerous! You might encounter opportunities for new experiences and new learning. Unhelpful rules and assumptions, and old negative core beliefs may or may not be confirmed, but there are possibilities for adjustments being made and increased flexibility in the way you see things. Finally, your threshold for at-risk situations might be increased. This means that you are not as sensitive to possible negative situations and will be more open-minded and balanced in how you view new situations.

Model of Healthy Self-Esteem

At-Risk Situation

Situation in which unhelpful rules & assumptions
Are under threat of being broken or are broken

Activation of Old Negative Core Beliefs

Develop Realistic Expectations	Develop Balanced Self-Evaluation
Use Thought Diaries	Use Thought Diaries

Engage in Helpful Behavior

- Approach challenges with open mind
- Stop avoidance, escaping & safety behaviors
- Treat yourself well
- Engage in life
- No withdrawal or isolation

Neglect Life Experiences (cannot change past)	Adjust Negative Core Beliefs - Develope new understanding of evidence for old negative beliefs	Adjust Unhelpful Rules & Assumptions -Question impact & helpfulness of unhelpful rules & assumptions

Change Unhelpful Behavior

- Put new rules into practice

Possible Consequence

- Opportunities for new experiences

Keep Practicing

Now that you have come to the end of this information package, the most important thing for you now is to keep practicing the strategies you have learned in all the Sections. This means continuing to apply all the useful skills and insights about yourself you might have gained. If you continue practicing the concepts and skills you have learned, they will become healthy habits that have been integrated into your lifestyle.

There are a few things to keep in mind now that you have learned some important skills in overcoming low self-esteem. One area to think about is how to maintain the gains that you have made. Another area to think about is how to minimize setbacks that might occur.

Maintaining Gains

It is important to recognize the progress that you've made, and as your self-esteem improves, it is helpful and appropriate to pat yourself on the back and celebrate your achievements. This will encourage you to keep going – to keep practicing and applying the new skills you have learned. Maintaining the gains you have made relies on you continuing to practice these skills. Remember, developing new skills to challenge what may be years' worth of old habits takes time and persistence.

So, there are some important things you will need to do in order to make the most of what you have learned to stay well or gain that extra improvement. The easiest way to summarize this is by looking at the "Healthy Self-Esteem" worksheet. It shows the main strategies you have learned to tackle low self-esteem and develop a more balanced view of yourself. Continuing to work on these strategies will help you continue maintaining your gains.

You will notice that on the "Healthy Self-Esteem" worksheet, there are some key things that you have learned over this series of Sections to manage low self-esteem:

- You have learned how to adjust your core beliefs and rules, so that they are more reasonable, flexible, balanced and realistic
- You have learned to question and test out negative thoughts (ex. biased expectations and negative self-evaluations) and address unhelpful behaviors in day-to-day situations
- You have learned to promote and support balanced self-evaluations by paying attention to your positive qualities and treating yourself well from day to day.

Minimizing Setbacks

Setbacks or slip-ups in progress can happen at any time and are to be expected. Try not to fall into the trap of believing that you are 'back to square one' as this will only make you feel worse. Change is not a steady process, it's more like the old saying: "Two steps forward, one step back" from time to time.

Think about how you learned to ride a bike. It probably took a few unsteady attempts and a few falls before you gained your balance. Even when you get your balance, you might still be unsteady when travelling over new ground, or on different surfaces. In the same way, different situations or times in your life may be more challenging, and may require extra effort and persistence (i.e., more challenging of biased expectations or negative self-evaluations, more pleasant activities, more paying attention to positive qualities, more experimenting with your behaviors, etc.). Even after much practice, there may be times when you think you've slipped back and feel a little off balance. Developing new skills is never a smooth process, you're always being faced with new challenges and different situations to apply those skills.

There are several reasons for setbacks occurring. There may be an increase in physical or mental stress. Just like riding a bike over challenging terrain, physical and mental stress can be challenges to the new ways of thinking and behaving that you have developed, and you may go back to old habits. Also, when we are physically unwell, we are less likely to have the mental or physical energy required to challenge or experiment with our negative thoughts, rule or beliefs, to treat ourselves well, or think of our positive qualities.

 It may help to remind yourself that most people have 'down days' or days where life's hassles are harder to deal with – it's part of being human! Use the Thought Diary skills you have learned to help when these situations occur. Also, you can use setbacks as a way of learning something new about yourself to help avoid similar problems in the future.

Preventing Major Setbacks

As you are progressing, try not to focus too much on small setbacks. If you are experiencing several small setbacks then there are some ways of preventing a major setback.

1. Identify Early Warning Signs

The first step is to look out for your own early warning signs. Some common examples are:

- Spending increased time expecting the worst or being self-critical
- Reverting back to unhelpful behaviors (e.g., avoidance, escape, safety behaviors, withdrawal, isolation, neglect, passivity, etc.)
- An increase in anxiety or depression.

2. Revise Skills

Think about the skills you have learned and what has been helpful in addressing your low-self-esteem (ex., challenging/experimenting with biased expectations and negative self-evaluations, paying attention to positive qualities, engaging in fun and achievement activities, treating yourself kindly, challenging/experimenting with your rules, challenging/experimenting with your negative core beliefs). Have you stopped practicing these skills consistently? You may wish to revise the Sections and techniques you have learned and perhaps increase practicing those skills.

3. Social Support

It is wise to find someone with whom you can sit down and have a good talk. This doesn't mean a therapy session where you pour out your heart but rather just a chance to talk through what's going on in your life, what your goals are, and generally just to ventilate with someone you trust. Often, problems seem bigger than they really are when a person tries to deal with them on their own. Hearing yourself talk through something can help to put it into perspective.

On the next page is a self-management plan for you to complete. Make a note of the early warning signs that might signal a setback then write down the strategies and tools you have learnt about that can help you to deal with a setback.

Self-Management Plan

What are the early warning signs that tell me that I might be heading for a setback and need to do something about it myself? Ex. I am more depressed or anxious OR I am more critical of myself OR I am expecting the worst more often OR I am *avoiding or withdrawing from things.*

What are some of my biased expectations, negative self-evaluations, unhelpful behaviors, unhelpful rules or assumptions, and negative core beliefs I need to watch out for?

If I do experience a setback, what will I do about it?

What are my future support options? *Ex, friends, family, GP, other, etc.*

What strategies/techniques have I found most helpful and need to continue to practice?

How can I build on what I have learned in this information package?

Chapter 9

Stone FIVE

Shame vs. Empowerment

Before you can live an abundant life, you must believe and accept your own self-image. You must be realistic and need to be able to trust yourself. Don't be ashamed. Accept yourself as the person that you're supposed to be, not particularly the one that you have acted out as.

Shame leads to creativity being blocked and leads to hostility, and hard to get along with behavior. In fact, shame would do things that go against our own character in the moment that we find ourselves saying, "who is that person?" in reference to our actions. We need to be asking, "What am I ashamed of, and what caused me to act like this?" When hide the truth about a feeling such as shame, guilt, anxiety, fear, self-hate and condemnation you limit your potential as a person and important thought benefits that come to self-image. You have the right to feel. You have the right to be yourself. You have the right to be good enough and deserving for whatever you think you should you have. You have the right to achieve your goals. You have the right to make mistakes. You have the right to be yourself and not be burdened about it. You have the right to say that God loves you (or any other higher power). So, you must identify what brought you to these shame-based feelings.

There are many active invaders that lead to shame-based reaction. It is difficult sometimes for us to look back at that. What we have to do is go back to being a child. We have to look at some things that created the feelings of shame. Open yourself up to the fact that you come with baggage, and that you have observed that you have perpetrated some behaviors that are unacceptable.

A quote that I once read is: "the people who live and love themselves and hold themselves in high esteem are those who give the most, contribute the most, and love the most."

Author unknown.

To let go shame, you must identify what it comes from. In order to do this, you have to open yourself up to the peace and empowerment of self-acceptance. You must retrain your mind of thinking thoughts that bring you up and put down the ones that bleed you. Do not allow others to tell you why you feel shameful; "you should have done this!"/ "You could have done that!"/ "you're not successful!"/ "you could've made more money". That is another person's opinion of you that you have taken out on your family. Do not allow other people to determine what your self-worth is!

Last year the suicide of a 15-year-old boy inspired a poet and mental health advocate who reduced the stigma surrounding mental illness and depression. Depression being so prevalent in lower self-esteem, you need to figure out a way to have longer visions of your contributions, and not of the things that you have failed. Failure is not necessarily a bad thing, it can always be a motivator, and can always get you to a place where you do better next time. Live and learn!!!

Empowerment refers to increasing the spiritual, political, social, educational, gender, or economic strength of individuals and communities.

Shame is a negative emotion that combines feelings of dishonor, unworthiness, and embarrassment

Do you have such a low opinion of your partner that you choose to treat them with such disrespect? If yes why?

_____

_____

_____

_____

_____

_____

_____

_____

When you were growing up, what are some things that you were most ashamed of?

_____

_____

_____

_____

_____

When you were growing up, what are some of the things you were most proud of?

_____

_____

_____

_____

_____

What are some of the past mistakes you have made?

_____

_____

_____

_____

_____

_____

Name three of some positive things you've done (or good decisions you've made)

_____

_____

_____

_____

_____

_____

What would you have to do to open yourself up to self-acceptance?

_____

_____

_____

How much do you worry about what people think of you?

_____

_____

_____

What do you think and feel about these things, and how has it changed since you are looking at yourself in a more positive way?

_____

_____

_____

_____

What? Me Worry!?!?

Introduction

"What? Me worry?" Well, everybody experiences general feelings of nervousness or a sense of being worried about something. In fact, a study has shown that almost 2 in every 5 people worry at least once every day. For some people though, worrying and feeling anxious is chronic and can seem to take over. Chronic worrying is a part of generalized anxiety, which can affect any kind of person at any stage of their life. It is estimated that about 1 in every 20 people experience significant generalized anxiety at some point in their lives. So remember, you are not alone. The aim of this Section is to provide you with some general information about anxiety and generalized anxiety disorder, to describe the types of symptoms common to generalized anxiety, and to discuss what causes generalized anxiety.

Understanding Anxiety

Let's begin this section by talking about what we mean by **anxiety**...

Feeling afraid is very much a part of the experience of being human. Fear is actually a survival instinct when it occurs in response to a realistically dangerous situation. Think about how you might react if a dangerous animal approached you. Most likely you would respond with fear. In fact, it is often helpful to respond with fear at times like this because when we become afraid, our body goes through a whole series of changes that ultimately serve to protect us. This fear response would probably lead us to either run for our lives or become sufficiently 'pumped up' to physically defend ourselves. As you can see from this example, the experience of fear is part of the process of survival.

Anxiety can also be experienced in less threatening situations. For example, athletes before a big game or race will feel some degree of anxiety. This is a good thing, as some anxiety in this situation will pump them up and get them ready to compete. Anxiety only becomes a problem when it is out of proportion to the situation, that is, when it often occurs in situations where there is no actual threat or danger. Some anxiety might be anticipated in certain situations (e.g., a job interview, making a sales pitch), but if the anxiety is so extreme that it stops you from doing what needs to be done, then it becomes a problem. When anxiety occurs at this extreme level, it interferes with your quality of life.

Different Types of Anxiety

Anxiety can be experienced in different ways, and you may find it helpful to be able to differentiate between different levels of anxiety…

Fear describes a very intense type of anxiety and tends to be a reaction to an immediate and specific situation. Sometimes this fear occurs in social situations or at the thought of an up and coming social event. We would call this type of fear "social anxiety". Other people experience intense fear in response to very specific things, for example spiders, heights, water. These fears are known as phobias. While others experience fear that feels like "sheer terror" that come out of the blue. These are known as panic attacks.

This information package addresses a level of anxiety that is described as **generalized anxiety, nervousness or chronic worrying**. This type of anxiety has similar physical and emotional characteristics to those of fear, but may be experienced at a different level of intensity. Instead of going straight to sheer terror, this anxiety builds up more gradually, has a high level of tension and gives you little peace of mind. The anxiety is often long-lasting and may appear when actually experiencing a negative event, or anticipating a future event.

Understanding Generalized Anxiety

While worrying and feeling nervous is something that all human beings experience, as with anything, too much of something can be bad for you. Normal anxiety can become a problem when it is:

- Excessive,
- feels uncontrollable,
- is experienced as intrusive in your life,
- is persistent – seeming to always be around,
- and causes you significant distress, or impairs your ability to go about your day-to-day life.

This is when normal anxiety becomes generalized anxiety.

Some common things people have told us they experience when they have generalized anxiety are:

1. Chronic worries running through their head. They occur over and over again like a broken record
2. Uncontrollable anxiety. Having a strong desire to be in control of their emotions, yet feeling as if the anxiety and worry has taken control over them and there is nothing they can do to stop it
3. Intrusive thoughts. No matter how much they try not to worry, not to think about things that make them nervous, these thoughts keep popping back into their mind against their will
4. Hating uncertainty. Wanting to know what is going to happen in the future and finding the experience of 'not knowing' very difficult indeed
5. Feeling restless, keyed up, on edge and unable to relax
6. Being physically tense. Feeling nervy or uptight, and having tightness or stiffness in the muscles of their body
7. Sleep disturbance. Having trouble falling asleep, maintaining sleep, or experiencing unsettled sleep, because their mind is constantly ticking over with worry
8. Problems concentrating and focusing on a task
9. Procrastinating about getting things done. Putting things off because it all feels too much and too overwhelming
10. Avoiding situations in which they worry or get anxious and nervous.

Take a moment to write down what it is that you experience when you have generalized anxiety.

_____

_____

_____

_____

One of the important features of generalize anxiety is that the anxiety is spread across a number of different areas such as health, work, interpersonal relationships, finances, and so on. This makes it different from other anxiety problems, such as social anxiety or phobias, where nervousness and worrying are more specific to particular situations.

Think about what areas of your life you tend to worry about? (Make a list of the different things you worry about).

_____

_____

_____

_____

_____

You may think that generalized anxiety is not as serious as other problems, such as social anxiety, phobias or panic, where the anxiety may appear to be more intense. However, generalized anxiety, nervousness, or worrying can significantly interfere in a person's life because it is long-term and chronic. In this way, it can be likened to having a condition like asthma or diabetes.

Unfortunately, people who have problems with generalized anxiety often do not seek treatment, as they might feel embarrassed to be seen as someone who cannot control their nerves. They may also believe that because they "have always been like this", they just have to live with it. Having these views may mean that they don't seek help for their worrying and nervousness, but it is important to remember that there are ways to break the worry habit.

It is also not uncommon for people experiencing generalized anxiety to also experience other types of anxiety disorders, or to experience mood disorders, such as depression, at the same time. Often when people do seek treatment it is for these other problems, rather than for their tendency to worry excessively.

Now that you know a bit more about generalized anxiety, take a moment to think about how serious your general anxiousness, nervousness, and worrying are to you. Tell us how serious the problem is by rating the two questions below. You will be asked to make these ratings again at the end of the "What? Me Worry!?!" information package, so you can see the impact the information contained in these Sections has on your generalized anxiety.

Overall, how distressing is your generalized anxiety?

(Circle the number that best describes you)

0   1   2   3   4   5   6   7   8   9   10

Not at all   Moderately   Extremely

Overall, how much of a problem is your generalized anxiety?

(Circle the number that best describes you)

0   1   2   3   4   5   6   7   8   9   10

Not at all   Moderately   Extremely

What Causes Generalized Anxiety?

So, how does one become a chronic worrier? There's no simple answer, of course, as everyone is different. However, there are some important factors that have been identified. These factors can generally be divided into biological and psychological causes.

Biological Factors

No single gene has been associated with generalized anxiety. Based on twin and family studies, it does seem that individuals may inherit a vulnerability to develop an anxiety disorder. These studies have reported a general vulnerability to develop an anxiety disorder, and interestingly, also a mood disorder. Notice that the researchers tell us that this is a general vulnerability, rather than a specific vulnerability for a specific type of disorder. In addition, it has been found that people born with a particular 'anxious' type of temperament, may be more likely to develop an anxiety disorder later in life.

Psychological Factors

However, it is important to remember that while our biology may make us vulnerable to developing an anxiety disorder, not all people with this vulnerability go on to develop problematic anxiety. A great deal depends on the lifestyle of that person, the types of life stressors they have encountered, and how they cope with such stressors.

Stressful, traumatic, and often uncontrollable life events may contribute to the development of generalized anxiety. When such events occur, some people may come to believe that life is dangerous and unpredictable, and that worrying about possible future negative events is a way of coping with the uncertainty of life. They may think that worrying helps them achieve a greater sense of certainty and control, because they would be better prepared for anything.

Anxiety may also develop when the people around you give you information about what is threatening and how to cope with those threats. For example, a child may have seen a parent constantly worrying about current circumstances and potentially negative future events, and may learn to follow the parent's behavior. Alternatively, you may have been told that "Worrying is good and shows that you are a conscientious and prepared person". These sorts of indirect and direct messages may increase your chances of developing generalized anxiety.

Finally, anxiety is made worse when one begins avoiding things they have some concern about. Avoidance will quickly make something that is initially a slight concern for a person, become a source of anxiety. If the people in your life (i.e., parents, siblings, peers, spouses/partners) support your avoidance of various things, this may make your anxiety worse in the long run. People usually support a person's avoidance because they don't want the person to feel any distress. However, experiencing a small amount of distress and learning how to solve or cope with the problem is likely to stop more severe anxiety in the long run.

Overview of Worrying

Introduction

Most clinicians and researchers agree that worrying is a central feature of generalized anxiety disorder. As we discussed one of the common things that people with generalized anxiety disorder experience is chronic worrying.

The aim of this section is to provide an overview of what worrying is, what triggers worrying, what keeps it going, and most importantly, how to treat it effectively.

Understanding Worrying

You can think of worrying as a self-talk activity, where we 'talk to ourselves' about possible future negative events that might happen and of which we are afraid. We discuss the event with ourselves and we think about how we might deal with it should the event happen. As such, worrying is a type of vigilance for threat, and an 'attempt' at mentally 'solving problems' that haven't yet happened. We say 'attempt' because often a good solution is not found, and people are left thinking they will not be able to cope should their worst fears happen. We say 'solving problems' because people often think that worrying is problem-solving, when in fact effective problem-solving is a very different type of activity.

"What If…" Worries

People with generalized anxiety are often having an internal conversation about things they fear might happen. In this way, worrying often occurs in the form of "What if…" questions. The questions play in your mind like a song and the words may sound like these:

"What if I can't get to my appointment on time?"

"What if I fail my exam?"

"What if I can't do the job?"

"What if I can't provide for my family?"

"What if something happens to my child?"

"What if my husband/wife/partner has an accident?"

"What if I get anxious during my interview?"

"What if my face turns red?"

"What if I get sick?"

As you will have noticed, the above examples of worrisome thoughts are about external things (e.g., work, family, etc) or internal physical things (e.g., illness).

What are the "What if…" questions you often ask yourself? (What external things or internal physical things do you tend to worry about?).

_____

_____

_____

_____

What Triggers Worrying?

Worrying can be triggered by various things. Some triggers may be more obvious and linked to external things, for example:

- Seeing a certain image (e.g., in the newspaper or on the T.V. news)
- Hearing certain information (e.g., on the radio or in a conversation)
- Being put in a certain situation (e.g., having to make decisions, perform a task, lead others)

Some triggers may be less obvious. These may be thoughts or images that seem to just pop into your head out of the blue. An initial "What if…" question that comes to mind for no apparent reason, can even be a trigger for worrying. For example, the thought "What if I left the iron on?" might pop into my head. If I think "I probably didn't" and decide not to worry about it, chances are I will forget about it, and the thought will slip my mind. However, if instead I start to 'chase' the thought further (e.g., "The ironing board might catch fire and that will spread to the whole house." "The house might burn down and then I will lose everything!"), then the original "What if…" question has now triggered a worry episode.

Write down any external images, information, and situations, or any internal images or "What if…" thoughts that have triggered worrying for you.

_____

_____

_____

_____

_____

_____

What Maintains Worrying?

People who describe themselves as chronic worriers are often disturbed that they seem to spend much of their waking hours worrying excessively about a number of different life circumstances. They do not understand why this activity continues. They often ask, "Why do I do it?" and "What keeps my worrying going?"

Negative Beliefs About Worrying

 In addition to the specific things people worry about, people with generalized anxiety disorder may also **worry about the fact that they are worrying**. In this case, such worriers are often concerned that worrying is "bad" and they hold negative beliefs about the activity of worrying. For example, they may believe that:

- Worrying is **uncontrollable**, and will take over and result in a loss of control (e.g., "I won't be able to control my worrying, and it will never stop").
- Worrying is **dangerous**, and will cause either physical or mental harm (e.g., "If I keep worrying like this I will go crazy/have a breakdown/become ill").

Holding these negative beliefs about worrying makes the process of worrying very distressing for you, and this will even keep your worrying going. Researchers believe that it may be these negative beliefs about worrying that are unique to people with generalized anxiety disorder.

What worries-about-worrying do you have? (What are the disadvantages of worrying?)

Positive Beliefs About Worrying

While worriers may hold negative beliefs about worrying (i.e., that worrying is uncontrollable and harmful), they also often hold positive beliefs that worrying is beneficial and "good". It is these positive beliefs about the usefulness of worrying that can keep worriers worrying. Some positive beliefs may be:

Worrying **motivates** me to do things

Worrying helps me find **solutions** to problems

Worrying **prepares** me for the worst

Worrying helps me **avoid** bad things

Worrying **prevents** bad things

What positive beliefs do you hold about worrying? (What are the advantages of worrying?)

_____

_____

_____

_____

Unhelpful Strategies

In an attempt to decrease or stop worrying in the short term, people often use certain strategies. However, in the long term, these strategies actually keep worrying going, making such strategies "unhelpful". There are two main types of unhelpful strategies.

The first type of unhelpful strategy is **avoidance**. This may take the form of avoidance of a feared outcome or avoidance of worrying itself. For example, if someone was given the opportunity to take on a new and important project at work, a person with generalized anxiety may worry "What if I can't do the job? What if I fail?" In order to avoid this feared negative outcome, they may pass the opportunity on to another colleague. An example of avoiding the act of worrying may be avoiding the television news because you know that the news tends to trigger episodes of worrying, or constantly contacting a loved one to allay fears that something bad has happened to them. This last example is known as reassurance seeking.

The problem with avoidance is that people limit their opportunity to be exposed to their worrying, and learn that the outcome isn't as bad as they thought, that worrying isn't uncontrollable or dangerous, and that there are other ways of coping besides worrying. Avoidance limits a person's opportunity to have experiences that disconfirm their worries and their beliefs about worrying. This keeps worrying going because their worries go unchallenged.

How have you avoided feared outcomes or avoided worrying itself?

_____

_____

_____

_____

_____

_____

_____

The second type of unhelpful strategy is thought control. People with generalized anxiety often attempt unsuccessfully to control their worrisome thoughts in a number of ways. These may include trying to suppress their worries (i.e., telling themselves to "Stop worrying"), trying to reason with their worrisome thoughts (i.e., "The likelihood of these things happening is so small"), distracting themselves (i.e., focusing attention on another task) or thinking positively (i.e., "Everything will be OK"). These attempts at controlling their worries often do not work for various reasons.

For example, it is widely known that trying to suppress a thought has the opposite effect of making that thought occur more. For example, try not to think of a pink elephant for the next 60 seconds and see **how well you do**.

Again, trying to reason with your worries is often useless, because no matter how small the chance is of something happening, your need for certainty will not be able to tolerate this small chance, and the answer to all your reasoning attempts will always be, "But it still could happen!" These ineffective thought control strategies not only keep the worrying going because they are not good at stopping the worrisome thoughts, more importantly they fuel one of your negative beliefs about worrying – that worrying is uncontrollable.

What thought control strategies have you tried for controlling your worries?

_____

_____

_____

_____

Treatment For Your Worrying

Let's recap and put all the information we now know about worrying together, and then have a look at how you can overcome your worrying. You can use the worksheet to summarize all the things you have written on the previous pages in one worksheet.

When your worrying is **triggered** by something external or internal:

1) Very specific worries related to the trigger are set off, and tend to take the form of "What if" questions. It is likely that the fact you respond with worrying so quickly, is because you believe that at times worrying can be helpful to you. That is, you hold some positive beliefs about worrying.
2) However, if you keep on worrying, your worries may start to focus more on worries-about-worrying and how uncontrollable and harmful your worrying is. This is

because you also hold some negative beliefs about worrying.

3) You experience distressing emotions and unpleasant physical sensations when you worry, which make you feel worse and make you believe even more that your worrying is harmful to you.

4) You engage in unhelpful strategies like trying to control your worrisome thoughts. These often don't work and will make you feel worse, making you believe even more that you're worrying is uncontrollable.

5) You may engage in other unhelpful strategies like trying to avoid worrying. This may make you feel better in the short term, but in the long run it will limit your opportunity to find better ways of coping with life than worrying.

From what you now know about the process of worrying, it makes sense that to overcome worrying and generalized anxiety, you need to do three things: 1) address your beliefs about worrying; 2) deal with the specific worries you have; and 3) learn to use helpful rather than unhelpful strategies.

Negative Beliefs About Worrying:

"Worrying Is Uncontrollable"

Introduction

Ask yourself this question: if you believed you had control over your worrying, how much would your worrying bother you? Chances are, you wouldn't feel as bad if you thought you were in control of your worrying, as opposed to thinking that your worrying is in control of you. So in this Section we will look at changing your beliefs that:

"I have no control over my worrying"

"Once I start worrying I can't stop"

"My worrying is uncontrollable"

"My worrying will never end"

"My worrying controls me"

"I can't do anything to stop my worrying"

Changing Your Belief

Before we start changing your belief that worrying is uncontrollable, we need to know how much you believe it. How convinced are you that your worrying is beyond your control? Do you believe it fully and whole-heartedly? Do you mostly believe it? Half the time? Occasionally? Or maybe this is not a belief you even hold? Even if you think you do not hold this belief, we encourage you to still work through this Section to be sure it is not a belief that is lurking at the back of your mind without you realizing. Chances are, you can move on quickly from this Section to the next.

How much do you believe that your worrying is uncontrollable?

(Circle the percentage that best describes the strength of your belief)

0% 10% 20% 30% 40% 50% 60% 70% 80% 90% 100%

To change your belief that your worrying is uncontrollable, you need to do two things.

Firstly, you need to **challenge** or dispute your belief. That means taking apart the belief that you can't control your worrying, by evaluating if it really is accurate and true, and examining what evidence you base your belief on. In this way you will be like a detective, trying to get to the facts of whether worrying really is uncontrollable.

Secondly, you need to **experiment** with your belief. That means doing things to see if worrying really is uncontrollable. If you are able to do things that show your belief isn't true – that in fact you can control your worrying – it is going to be hard to hold on to your belief. In this way you will be like a scientist with a prediction that worrying is uncontrollable, which needs to be tested.

Challenging Your Belief

Below is a list of questions you can ask yourself to challenge whether your belief that worrying is uncontrollable is really true. By using these questions you will become a detective, examining the evidence for and against your belief. An example is given below of how to use these questions to challenge your belief, you will find a worksheet to help you do this for yourself.

Evidence For

- What makes you think worrying is uncontrollable?
- What's the evidence for your belief?
- Is the evidence for your belief good/solid/reliable?
- Is there another way you could view the evidence for your belief?

Evidence Against

- Is there any evidence that goes against your belief?
- Have there been times when your worrying has been interrupted by something that has distracted you (e.g., phone rings, having to interact with someone)? What does this experience tell you about your worrying being uncontrollable?
- Have there been times when you normally would have worried about something, but couldn't because you had to do something else? What does this experience tell you about your worrying being uncontrollable?
- Have you ever tried to properly postpone your worrying (that is, not suppress it, but instead allow yourself to have a worrisome thought, and decide not to worry about it at that particular moment)? If you have done this, what does this tell you about your worrying being uncontrollable? If you haven't done this, how do you truly know your worrying is uncontrollable?
- Does your worrying stop eventually? How can this be if it is uncontrollable? Shouldn't it just go on forever if it can't be controlled?

Challenging Your Belief

Belief: *"My worrying is uncontrollable"*	
Evidence For	Evidence Against

Experimenting With Your Belief

Now it's time to do a bit of experimenting with your belief that worrying is uncontrollable. Like any good scientist, if you have a prediction about something, the best thing to do is to conduct an experiment to see if it is true.

You will have noticed in the previous example for challenging your belief that a distinction was made between suppressing thoughts, and postponing worrying. Remember earlier you did an experiment where you were asked to suppress a thought:

Try not to think of a pink elephant for the next 60 seconds.

Try it again right now!

Chances are you can't, and thoughts of pink elephants keep popping into your head.

Suppressing worrisome thoughts means trying to get all thoughts related to whatever you are worried about out of your mind – trying not to think about any of it. However, doing this is just not possible, as the pink elephant activity will have shown you.

Postponing worrying is something different. Postponing worrying means that it is alright for an initial worrisome thought to be in your mind (e.g., "What if I fail my exam?"), but you make a decision not to 'chase' the thought any further at that particular time. Not chasing the worrisome thought further means that you don't try to anticipate the worst or run scenarios and solutions related to your initial thought through your head over and over again (e.g., "It will be a disaster, I will be a failure, I will get kicked out of uni, I won't be able to find a job, maybe I should pull out of my course," etc.). Instead, you postpone your worrying until a later time. Can you see the difference between suppressing thoughts and postponing worrying?

It makes sense that if you are able to postpone worrying, then your worrying can't be uncontrollable, and this belief is not true.

Experiment: Postpone Worrying

Every day over the next week, try to postpone your worrying. Here's what to do:

- Pick a 'worry period'. This is a set time, place, and length of time to do all your worrying. Plan when, where, and for how long you will do all your worrying. Try and keep your worry period the same everyday (e.g., 6pm, dining room, 20mins) and don't do your worrying in bed or before you go to sleep
- When you notice yourself worrying about something or other during the day, list your worries briefly (in a couple of words only)
- Make the decision not to worry about it then and there, but save the worry for your set worry period. Bring your attention back to the present and what it was you were doing, reassuring yourself that you will deal with your worries later
- When you get to your worry period, only worry about the things you've listed if you feel you must (you don't have to worry about them if they no longer bother you, or if they no longer seem relevant to you). If you do need to worry, only worry for the set amount of time specified.

Before you start the experiment, complete the worksheet in as much detail as you can and then continue filling it out as you go along.

Instructions for completing the worksheet:

First, write down the details of your worry period (start time, end time, and place). Then, write down what you think will happen when you try to postpone your worrying. After that, rate how confident you are of your ability to postpone your worrying (between 0 and 10).

Now just give the experiment a go and see what happens.

For each of the next 7 days, fill in the day and the date, list what your worries were for the day, and underline the things you did worry about during your worry period. Record what actually happened during the day (e.g., did you manage to stop chasing worrisome thoughts and to postpone worrying?). Rate how much of the time during the day you were able to postpone worrying.

Then, compare what you predicted would happen with what actually happened on those 7 days. Typically people predict that they won't be able to postpone their worrying, and that their worrying will be out of control when they try this new strategy. Often people are surprised that they are actually able to postpone their worrying, and experience a sense of control. What did you find?

While postponing worrying is used here as an experiment to tackle your belief about worrying being uncontrollable, it is also just a really good strategy to stop your worries interfering in your day-to-day life. So, try to continue with the postponing worrying activity indefinitely. A later experiment recommended in this information package may require that you stop the postponing worrying experiment for a certain period of time. But unless another experiment gets in the way of you postponing your worrying, treat this technique as your new way of dealing with worrying generally, and use it for as long as worrying is still a problem for you.

Now that you have challenged and experimented with your belief that worrying is uncontrollable:

Rate again how much you believe your worrying is uncontrollable?

(Circle the percentage that best describes the strength of your belief)

0% 10% 20% 30% 40% 50% 60% 70% 80% 90% 100%

If there is some weakening (however small) of your belief that your worrying is uncontrollable compared to what it was at the start of this Section, congratulate yourself. If there's no change yet, that's okay. Remember, changing your beliefs takes time and persistence. Just going over the evidence for and against your belief once or experimenting with your belief once may not be enough. These are ongoing strategies you can practice until the evidence for your belief is weak, the evidence against your belief is strong, and you are successfully able to postpone worrying. A good gauge of when you have done enough work on this belief may be when your belief is relatively weak– let's say only 20%.

Postpone Worrying Experiment

My Worry Period:

Start Time:	End Time:	Place:

Prediction (What do you think will happen if you postpone worrying?)

_____

_____

_____

_____

How confident are you of your ability to postpone worrying?

0	1	2	3	4	5	6	7	8	9	10

I cannot postpone   I am moderately confident   I am extremely confident

Day: Date:	day	day	day	day	day	day	day
List of worries during the day							
What happened (Did you postpone the negative thoughts?							
How much time were you able to post pone worrying? (0% to 100%)							

Compare prediction with what happened

_____

_____

_____

Negative Beliefs About Worrying: "Worrying is Dangerous"

Introduction

Ask yourself the question: if you felt your worrying couldn't harm you or wasn't dangerous, how much would your worrying bother you? Chances are, you wouldn't feel as bad if you thought your worrying was harmless, as opposed to thinking your worrying is harmful. So in this Section we will look at changing your beliefs that:

"Worrying will make me go crazy"
"If I keep worrying I will have a nervous breakdown"
"I'll get sick if I don't stop worrying"
"Worrying will damage my body"
"I'll go nuts if I keep worrying"
"Worrying will make me ill"

Changing Your Belief

As in the previous section, before we start changing your belief that worrying is dangerous and harmful, we need to know how much you believe it.

How much do you believe your worrying is dangerous/harmful?

(Circle the percentage that best describes the strength of your belief)

0% 10% 20% 30% 40% 50% 60% 70% 80% 90% 100%

If you do not think you hold this belief at all, still work through this Section just to be sure, but chances are you can move on quickly from this Section to the next.

To change your belief that your worrying is dangerous, you need to do something you are already familiar with. That is, challenge or dispute your belief. This means dissecting the belief that your worry will cause you physical or mental harm, by evaluating if it really is accurate and true, and examining what evidence you base your belief on. In this way you will be like a detective, trying to get to the facts of whether worrying really is dangerous to you.

Often people can experiment with this belief too, just as you did in the last Section. Such an experiment might involve pushing your worrying to the 'max'. This means trying your hardest to lose control of your worrying. Typically people predict that trying to push their worrying to the limit will be awful, and that something terrible will happen. Often people are surprised that nothing bad actually happens and they experience their worry as harmless. However, it is recommended that this approach be used with the guidance of a mental health professional, and so is not used in this information package.

Challenging Your Belief

Below is a list of questions you can ask yourself to challenge whether your belief that worrying is dangerous is really true.

Remember, you are a detective examining the evidence for and against your belief. An example is given below of how to use these questions to challenge your belief, and you will find a worksheet to help you do this for yourself.

Evidence For

- What makes you think worrying is dangerous/harmful?
- What's the evidence for your belief?
- Exactly how does worrying cause mental/physical harm (be specific)?
- Is the evidence for your belief good/solid/reliable?
- Is there another way the evidence for your belief could be viewed?

Evidence Against

- Is there any evidence that goes against your belief?
- How long have you worried for? What specific physical or mental harm has resulted over this time?
- During a worry episode have you ever become ill or gone crazy?
- Can you think of other people/professions that are constantly under intense stress or anxiety, have they been harmed physically or mentally by their worry? (e.g., students studying for exams, people in stressful jobs – army officers, police, emergency department staff, etc).
- How can you believe that worrying is both dangerous on the one hand and has many positive benefits (motivates, prepares, prevents, etc) on the other hand?

EXAMPLE:

Evidence For	Evidence Against
I don't know how exactly how it will make me sick, but I have heard stress isn't good for you, so it must be something to do with that. [I haven't got a very strong argument for worrying being harmful. Maybe I need to look into it more, and get the facts.]	*How can something be both dangerous and helpful at the same time?* [My beliefs about worrying don't match up. Maybe I need to re-think.]
It just feels like I am going to go crazy, therefore I must be. [This isn't very solid evidence that worrying is going to harm me. It has never actually happened, it is just that it feels so bad at the time, so I assume something bad will happen. Just it is true, isn't really evidence it is true.]	*I have never actually gone crazy or gotten really sick from worrying.* [What I am worried about has never actually happened.]
Where I worry a lot, I get a cold, so worrying must be bad for my health. [There have been times when I haven't worried and have gotten sick. Also when I have worried a lot and gotten sick, I guess I haven't been sleeping well, easting right or exercising. So I guess it might not be the worrying itself that caused it, but how my lifestyle changes when I worry.]	*Plenty of people have worry and stress in their lives. While it doesn't feel great, these people don't break down physically or mentally.* [It doesn't tend to happen to other people, so why should it happen to me.]

Challenging Your Belief

Belief: *My worry is dangerous*	
Evidence For	**Evidence Against**

Now that you have challenged your belief that worrying is dangerous/harmful:

Rate again how much you believe your worrying is dangerous/harmful?

(Circle the percentage that best describes the strength of your belief)

0% 10% 20% 30% 40% 50% 60% 70% 80% 90% 100%

If there is some weakening (however small) of your belief that your worrying is dangerous compared to what it was at the start of this Section, congratulate yourself. If there's no change yet, that's okay. Remember, changing your beliefs takes time and persistence. Just going over the evidence for and against your belief once may not be enough. You need to practice this strategy until the evidence for your belief is weak and the evidence against your belief is strong. A good gauge of when you have done enough work on this belief may be when your belief is relatively weak – say about only 20%

Positive Beliefs About Worrying

Introduction

Ask yourself the question: if you believed your worrying has many benefits, how willing would you be to give it up? Your answer is probably that you wouldn't be very willing, as you might feel like you would be losing something valuable and that giving up worrying would be very costly to you. So in this Section, we will look at changing your positive beliefs about worrying, such as:

"Worrying helps me cope with things"
"If I keep worrying, bad things will not happen to me"
"Worrying helps me solve problems"
"If I worry, I will be motivated to do things"
"Worrying prepares me for anything"

Changing Your Beliefs

By now you know the drill. Before we start changing your positive beliefs about worrying, we need to know how much you believe them.

How much do you believe your worrying has positive benefits?

(Circle the percentage that best describes the strength of your belief)

0% 10% 20% 30% 40% 50% 60% 70% 80% 90% 100%

Through the work you have already done, you may have already come to the conclusion that worrying has little benefit. Do continue to work through this Section just to be sure.

As with your negative beliefs about worrying, to change your positive beliefs about worrying, you can do two things.

Firstly, you can challenge or dispute your beliefs. That means dissecting your beliefs about the benefits of worrying, by evaluating if they really are accurate and true, and examining what evidence you base your beliefs on. In this way you will be like a detective, trying to get to the facts of whether worrying really is beneficial to you.

Secondly, you can experiment with your beliefs. That means doing things to see if worrying really does have many positives. If you are able to do things that show your beliefs are not true, that in fact your worrying has no benefits or can get in the way at times, it is going to be hard to hold on to your beliefs. In this way you will be like a scientist with a prediction that worrying is beneficial, which needs to be tested.

Challenging Your Beliefs

Below is a list of questions you can ask yourself to challenge whether your positive beliefs about worrying are really true. Remember, these questions are to help you do your detective work. An example is given below of how to use these questions to challenge your beliefs, and you will find a worksheet to help you do this for yourself.

Evidence For

What makes you think worrying is beneficial?

What's the evidence for your positive beliefs?

Exactly how does worrying help you prevent or avoid bad things?

Exactly how does worrying help you cope/solve problems?

Is the evidence for your beliefs good/solid/reliable?

Is there another way the evidence for your beliefs could be viewed?

Evidence Against

Is there any evidence that goes against your positive beliefs about worrying?

What are the disadvantages of worrying?

How can you believe that worrying has many positive benefits on the one hand (motivates, prepares, prevents, etc) and many disadvantages on the other (distressing, interferes, doesn't help, makes things worse)?

Have there been situations where you haven't worried, and things have still turned out okay?

EXAMPLE:

Evidence For	Evidence Against
Worrying prepares me, so that if bad things happen I can cope better. [What is the good in always being prepared for the worst, which never seems to happen… It just ends up making me feel awful all the time – and how can that be good coping? Maybe if I didn't worry, I would still have been able to cope if something had happened.]	*Worrying makes me upset, interferes with my ability to concentrate and make decisions, and makes me procrastinate.* [What my worrying actually does to me does not match with my positive beliefs that worrying makes me cope, helps solve problems and motivates me- maybe I need to rethink things.]
Worrying helps me get everything done properly and on time. [Sometimes I worry so much that I am unable to do things, so how does this fit with my beliefs? Maybe if I didn't worry, I would still get things done well- maybe I should try and see.]	*There have been times when I haven't worried and bad things haven't happened. I have been able to cope. I have gotten things done properly and on time.* [I guess these experiences show that the benefits I thought worrying gave me may not be real.]
I don't know how worrying stops bad things from happening…I just feel it does. [I don't have any strong, specific or scientific evidence to break my belief. What I am thinking is really superstitious.]	*The things I worry about are unrealistic things that I have such a small chance of happening.* [How can worrying about unrealistic things occurring be positive, helpful, and beneficial to me?]
The fact that nothing bad ever happens is because I worry. [I have no explanation for how this is possible. How can my worrying actually effect what happens in the world?]	

Challenging Your Beliefs

Belief: *My worrying has positive benefits*	
Evidence For	**Evidence Against**

One thing you may have written down when challenging your positive beliefs about worrying, is that the things you worry about are unrealistic and never happen in reality, and so how can worrying about these things be in any way helpful to you? Here's something you can do that will strengthen this particular challenge to your beliefs.

- Pick a situation that you have worried about either in the past or the present
- Write out in detail all the things you worried would happen – all the disastrous scenarios and outcomes you had going through your head
- Once the situation you worried about has passed, write out in detail what actually happened – the facts
- Now compare what you predicted would happen to what actually happened. Chances are, what you predicted was pretty inaccurate and did not happen in reality
- You might want to do this with a few worry situations you have had
- When you have finished ask yourself, "If what I worry about is inaccurate and unrealistic, how can it be helpful, valuable or beneficial to me?"

Try recording this exercise in this mini worksheet

Worries vs. Facts Exercise

What's a situation you were (are) worried about?
What did (do) you think would happen? (Write down all the things that went through your mind- the disastrous scenarios and possible things that might have happened)
What actually did happen? (Write down all the facts about what happened)
Compare what actually happened with what you were worried would happen
What conclusion can you make from this? What can you learn from this?

Experimenting With Your Beliefs

Having challenged your beliefs, it is now experiment time!

If you believe that worrying is helpful, beneficial, and valuable to you, then you need to compare what happens when you increase your worrying with what happens when you decrease your worrying.

It makes sense that if things don't change between when you worry and when you don't worry, or if things are worse when you worry and better when you don't worry, then your beliefs about the positive benefits of worry are false.

Experiment: Up & Down Worrying

In this experiment we want you to alternate between each day of the week, turning down the volume on worrying on one day, then turning up the volume on worrying the next day.

Day 1 (**Down**): On the first day, attempt not to worry at all or worry only very minimally for the whole day. You may want to use the "postpone worrying" strategies you have developed, to enable you to turn down your worrying and leave it till the next day. Note: in this experiment, postpone your worrying until the next day rather than until a certain time the same day as you have been doing until now.

Day 2 (**Up**): On the next day, now increase your worrying and re-visit that old habit of excessively worrying about everything, which you had been doing very regularly prior to commencing this information package. Use the worries you collect over the previous day, as well as worries that present themselves on this day, and have a field day chasing these worrisome thoughts.

Day 3 **(Down)**: Then the next day, attempt not to worry again (or worry only very minimally).

Day 4 **(Up)**: Then the next day go back to worrying excessively again. And so on.

The idea is to turn the volume down on your worrying one day, and then turn the volume up on your worrying the next day. Keep alternating each day between turning down your worrying and turning up your worrying.

Before you start the experiment, complete the worksheet in as much detail as you can and then continue filling it out as you go along.

Instructions for completing the worksheet:

First, write down what you think will happen on the days you worry, and what you think will happen on the days you don't worry. If you think worrying has many positive benefits, then you should predict better outcomes on the days you worry, namely that bad things won't happen, you will be able to cope better, you will solve problems more effectively, you will be more motivated, you will do a better job and get more things done, etc.

Now just give the experiment a go and see what happens.

For each of the next 7 days, fill in the day and the date. Make sure you take note of whether it is a turn down or turn up worrying day. At the end of your day, assess whether positive things happened, negative things happened, you coped during the day, you solved problems that arose, and you got things done. Also rate how much you believe your worrying has positive benefits. Then, compare what you predicted would happen with what actually happened on those 7 days. Typically people predict that if they don't worry they will not experience any of the benefits worrying has to offer. Often people are surprised that there is either:

- No difference in terms of bad things happening, getting the job done, coping, etc, between days they worried and days they didn't, **OR**
- That in fact the reverse is true, and they experienced more benefits on the days they didn't worry (e.g., being better able to concentrate and therefore more and better work was accomplished).

What did you find?

Now that you have challenged and experimented with your beliefs that worrying is beneficial:

Rate again how much you believe your worrying has positive benefits?

(Circle the percentage that best describes the strength of your belief)

0% 10% 20% 30% 40% 50% 60% 70% 80% 90% 100%

If there is some weakening (however small) of your belief that your worry is beneficial compared to what it was at the start of this Section, congratulate yourself. If there's no change yet, that's OK. Remember, changing your beliefs takes time and persistence. Just going over the evidence for and against your beliefs once or experimenting with your beliefs once may not be enough. These are ongoing strategies you can practice until the evidence for your beliefs is weak, the evidence against your beliefs is strong, and you have shown yourself that worry does not have the positive benefits you first thought, and therefore you wouldn't be losing anything valuable by giving up worrying. A good gauge of when you have done enough work on these beliefs may be when your beliefs are relatively weak–about 20%.

Up & Down Worrying Experiment

Prediction 1: What do you think will happen on the days you worry?

_____

_____

_____

_____

_____

Prediction 2: What do you think will happen on the days you <u>don't</u> worry?

Day: Date:	day	day	day	day	day	day	day
Worry Volume	Down	Up	Down	Up	Down	Up	Down
Did Positive things happen?							
Did you cope during the day?							
Did you solve problem that arose?							
Did you get things done?							
How much do you believe your worry has positive benefits? (0% to 100%)							

Compare your two predictions with what actually happened

_____

_____

_____

_____

Challenging Worries

Introduction

In this section, you will learn an active way of dealing with the specific worries you have by challenging them head on. In the next Section, you will learn a different technique, which is a more passive way of dealing with your specific worries, that is, letting them go. Both techniques are useful. Some people prefer one over the other and some find that they like to use both at different times. This is for you to decide. The main thing is that you will have a couple of techniques up your sleeve to deal with your specific worries when they start to hassle you.

The Thinking-Feeling Connection

What you think, and the thoughts that go through your mind, are very important in determining how you feel. Stop for a moment and think: when you are feeling good, what sorts of thoughts roam around in your head? Conversely, when you are feeling bad, what sorts of thoughts are you having?

It makes sense to most people when we say that:

It is not the situation you are in that determines how you feel, but the thoughts, meanings, and interpretations you bring to that situation.

Here is an example of what we mean. Imagine you are told that you will have a pop quiz on Monday. Below are three different ways of thinking about this same situation and the different emotions, behaviors, and physical sensations that would result from thinking in these different ways.

Example event: *Being told you have a pop quiz*			
	Emotions	Behavior	Physical
Thought 1 I love quizzes! I know this stuff quite well so I think I'll do fine.	Happy	Do a bit of revision	Quite Relaxed
Thought 2 I don't know anything. 7	Anxious Sad	Try to study hard, can't concentrate don't get much done	Sick in stomach
Thought 3 So what? I don't care. This subject isn't important anyway.	Neutral	Do not study	Quite Relaxed

Can you see how what we think can be so important in determining how we feel emotionally and physically, and can influence what we do?

As we have already explained, worrying is a type of thought process where you engage in negative and catastrophic thinking about things you predict could happen. When such a negative thinking style is constantly hassling you, emotions like anxiety may result, and you may experience unpleasant physical sensations and avoid doing certain things. One way to lift those negative emotions and unpleasant bodily sensations and get you back to doing things, is to challenge those worrisome thoughts. This means that you don't just accept them as true, but analyses and take them apart, just like the previous detective work you did with your beliefs about worrying. However this time, we will try something a little different.

Your Worry Diary

We would like you to start using what we call a 'Worry Diary'. A good time to use a Worry Diary might be during your worry period, after having postponed your worrying. By using a Worry Diary, you get all those worrisome thoughts that are going round and round in your head out on paper. Just putting them all on paper can be very helpful in itself, as it frees your mind, making it less cluttered so you are able to think more clearly. Remember, writing your worries down on paper is a good strategy to use when you find that your worries are interfering with your sleep or work.

On the next page is an example of how to complete a Worry Diary, and following that is a blank Worry Diary for you to practice on. The Worry Diaries guide you through how to get your worrisome thoughts out on paper. The Worry Diary will first ask you to write down information About Your Worries. For example:

- What am I worrying about?
- List my worrisome thoughts.
- After seeing these worrisome thoughts written down, you'll then need to ask yourself:
- What am I predicting is going to happen? Usually you are predicting that something bad is going to happen, so be specific and write down exactly what it is you fear might happen.
- How strongly do I believe this will happen? Rate the strength of your belief between 0 and 100%
- What emotion(s) am I feeling?
- How intense are these emotions? Rate the intensity of your emotion(s) between 0 and 100%

You are not just going to get those worrisome thoughts out on paper, you are also going to start Challenging Your Worries on paper. Here are the questions asked in your Worry Diary to challenge your worries:

- What is the evidence for my prediction?
- What is the evidence against my prediction?
- How likely is it that what I am predicting will actually happen (Rate 0-100%)?
- What is the worst that could happen?
- What is the best that could happen?
- What is the most likely thing that will happen?

- How helpful is it for me to worry about this?
- If the worst did happen, what would I be able to do to cope?
- How else could I view the situation?

Based on your answers to the questions in your Worry Diary, you will then engage in more Balanced Thinking by asking:

- What would be a more balanced and helpful thought to replace my worry? The final step is to:
- Re-rate how much you now believe the original prediction you were making.
- Re-rate how intense the emotions are that you were originally feeling.

If you follow through with this strategy of challenging your worries, it is likely that you will experience a decrease in your belief in the negative predictions you were making and a decrease in the intensity of your emotions. Keep chipping away at your worries. It will take time, persistence, and practice, but combating your worries will be very rewarding.

Worry Diary

About Your Worries

What am I worried about? List my worrisome thoughts	What am I predicting? How much do I believe it will happen (0-100%)?	What emotion(s) am I feeling? (Rate the intensity 0-100%)

Challenging Your Worries

What is the evidence for my prediction?	What is the evidence against my prediction?
How likely is it that was I am predicting will actually happen?	
What is the worst that could happen?	What is the best thing that could happen?
What is the most likely thing that will happen	How helpful is it for me to worry about this?
If the worst did happen, what I be able to do to cope?	
How else could I view this situation?	

Balanced Thinking

A more balanced and helpful thought to replace my worry is:	
How much do I believe my prediction now (0-100%)	How intense are my emotions now (0-100%)

Letting Go of Worries

Introduction

In the last Section, we took a more active approach to dealing with your worries – we challenged them. Now we will take a different approach to dealing with the specific worries you have. This approach could be seen as more passive in nature, as it involves letting go of your worries. Just because it may be more passive doesn't mean that this technique is any less effective or requires any less practice, effort, or skill. Mastering this technique will take some practice and it can also be an effective way of dealing with your worries.

What Is 'Letting Go'

So, what do we mean by 'Letting Go" of your worries? To let go of your worries means you are doing the opposite to what you would normally do with your worries, which is to engage with them, chase them, react to them, try to control them, and try to reason with them. Instead, letting go is about releasing your worries, letting your worries pass, and not engaging with or reacting to your worries.

We established that worrying does not have the positive benefits you may have once thought. In fact, worrying is unhelpful and of little use or value. It is important to remember this throughout the Section, so you know that you are not losing anything valuable by letting go of worries and giving up worrying.

In some ways you have already done a bit of letting go of your worries, when doing your postponement of worrying experiment. In order to postpone your worrying, you had to make the decision not to worry about something at that particular moment. Instead, you had to bring your attention back to the present and what it was you were doing, with the aim of going back to the worrying some time later. In this Section we will take this one step further. The aim will be for you to let go of your worries indefinitely (that is, not plan to return to thinking about them later), and we will focus more on the attitude you will need to have towards your worries to be able to let go of them.

How To Let Go Of Worries

Now that you know what "letting go" is all about, there are a number of things that you can do to let go of your worries.

Be Aware

The first thing is to be aware and acknowledge the presence of worries. You can't let go of something if you don't know you have it in the first place. So, the first thing you should do is just notice and acknowledge that you are worrying. You might do this by saying to yourself: "Here comes a worry…" or "A worry has arrived…" or "I notice I am worrying…"

Don't Respond

The next thing to do is not to respond to your worries. As we have already said, normally you would engage with your worries, chase them around, or try and control them in some way. Instead, don't do anything to your worries. Just observe your worries with interest. Don't judge them or react to them. Describe to yourself the thoughts, feelings, and sensations you are experiencing right at that moment. Just allow the worries to be, without responding to them or trying to change them in any way

Let Go

Only after fully acknowledging, observing, and describing the worries you have in your mind, can you then make the decision to let the worries go. Think of letting the worries just pass by like clouds moving slowly across the sky or leaves floating in a stream. Release the worries and let them wash over you – let them go. You might do this by saying to yourself: "My worries are not facts, realities, or truths…they are just thoughts…they aren't helpful to me…I'll just let them go".

Be Present-Focused

Once you have told yourself to let the worries go or pass, it is important to focus your attention on the present moment. When you worry, you are focused on the future and bad things that could happen. Instead, if you focus on the simple things happening in the present moment, it is impossible to worry.

Let's give it a try. Why don't you start by noticing your breathing and what it is like at that moment. Draw your attention to all the different physical sensations you might feel as you inhale and exhale. Notice the physical sensations you have in your body as you are standing or sitting. Become aware of how your body makes contact with the environment around you (e.g., the chair, the ground, the air) and what these sensations of touch and pressure feel like. For example, notice how your feet feel in your shoes or sandals. Do they feel warm or cool? Do they feel dry or a little clammy? Wiggle your toes a little – how does that feel?

Now … what did you observe about yourself as you did this exercise? Did you notice that there probably wasn't a lot of room in your mind for worries?

Being present in the moment may seem a strange concept at first, but it is about increasing your awareness of your breathing, body, and surroundings in the moment as they are happening – something we rarely stop to focus on. This is something that requires a lot of practice, but by focusing on the present moment, you will allow your worries to pass you by.

Dealing With A Wandering Mind

When being focused on the present, people might get frustrated when they find their mind wandering away from their focus on their breathing or bodily sensations, and back to worrisome thoughts. This is natural and normal. The important thing to do is to congratulate yourself for recognizing your mind has wandered, and just return your attention to the present again and what it was you were focused on. Do this as often as you need to.

On the next page is an example of how you could 'let go' next time worrying is a problem for you.

EXAMPLE

You have a big dinner party planned for the weekend and are worried that everything will go wrong. You are thinking, "Everything will go wrong, I won't do a good job, they'll have a bad time." You are preoccupied by such thoughts and can't seem to get other important things done. You feel uptight and on edge.

Be Aware	*I am worrying about this dinner party.*
Don't Respond	*It is interesting to notice that right now my thoughts are predicting bad things. I am feeling anxious, I can't concentrate, and I feel tense in my stomach and in my hands. I'll just sit with these feelings a little while... observing and noticing them for a bit.*
Let Go	*My worries about the party are not facts...they are just thoughts...they aren't helping me...I'll just let them go.(Visualize these thoughts floating past you like clouds in the sky or as you breath out, say under your breath Let go or Release)*
Be Present-Focused	*I need to bring my attention to the present. I'm noticing my breathing right now. When I inhale I can feel a slight pressure on my stomach as the air fills my lungs. As I exhale I feel a release as the air flows out of my lungs...ect. I now notice my body sitting in this chair, how the seat supports by shoulders, spine, buttocks and backs of my legs...ect.*
Deal With A Wandering Mind	*Ah my mind has wondered back to worrying about the party. That's okay. I'll just bring my attention back to focusing on the present now. Back to noticing my breathing.*

Letting go of worries may appear simple, but it will take practice. The worksheet is designed to help you practice this technique.

Instructions for completing the worksheet:

First, write down what you think will happen when you try to let go of your worries. After that, rate how much of the time you think you will be able to let go of your worries (between 0% and 100%).

Now, try letting go of your worries for at least the next week and see what happens.

For each day of the next 7 days, fill in the day and the date. Follow the prompts on how to let go of your worries every time a worrisome thought rears its ugly head. Record how many times during the day you tried to let go of worries. Write down what happened and whether or not you were able to let go of your worries. Also, rate how much of the time during the day you were able to let go of your worries.

Then, compare what you predicted would happen with what actually happens on those 7 days. Typically people predict they won't do well, but with some practice they surprise themselves. What did you find?

It is important to remember that **challenging** and **letting go** are two different techniques you can use to deal with the specific worries you have. Certain people prefer one technique over the other, and this will be something you will discover after trying both. Some people like to have both techniques up their sleeve, in case their preferred technique isn't as helpful for them with particular worries. Also some people like to do the challenging technique first, and then finish by using the letting go technique afterwards. Try both techniques and see which works better for you. But remember, both are skills that require effort and lots of practice to be effective in dealing with the specific things you worry about.

Letting Go Of Worries

Prediction (What do you think will happen if you try letting go of your worries?)

_____

_____

_____

_____

How much of the time do you think you will be able to let go of your worries?

0% 10% 20% 30% 40% 50% 60% 70% 80% 90% 100%
None of the time   Half of the time   All of the time

Remember when letting go of worries:

Be aware of your worries and acknowledge their presence.

Don't respond to your worries, but instead observe and describe them.

Let go and acknowledge that your worries are neither real nor helpful.

Be present-focused by moving your attention to the present moment, focusing on your breathing, bodily sensations, and surrounding environment.

Deal with a wandering mind by not getting frustrated, but acknowledging it and drawing your focus back to the present.

Day: Date:	day	day	day	day	day	day	day
How many times during the day did you try to let go of your worries?							
What happened? (Did you let go of your worries?)							
How much of the time were you able to let go of your worries? (0% to 100%)							

Compare what you predicted with what actually happened

_____

_____

_____

_____

Accepting Uncertainty

Introduction

In earlier Sections, we mentioned that the inability to tolerate uncertainty tends to be a unique feature of people who experience generalized anxiety and excessive worrying. This Section aims to examine your need for certainty, to look at how this need keeps worrying going, to describe ways of challenging this need, and to discuss how to ultimately accept uncertainty in your life.

Intolerance Of Uncertainty

The inability to tolerate uncertainty is an attitude many people have towards life. When one has this attitude, uncertainly, unpredictability, and doubt are seen as awful and unbearable experiences that must be avoided at all costs. People who hate uncertainty and need guarantees may:

- Say things like: "I can't cope not knowing," "I know the chances of it happening are so small, but it still could happen," "I need to be 100% sure."
- Prefer that something bad happens right now, rather than go on any longer not knowing what the eventual outcome will be
- Find it hard to put a plan or solution in place, because they first need a guarantee that it will work.

If you have this attitude of being unable to stand uncertainty, then you may perceive worrying to be useful to you. You may think that worrying is a way of preparing yourself for the worst – getting you ready for anything that might happen. Worrying is seen as a way of attempting to predict life so that there are no nasty surprises. As such, worrying reduces your experience of uncertainty and unpredictability. And because worrying reduces your feelings of uncertainty, you will continue worrying and worrying and worrying. In other words, you keep worrying because you believe it is your only strategy for making things in life more certain and more predictable – it helps you believe that you have more control.

In reality, has your worrying made anything more certain or more predictable? By worrying, does it change the outcome of what will happen? Isn't life still as uncertain and unpredictable as it ever was? It is only your perception that you somehow have more control by worrying. But is this really true? In fact, all you have done is think of all the worst case scenarios and worked yourself up and made yourself feel really bad in the process. So, ask yourself, is it really worth it? Does having a 'fake' sense of certainty justify all the negative consequences of worrying?

If your answer is 'No', then there are two ways you can tackle your intolerance of uncertainty, which require skills taught in the last two Sections. You can:

Challenge your intolerance of uncertainty
and
Let go of your intolerance of uncertainty (or **Accept** uncertainty)

By addressing your need for certainty, you are dealing with a key factor that drives you to keep worrying. So by reducing your need for certainty, you will reduce the drive to worry.

Challenging Intolerance Of Uncertainty

You should be quite familiar with the challenging process by now. You can use this process to dissect your intolerance of uncertainty and question your need for certainty. Do the exercise below and ask yourself some questions to chip away at your need for certainty. These questions can help you to see that trying to eliminate uncertainty and unpredictability from your life is both impossible and unhelpful.

Can you be absolutely certain about everything in life?	
What are the advantages of requiring certainty in life? *How has needing certainty in life been helpful to you?*	**What are the disadvantages of requiring certainty in life?** *How has needing certainty in life been unhelpful to you or detrimental to your life?*
Do you tend to predict that something bad will happen just because you are uncertain? *Is this a reasonable thing to do? Could something good or neutral just as likely happen?*	**What is the likelihood that the things you predict will happen?** *If the likelihood tends to be low, could you live with this small chance?*
Are there some uncertainties in your life that you can live with? *How do you do this? Can you do the same thing in situation where you have difficulty tolerating uncertainty?*	**Talk to the people you know. Ask how they cope with the uncertainty and unpredictability of life?** *Could you do the same thing they do in situations where you have difficulty tolerating uncertainty?*

Accepting Uncertainty

What was your answer to the last two questions in the 'Challenging Intolerance Of Uncertainty' worksheet? One question asked about how you tolerate uncertainty in certain areas of your life. The other question asked about how other people tolerate uncertainty in their lives. Chances are you came up with a similar answer to both questions, which might sound something like: There is nothing I can do about it, so I just have to accept it and move on.

Demanding certainty and predictability is a very future-focused task, just like worrying. In the last Section, we looked at how to deal with worrying through acceptance and letting go of worries. This technique can be applied here to let go of your intolerance of uncertainty and accept uncertainty as being an inevitable part of life. You can do this by recognizing or acknowledging it, then letting go of your intolerance and accepting uncertainty, and finally being more present-focused rather than future focused. Being more present-focused can help bring about an acceptance of uncertainty. If you are focused on the present rather than the future, then uncertainty about the future is less likely to bother you.

You already know the steps for being able to achieve acceptance, but let's look at these steps again, and use them specifically to accept uncertainty in your life. Below is an example for you, but use the worksheet to put in your own words what would help you let go of your need for certainty and accept uncertainty.

EXAMPLE

Be Aware	" *I tell myself how terrible or unbearable not knowing is"; I seek reassurance"; "I get this agitated and restless feeling that comes with not knowing what will happen"; I worry about things you can't be certain of"; "I can't made decisions because I need to be sure of the outcome first. "*
Don't Respond	*"It is interesting to notice that in this situation I have a need for certainty, predictability a guarantee... this need is leading me to worry. I'll just sit here with these feelings a little while...observing and noticing them for a bit".*
Let Go	*"My need for certainty is unnecessary... uncertainty is just a part of life...I'll just let me need for certainty go, and accept uncertainty" (Visualize your need for certainty floating past you like clouds in the sky or as you breathe out say under your breath "let go" or "accept")*
Be Present-Focused	*I need to bring my attention to the present. I am noticing my breathing right now. When I inhale I can feel slight pressure on my stomach as the air fills my lungs. As I exhale I feel a release as the air flows out of my lungs...ect. I now notice my body sitting in this chair, how the seat supports my shoulders, spine, buttocks and backs of my legs...ect".*
Deal With A Wandering Mind	*"Ah my mind has wandered back to demanding certainty. That's okay. I'll just bring my attention back to focusing on the present now. Back to noticing my breathing..."*

Once you have completed both worksheets, remember that challenging and acceptance are two different techniques you can use to address your need for certainty. Try both techniques and see which works better for you. Use either of them, or a combination of the two. But remember, both require effort and lots of practice to be effective in addressing your need for certainty.

Accepting Uncertainty

Be Aware

What do you notice yourself doing when you are in needing certainty?

Don't Respond

What can you tell yourself to help you not respond to your need for certainty?

Let Go

What can you tell yourself to help you let go of your need for certainty?

Be Present-Focused

What can you tell yourself to help you be more present focused?

Deal with a Wandering Mind

What can you tell yourself to help you when your mind wanders back to needing certainty?

Problem - Solving

Introduction

You may have once thought that worrying and problem-solving are one and the same. This Section will show you that, in fact, worrying and problem-solving are two very different things. The aim of this Section is to teach you some valuable strategies for being able to effectively solve problems that you encounter in your day-to-day life, and hence reduce your need to worry about these problems.

Worrying Versus Problem-Solving

As we've mentioned many times, worrying is a negative thought process. When we worry, thoughts involving worst case scenarios and all the possible problems that might happen in the future go round and round in our heads like a broken record. We may often ask ourselves what we would do if this terrible thing ever happened, but often we are so anxious that we can't think clearly, and so can't find any real solutions. Instead, we just dwell on our worst fear. In this way, worrying makes us anticipate and fear something that is typically unlikely to happen in the future, yet leaves us unprepared and without a plan to deal with this unlikely occurrence even if it did happen.

Problem-solving is different. It is a constructive thought process focused on how we can flexibly and effectively deal with a problem at hand. It involves identifying what the problem is and thinking of possible ways of dealing with the problem. We then choose which of these suggestions seem the best solutions and examine the pros and cons for each. Based on our evaluation of the solutions, we can then develop a plan of how best to deal with the situation by using one or more of the strategies we have thought of. The next step is to put this plan into place. At the end of this process, we step back and evaluate how well we have done in dealing with the problem.

Can you see how worrying can be an unhelpful and futile process, which focuses on things that haven't happened and yet doesn't produce any real solutions if they did happen? In contrast, problem-solving is a practical and helpful process, which focuses on problems at hand that need to be dealt with, by devising a clear plan to tackle them. Since worrying doesn't seem to be useful for us, it might be more helpful to learn a skill like problem-solving.

Preparing For Problem-Solving

Before you start trying to solve a problem, there are a couple of things you need to consider.

The Right Set Up

When you decide to adopt the problem-solving strategy recommended here to deal with problems in your life, you need to give yourself the best chance of doing it well. Consider setting up the activity of problem solving by doing the following:

- **Set aside time**. Problem-solving takes energy and concentration, and isn't something that can be done on the run. You will need to give it the time and attention it deserves to gain the most benefit.
- **One by one**. Make sure you deal with one problem at a time. Don't try to find solutions to everything all at once, as the quality of your solutions will suffer.
- **Use paper**. Finally, make sure you tackle a problem on paper, that is, write it down. Don't try and solve problems in your head. You will find that things get too cluttered when you try to hold a number of things in your head at one time. Many things will become clearer when putting pen to paper.

Is There A Problem?

This is something you need to ask yourself before launching into problem-solving. Is there actually a problem that requires solving? Whatever it is you are worrying about ask yourself:

- Is it a real and likely problem I am concerned about?
- Is the problem something happening now?
- Is the problem something I have some control over?

If the problem you are worried about is an unrealistic and unlikely prediction of the future, of which you have little control over, then although it might appear that the problem is "real", it is not an actual problem that requires a solution. In these cases, it will be the challenging and letting go strategies that will be most useful in dealing with your worry. However, if it is a real problem in the here-and-now that you can do something about, then using problem-solving strategies may be a useful way to deal with the problem.

Below are some examples of things you may worry about that are real problems to be solved, compared to those that cannot be solved.

Solvable Worries	Unsolvable Worries
<ul><li>The phone and gas bill are due, and I don't have enough money for both</li><li>I have too many tasks to finish at work/home by the end of the week</li><li>I had a flight with my spouse/partner</li><li>My child disobeys me a lot</li></ul>	<ul><li>My spouse/partner might have an accident</li><li>My child might join the 'wrong crowd' and start doing drugs</li><li>There could be a terrorist attack</li><li>Interest rates might go up</li><li>I might become seriously ill</li></ul>

Can you see from these examples how some of your worries are not real problems requiring a solution, while others are?

Now, try writing down which of your worries are solvable problems and which are not. Use the criteria of whether they are realistic, likely, in the here-and-now, and within your control to figure out which are real problems you can try to solve.

Solvable Worries	Unsolvable Worries

How To Solve Problems

There are 6 steps to effective problem-solving. Let's go through each of these steps now, using an example.

Let's use the example that you are worried because the gas and phone bills are due at the same time, you don't have enough money to cover both, and you don't know what to do. This is a real problem that is occurring in the here-and-now, which you can do something about. Therefore, it is a problem we can use to try out this 6-step problem-solving process.

Step 1: Identify/Define Problem

Try to state the problem as clearly as possible. Be objective and specific about the behavior, situation, timing, and circumstances that make it a problem. Describe the problem in terms of what you can observe rather than subjective feelings.

Problem Definition

The gas and phone bills are due at the same time. I don't have enough money to cover both this month.

Step 2: Generate Possible Solutions/Options

List all the possible solutions. Be creative and forget about the quality of the solutions. If you allow yourself to be creative, you may come up with some options that you would not otherwise have thought of.

List All Possible Solutions

- *Ring both companies – see if I can negotiate to pay it off gradually*
- *Priorities – I can live without the phone for a while, but not the gas, so I will pay the gas bill first*
- *Borrow money from family or friends to pay both bills*
- *Pay bills on my credit card – then pay that off later •*
  See a financial counsellor – they may be able to help me sort it out
- *Get a second job*
- *Sell some of my possessions to pay the bills*
- *Don't pay the bills and move in with a friend instead*

Now eliminate the less desirable or unreasonable alternatives only after as many possible solutions have been listed. Then, list the remaining options in order of preference.

Preferred Solutions/Options

1. <u>Ring both companies – see if I can negotiate to pay it off gradually.</u>
2. <u>See a financial counsellor – they may be able to help me sort it out.</u>
3. <u>Priorities – I can live without the phone for a while, but not the gas, so I will pay the gas bill first.</u>
4. <u>Get a second job.</u>

Step 3: Evaluate Alternatives

Evaluate the top 3 or 4 plans in terms of their advantages and disadvantages

	Advantages	Disadvantages
Potential Solution #1	I may be able to keep both the phone and gas on. I will feel I have done something.	I will feel embarrassed having to ring the companies. I may
Potential Solution #2		
Potential Solution #3		
Potential Solution #4		

Step 4: Decide On A Plan Decide on one, two or more of the plans. Specify who will take action, when the plan will be implemented and how the plan will be implemented.

Action Steps	Who	When
Contact gas and phone companies to negotiate options for paying the bills (pay off gradually or extend payment).	*Me*	*Monday Morning*
If that doesn't resolve the problem contact centerlink to ask about free financial counselors.	*Me*	*Monday Afternoon*
Visit financial counsellor for advice	*Me*	*Tuesday*
If that doesn't resolve the problem, pay gas bill and use pay phone temporarily.	*Me*	*Wednesday*

Step 5: Implement Plan

Implement your plan as specified above.

Step 6: Evaluate the Outcome

Evaluate how effective the plan was. Decide whether the existing plan needs to be revised, or whether a new plan is needed to better address the problem. If you are not pleased with the outcome, return to Step 2 to select a new option or revise the existing plan, and repeat the remaining steps.

Remember, this problem-solving strategy needs some practice, but it can help you deal with difficult situations. So next time you find yourself worrying about a real problem that is in the here-and-now and you have some control over, instead of worrying about it, why not sit down with a piece of paper and try problem-solving? It is more productive than worrying, it will reduce your anxiety, and by the end of it you will have a better plan of action. Following is a problem-solving worksheet for you to work through the 6 steps. Try it out and see how you go.

Problem-Solving

1. **Identify and Define Problem Area/Issue**

Problem Definition

2. **Generate Possible Solutions/Options**
   Preferred Solutions/Options
       List All Possible Solutions

   1._____

   2._____

   3._____

   4._____

   5._____

   6._____

3. **Evaluate Alternatives**

	Advantages	Disadvantages
Potential Solution #1		
Potential Solution #2		
Potential Solution #3		
Potential Solution #4		

4. **Decide on a Plan**

Action Steps	Who	When

Step 5: Implement Plan

Implement your plan as specified above.

Step 6: Evaluate the Outcome

- How effective was the plan?
- Does the existing plan need to be revised or would a new plan be needed to better address the problem?
- If you are not pleased with the outcome, return to Step 2 to select a new option or revise the existing plan, and repeat Steps 3 to 6.

Relaxation

Introduction

As previously discussed, you will remember that worrying often comes with some unpleasant physical sensations, particularly, feeling uptight, tense, and unable to relax. When we worry, changes in our breathing and the tension of our muscles bring on these bodily sensations, and contribute to our experience of nervousness and anxiety. This Section will target the physical arousal and bodily sensations you experience when you worry. You will be taught relaxation strategies that will reduce these sensations and help you feel calmer and more relaxed. Feeling calmer and more relaxed physically will help to decrease your worrying, make you better able to cope with worry, and reduce the nervous and anxious feelings that result from your worrying. The particular relaxation techniques you will learn in this Section focus on both your breathing and on muscle relaxation.

Breathing

We all need to breathe oxygen to survive. The lungs take in oxygen, which is used by the body, and produces carbon dioxide (CO_2), which we breathe out. In order for the body to run efficiently, there needs to be a balance between oxygen and carbon dioxide. This balance is maintained through how fast and how deeply we breathe. Breathe in too much and the balance tips so that there's increased oxygen. Breathe in too little and there's increased levels of carbon dioxide.

When you are anxious, nervous or worried, an increase in the rate and depth of your breathing often occurs. That is, we 'over breathe', and take in more oxygen than the body needs. This upsets the balance between oxygen and CO_2. When our breathing rate increases, a number of other physical changes occur in the body to make up for the imbalance. These changes cause the unpleasant physical sensations we experience when anxious. Most of the body's mechanisms, including breathing, are automatically controlled, but we can also actively control our breathing. For example, we can hold our breath when swimming, or speed up our breathing when blowing up a balloon. Stress and our general mood (such as worrying) also affect our breathing. By learning how to maintain a calm and relaxed rate of breathing, it is possible to stop many of the unpleasant physical symptoms we experience when feeling nervous and worried.

Your Rate Of Breathing

To gain control of your breathing, it is important to know more about your rate of breathing. The rate of breathing when feeling calm and relaxed is around 10 to 14 breaths per minute. How does this compare to your rate of breathing generally and when you are worrying? (Count how many breaths per minute you take).

My rate of breathing generally is _____

My rate of breathing when worried is _____

Your Depth Of Breathing

To gain control of your breathing, it is also important to know more about your depth of breathing. Generally, when you breathe you either use (1) 'chest-breathing' or, (2) 'stomach-breathing'.

Chest breathing:

If you are troubled by nerves, worries, and anxiety in your life, chances are you're a 'chest-breather'. Chest breathing is shallow and often irregular and rapid. Anxious people may experience breath-holding, hyperventilation, or shortness of breath when breathing in this manner.

Stomach Breathing:

The second type of breathing is usually used by people with little anxiety in their life, or those who are coping better with anxiety. Stomach breathing (abdominal/ diaphragmatic breathing) is used by newborn babies and sleeping adults. Breath is drawn into the lungs and exhaled as the diaphragm becomes smaller and expands. Breathing is even and not limited. The breathing system is better able to do its job of producing energy from oxygen and removing carbon dioxide.

Do you breathe with your chest or your stomach?

Place the hand you write with on your stomach between your lower ribs and belly button (navel). Put the other hand on your breastbone, just below the collarbones. Take a deep breath and notice:

"Which hand moves the most? The hand on your chest or the hand on your stomach?" "Did you breathe in through your mouth or nose?"

I breathe through: - my mouth   -my nose

I am a: - chest-breather   -stomach-breather

If you breathed through your nose, your stomach probably expanded first, with little upper chest movement. This is the type of breathing that is most helpful for your body. On the other hand, if you breathed in through your mouth, your upper chest probably raised first with little or no movement under the hand located on your stomach. This would indicate an unhelpful breathing style and might be contributing to the anxiety you may experience.

Calming Technique

Gaining control over your breathing rate and depth is an important skill to develop. This calming technique will help you to (1) decrease some of the physical sensations you experience when you worry, and (2) facilitate general relaxation through your breathing.

* Note: if you have breathing problems related to a physical illness, you should consult your doctor before doing breathing exercises if you have any concerns about the effects.

Breathing Pattern

When you do the exercise, try to find a comfortable chair and eliminate any potential interruptions. Sit comfortably, without crossing your legs. How you breathe is important, so consider the following:

- Relax your shoulders and upper chest
- With jaw relaxed, draw air slowly in through your nose.
- Breathe in by relaxing and expanding your waist so your stomach puffs up. Check that you are using stomach/diaphragm breathing by placing one hand on your stomach and the other hand on your chest
- Do not take in deep breaths, just stick to your own natural depth of breath that is smooth and easy
- Breath out through your mouth, and let the air 'fall' out of your chest as the elastic recoil of your lower chest and diaphragm breathes air out effortlessly
- If you find it hard to keep breathing low and slow, place a book on your stomach. This will help focus your effort.

Breathing Timing

Once you're confident about your breathing pattern, it's important to concentrate on how many breaths per minute you are taking.

- Aim for a 4-in, 2-hold, 6-out cycle. Breathe in for 4 seconds, hold for 2 seconds, then breathe out for 6 seconds

- If you have been breathing rapidly for some time, and this timing is difficult to start with, you might try a 3-in, 1-hold, 4-out cycle. Start with what you can most comfortably slow down to, and then work your way up to the 4-in, 2-hold, 6-out cycle
- When counting, you can add the word 'hundred' after each number so it roughly equals one second (i.e., one-hundred, two-hundred, etc).

Remember to focus on the evenness of your breathing pattern. Breathing out usually takes slightly longer than breathing in, with a relaxed pause at the end of the exhalation. As you do the breathing exercise, try to keep count in your head – not only will it help to keep your breathing on track, it's also an important meditative aspect of the calming technique. What you might find if you stop counting is that your mind wanders, and it might wander right back to some worrisome thoughts! If it does start to wander, just allow yourself the thought and then return to the counting.

Breathing Practice

Calming Technique
Ensure that you are sitting on a comfortable chair
Take a breath in for 4 seconds (through your nose if possible)
Hold the breath for 2 seconds
Release the breath taking 6 seconds (through your mouth if possible).

With practice, this new breathing pattern will eventually become second nature and a good habit. At first, if you've been using the mouth/upper chest breathing habit, you might find the nose/stomach breathing technique somewhat unnatural. It usually takes quite a bit of practice to train your stomach muscles to be accustomed to this kind of breathing. It is important not to be hard on yourself if you fall back into unhelpful breathing habits. It is far better to concentrate on both the next breath and getting it correct.

Muscle Tension

Learning to change your breathing habits can help to reduce general levels of anxiety. In addition, muscle relaxation can be particularly helpful for people who worry, as worrying is commonly associated with muscle tension. This type of relaxation can help to interrupt the development of anxiety and tension by providing you with the skills to respond differently to muscle tension.

Think about what happens when you worry. Do you "tense up"? Sometimes the change may be so subtle that you don't even notice it happening. Perhaps you clench your teeth slightly so your jaw ends up feeling tight, or maybe your shoulders become tense, resulting in a feeling of tightness in your neck and shoulders. Muscle tension can also be associated with backaches, muscle spasms and tension headaches, and it can also leave some people feeling exhausted. Different people respond to worry with muscle tension in different parts of the body and to different extents.

Muscle Tension Scan

Consider your own body for a moment. You may have noticed that in the past certain parts of your body felt tense, especially after worrying or being nervous. Where do you often feel tension and "tightness" in your body?

- Forehead	- Shoulders E	- Lower legs
- Mouth and/or jaw	- Arms	- Other
- Neck	- Back	- Other
- Chest	- Upper legs	- Other

The places you notice tension the most may be those you will want to focus particular attention on when doing your muscle relaxation.

Progressive Muscle Relaxation

One particular method of reducing muscle tension is through a technique called Progressive Muscle Relaxation. During progressive muscle relaxation, you tense particular muscles and then relax them or let go of the tension. Many people find this process of tensing and relaxing their muscles helpful in reducing muscle tension that has resulted from prolonged periods of worry.

There are a few important steps involved in learning progressive muscle relaxation.

- Differentiating between muscle groups. For those of us who don't think about our muscles very often, when we try to tense up our hand and forearm, we may end up tensing our whole arm. Learning this technique involves learning to tense and relax specific parts of our body
- Learning how to tense different muscle groups and what that tension feels like
- Allowing yourself to relax and let go of the tension
- Practice, practice, practice and more practice.

The following section describes progressive muscle relaxation. This includes the general procedure, a full description of how to tense particular muscle groups, and the order in which to tense and relax them. You will see that this is quite a lengthy technique, as it involves working through each group of muscles in the body in a systematic way. Once you are familiar with the technique, you could shorten the exercise, and focus on tensing and relaxing only those areas of the body that you sense a buildup of tension.

*Note: If you have any injuries, such as sporting injuries, or have a history of physical problems that may cause muscle pain, you should consult your doctor before attempting any muscle relaxation exercises. Talk to your doctor if you have any concerns or queries about how these exercises may affect you.

General Procedure

- Choose quiet surroundings and make yourself comfortable.
- Use the calming technique to help you let go of the stress, worry, and anxiety that may have existed in your day so far. Do this for 3 to 5 breaths.

Calming Technique:

- Breathe in for 4 seconds (through your nose)
- Hold for 2 seconds
- Breathe out for 6 seconds (If you are still getting used to changing your breathing, use a 3-in, 1-hold, and 4-out cycle).
- When you are ready to begin, tense the muscle group described:
- Make sure you can feel the tension, but not so much that you feel a great deal of pain
- It is more important to focus on what the tension feels like and how the tension builds up, rather than trying to overstrain the muscle
- Keep the muscle tensed for approximately 5 seconds.
- Relax the muscles:

- Relax the muscle and keep it relaxed for approximately 10 seconds
- It may be helpful to say something like "Relax" as you relax the muscle
- Focus on the difference between how the muscle feels when it is relaxed compared to when it is tense.

You can tense and relax each muscle group twice before moving on to the next muscle group.

When you have finished the relaxation procedure, remain seated for a few moments allowing yourself to become alert. Continue your breathing exercises using the calming technique, and get up slowly.

Relaxation Sequence

1. **Right hand and forearm**. Make a fist with your right hand. Focus on the tension in your hand and your arm (below the elbow) and hold the tension for 5 seconds. Relax your hand and arm, releasing the tension for about 10 seconds. Notice the difference between the tension and the relaxation.
2. **Right upper arm**. Bring your right forearm up to your shoulder. The closer you bring your hand to your shoulder, the more tense your upper arm will become. Focus on the muscles in between your elbow and your shoulder - try not to tense your forearm or your hand too much. Hold the tension for 5 seconds, then release for 10 seconds.
3. **Left hand and forearm**. Repeat as for the right hand and forearm.
4. **Left upper arm**. Repeat as for the right upper arm.
5. **Forehead**. Focus on your face now, raising your eyebrows as high as they will go, as though you were surprised by something. Feel the tightness in the muscles above your eyes. When you release the tension of the muscles around your forehead, focus on them becoming smooth and relaxed.

6. **Eyes and cheeks.** Squeeze your eyes tight shut. Focus on the tension around your eyes and your cheeks. Notice how the tension is released as you relax those muscles.
7. **Mouth and jaw.** Open your mouth as wide as you can, as some people do when they have a big yawn. Feel all the muscles in the hinge of your jaw tightening, and notice the tension around your mouth. When you relax your mouth and jaw you can leave your lips slightly apart and just let your jaw hang freely.
8. **Neck. !!!** Be careful as you tense these muscles. Focus on the muscles in your neck by facing forward and then pulling your head back slowly, as though you are looking up to the ceiling. Feel the tension in the muscles in the back of your neck, as this is often an area that becomes tense. Relax these muscles by bringing your head back down to a loose, resting position, noticing how the tension is released.
9. **Shoulders.** Tense the muscles in your shoulders as you bring your shoulders up towards your ears. Focus on the tightness in your shoulders. Hold it for 5 seconds, and then let go of the tension by dropping your shoulders right down to a relaxed position. It is very common for people to keep tension in their shoulders, so notice the comparison between tensed and relaxed.
10. **Shoulder blades/Back.** Push your shoulder blades back, trying to almost touch them together, so that your chest is pushed forward. Hold the tension in the muscles, feeling the tightness in your upper back and in your shoulder blades. Release the tension by dropping your shoulders into a resting, relaxed posture, feeling the tension fade away.
11. **Chest and stomach.** Breathe in deeply, filling up your lungs and chest with air. Feel the tension in your chest and stomach muscles. Hold it for 5 seconds, and as you slowly breathe out, feel the muscles relaxing.
12. **Hips and buttocks.** Squeeze your buttock muscles, noticing the tension in your buttocks and hips. Try not to tense up your legs, just focus on tightening up the buttock and hip muscles. Relax the muscles, and feel them loosen up.
13. **Right upper leg.** Tighten your right thigh, concentrating on the tension in that area. You may get some tension in your hip and in your calf muscle, but try to focus most of the

tension in your thigh muscle. Release the tension and feel the muscle relax.

14. **Right lower leg**. !!! Do this slowly and carefully to avoid cramps. Pull your toes towards you to feel the tightness in your calf muscle. Hold it, then relax it and notice all the tension fade away from the muscle.
15. **Right foot**. Curl your toes downwards to feel the tension in your right foot. Hold the tension and then relax your toes, bringing them into their normal resting position.
16. **Left upper leg**. Repeat as for the right upper leg.
17. **Left lower leg**. Repeat as for the right lower leg.
18. **Left foot**. Repeat as for the right foot.

Additional Points

Here are some additional points to consider when doing relaxation…

Calming & Muscle Relaxation

It is important not to treat the calming technique for breathing and the muscle relaxation technique for muscle tension as separate relaxation exercises. These two techniques can be used in combination. For example, you can start by focusing on the calming technique, then move your focus to muscle relaxation, and finish by re-focusing on the calming technique again. In addition, when doing the calming technique you can scan the muscles in your body for signs of tension during the 4 count inhalation, and focus on releasing this tension during your 6 count exhalation.

Practice, Practice, Practice

The most important thing of all to remember is that relaxation through controlling your breathing and releasing muscle tension is a skill. To develop any skill, and become good at that skill, you need to practice. Try to practice the relaxation techniques as often as you can. When you start, practice in safe situations such as in the lounge room at home…rather than at times you are worried. Once you've mastered the technique you can try to use it to reduce feelings of nervousness, worry, and anxiety. It's a bit like sports practice – you want to master your skills before you get to the finals. For now, become as well-practiced as you can.

Once you have practiced these skills a lot and are good at them, remember that the calming technique and your shorter version of progressive muscle relaxation are 'portable' relaxation techniques. This means you will be able to use them in any situation when you start to worry, because no one will know you are using them.

Some people experience some unusual physical sensations when they first try these relaxation techniques. This is a normal part of becoming more attuned to your body. Keep practicing the techniques, and you will find that these sensations no longer bother you after a while.

Over the page is a worksheet for monitoring your relaxation. This will help you keep track of your relaxation, help remind you to regularly practice your relaxation, and will be the written proof that you are constantly improving this new and valuable skill for dealing with your worrying.

Monitoring Your Relaxation

As explained, it's important to practice relaxation to achieve the best results, as this is a new skill you're learning. It is useful to monitor your own progress by keeping a relaxation diary that records the when, where, and how of your practice.

The following table is an example of a recording method that might be useful. Record the date and time you practice your relaxation, any comments about your relaxation experience, and rate your level of relaxation following the activity.

When rating your relaxation level:

10 represents the most tense or anxious you have ever been

0 represents the most relaxed or calm you have ever been

Date & Time	Comments/Reactions	Relaxation Level 0-10

Comments/Reactions:

- What type of relaxation did you do (calming technique, progressive muscle relaxation, or both)?

- What was your breathing like?
- What parts of your body relaxed easily?
- What sensations were you aware of in your body?
- Was your mind relaxed?
- What was your worrying like when doing the relaxation?

Self-Management

Introduction

Congratulations on making it to the end of this information package! We're glad you stayed on with us. If you haven't read all the Sections, it might be good to go back to the ones you missed. However, the most important thing for you now is to keep practicing the strategies you have learned through reading the Sections in the "What? Me Worry!?!" information package. This means continuing to apply all the useful skills and insights about yourself you might have gained. If you continue practicing the concepts and skills you have learned, they will become like habits that have been integrated into your lifestyle.

There are a few things to keep in mind now that you have learned some important skills in managing your worrying. One area to think about is how to maintain the gains that you have made. Another area to think about is how to minimize setbacks that might occur.

Maintaining Gains

In the beginning of "What? Me Worry!?!" we got you to make a couple of ratings about your generalized anxiety. We want you to make these ratings again and compare them to your ratings. How did you go? What progress have you made?

Overall, how distressing is your generalized anxiety?

(Circle the number that best describes you)

0   1   2   3   4   5   6   7   8   9   10

Not at all   Moderately   Extremely

Overall, how much of a problem is your generalized anxiety?

(Circle the number that best describes you)

0   1   2   3   4   5   6   7   8   9   10

Not at all   Moderately   Extremely

It is important to recognize the progress that you've made, and when you are reaching your goals it is useful to pat yourself on the back and celebrate those milestones. This will hopefully encourage you to keep going, to keep practicing, and to keep applying the new skills you have learnt. Maintaining the gains you have made relies on you continuing to practice these skills. Remember, developing new skills that are designed to challenge what may be years' worth of old habits takes time and persistence.

So there are some important things you will need to do in order to make the most of what you have learned to stay well or gain that extra improvement.

The easiest way to summarize this is by looking at the "Healthy Me "worksheet. It shows the main areas of your life that you should give some attention to in order for you to continue maintaining your gains.

You will notice that on the "Healthy Me" worksheet, each heading has spaces left blank for you to write in what you will need to attend to. For example, under Self-Care you might write: "I will shop every week and purchase fruit and vegetables, and avoid eating take-out". Under Social Activities you might write: "I will visit friends at least once each week." You may want to update this worksheet on a regular basis when you need to extend your goals or modify them. We really encourage you to do this, as it will enable you to keep track of things.

Healthy Me Worksheet

Helpful Thoughts

_____

_____

_____

_____

_____

_____

Setbacks

Setbacks or slip-ups in progress can happen at any time and are to be expected. Try not to fall into the trap of believing that you are 'back to square one' as this will only make you feel worse. Change is not a steady process, it's more like the old saying: "Two steps forward, one step back "from time to time.

Think about how you learned to ride a bike. It probably took a few unsteady attempts and a few falls before you gained your balance. Even when you get your balance, you might still be unsteady when travelling over new ground, or on different surfaces. In the same way, different situations or times in your life may be more challenging, and may require extra effort and persistence (i.e., more thought challenging, more letting go, more problem-solving, more relaxation, etc.). Even after much practice, there may be times when you think you've slipped back and feel a little off balance. Developing new skills is never a smooth process, you're always being faced with new challenges and different situations to apply those skills.

Reasons for Setbacks

There are several reasons for setbacks occurring. There may be an increase in physical or mental stress. Just like riding a bike over challenging terrain, physical and mental stress can be challenges to the new ways of thinking and acting that you have developed. Also, when we are physically unwell, we are less likely to have the mental or physical energy required to challenge or let go of our worries and use helpful strategies.

It may help to remind yourself that most people have 'down days' or days where life's hassles are harder to deal with – it's part of being human! Use the skills you learned for dealing with worrisome thoughts to help when this situation occurs. Also, you can use setbacks as a way of learning something new about yourself to help avoid similar problems in the future.

Preventing Major Setbacks

As you are progressing through your goals, try not to focus too much on small setbacks. If you are experiencing several small setbacks then there are some ways of preventing a major setback.

Identify Early Warning Signs

The first step is to look at your own early warning signs. Some common examples are:
  • Spending increased time worrying about things
  • Reverting back to unhelpful strategies (e.g., avoidance or thought control).
  • An increase in physical symptoms of anxiety, especially tension.

Revise Skills

Think about the skills you have learned and what has been helpful in reducing your worry (e.g., challenging/experimenting with beliefs about worrying, challenging worries, letting go of worries, accepting uncertainty, problem-solving, relaxation). Have you stopped practicing these skills consistently? You may wish to revise the Sections and techniques you have learned and perhaps increase practicing those skills.

Social Support

It is wise to find someone with whom you can sit down and have a good talk. This doesn't mean a therapy session where you pour out your heart but rather just a chance to talk through what's going on in your life, what your goals are, and generally just to ventilate with someone you trust. Often, problems seem bigger than they really are when a person tries to deal with them on their own. Hearing yourself talk through something can help to put it into perspective.

On the next 2 pages is a self-management plan for you to complete. Make a note of the early warning signs that might signal a setback then write down the strategies and tools you have learnt about that can help you to deal with a setback.

Self-Management Plan

What are the early warning signs that tell me that I might be heading for a setback and need to do something about it myself? Ex. I am spending more time worrying OR I am spending more time avoiding or trying to control my worries OR I have more physical symptoms of anxiety

What are some of my negative or positive beliefs about worrying and unhelpful strategies that I need to watch out for?

What situations are potential problems for me?

What are my future support options? Ex, friends, family, GP, other, etc.

What strategies/techniques have I found most helpful and need to continue to practice?

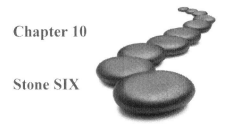

Chapter 10

Stone SIX

The Power and Control Wheel!

Where would you fit on this wheel of power and control? The wheel is a way of visually representing the tactics typically used by men who batter and the ongoing pattern of violence and abuse in intimate relationships. The graphic was created in 1982 by Penn State. It is part of the curriculum for court-

ordered Batterer Intervention Program. It was developed out of experience of attending support and educational groups.

Victims were asked "what do you want taught in a court ordered group for those who batter?" Their answer spoke to the need to bring the complex reality of "battery" into the open. That is where victims began to talk of their tactics. It became obvious that it was more important for the abuser to address this.

The wheel is not a theory, it is a conceptual tool. It will help you look at the patterns of behavior and their significance. It is not intended to capture every tactic of control, just the primary tactic. Your job is to review and personalize them

The wheel was based on victim's experiences. The battered victims did not identify a desire for power and control. It became motivation for their partners who engaged in these behaviors to gain the power to be able to look at themselves and change.

By 1984 it was concluded that identifying the positive and not just negative behaviors in training programs help batterers to change. Following this method they developed the equality and will to describe the characteristics of an abusive relationships and adapted the shapes of the power control.

Physical, spiritual, mental and emotional control. How have you displayed these behaviors and why were they wrong?

_____

_____

_____

_____

Everyone has heard the expression "male privilege". This is when you treat your partner as though you were the master and they were servant. You make the big decisions without asking their input. You act like the king of the castle without a queen; being the one in charge all the time.

Explain how and why you have displayed behaviors of *male privilege*:

_____

_____

_____

_____

_____

_____

_____

Power can control can be used in other ways such as using the children to make your partner feel guilty. Threatening to take the children, hurt the children or keep the children from your partner. Using the fact that the house may not be clean enough or meals may not be cooked to your liking.

List how you have used your children to harass and control your partner.

_____

_____

_____

_____

Minimizing, denying, blaming or making light of the abuse and not considering your partners concerns is serious. Saying that you're sorry or taking your partners concerns and making a joke out of it as if he/she deserved to be treated the way you been treating him/her is also serious. This is a good time to go back and review the section on denial.

Isolation

Isolation comes from controlling what your partner does; who he/she sees; who he/she talks to; what he/she reads, calling him/her 15 times a day while he/she is at work to ask what he/she is doing, when you know exactly what she's doing. By doing this you threaten his/her job by calling so often.

I want to tell you a story that was told to me that I believe is so relevant.

There was a man and his wife who went shopping in a local store. When they went outside, a young man ran up to the wife and put his arms around her, picked her up, turned and swirled her around and then planted a kiss on her cheek. The husband walked over to his truck, took out a gun and shot the man. It turned out that the young man was her brother who had been in Iraq for two terms. He went to surprise them. You see the partner never know the brother and he didn't look the same as he was full bearded and very bulked out. The last time the woman saw her brother was eight years earlier so he was aged. Think about this; how would you have reacted if this were your wife and this happened to you?

Coercion and threats or making her do illegal things like drugs, driving when drunk (even though you both had a few drinks she's the one who drives home), sending her to the store after she's already taken her medication, making her drop charges time and time again after you have abused her threatening to do something to her to hurt her hurt her family or hurt the children if she doesn't. Threatening to commit suicide or reporting her to the Department of Children and Families. Generally, anything to scare her, intimidate her and/or bully her.

Have you done this? Have you looked at it now as the behavior that needs to be changed?

_____

_____

_____

_____

The Cycle of Abuse

Although not all abusive relationships follow the same pattern, there is a cycle that is similar in many abusive relationships. It looks something that this:

The Honeymoon Stage:

Even the most abusive relationships usually start out romantic and loving. Many abusers act very sweet and kind, express a lot of love and make their partner feel special and cared for.

The Tension Building Stage:

During this phase tension builds in the relationship. There may be arguments, emotional abuse or minor physical abuse like grabbing or pushing.

The Blow Up Stage:

This is when the abuse is at its worst, and it may include extreme physical or sexual violence.

Back to the Honeymoon Stage:

After the 'blow up' the abuser may apologize, be very loving and kind, and promise it won't happen again. Because the abuser is so convincing the partner will often try to 'forgive and forget.' Unfortunately, the cycle usually repeats itself and abuse gets worse.

Have you experienced this cycle in your relationship? If so, briefly write down the behaviors you saw during each of the phases or think of a relationship from a movie, book or television and write down example of behaviors you saw at each stage of the relationship.

1. The Honeymoon Stage (beginning of the relationship):
2. The Tension Building Stage:
3. The Blow Up Stage:
4. The Honey Moon Stage (after the blow up):

Chapter 11

Stone SEVEN

Economic abuse

Do you prevent her from getting or keeping a job? Do you make her turn all her money over to you, not letting her know about or have access to any of your income? Not sharing your whereabouts, or who your friends are? Do you have affairs and justifying them? Do you sell things that aren't yours?

Have you been guilty of this? If so explain:

_____

_____

_____

_____

_____

_____

Relationships, Violence and Culture

A violent relationship may have cultural factors that contribute to their perpetration. In the center of the wheel a larger environment exists known as society. The culture itself are the actions of individuals, institutions and environments. This includes the use of language. All are cultural factors that look and sound the same, but yet are interpreted differently by the surroundings and the people who are instrumental to that culture. These cultural factors are integrated in us from the day we were born and can play roles in either ending or perpetrating violence. For example domestic violence was not considered a crime in West Virginia until 1992. Prior to that, violence against a stranger was considered a serious and prosecutable matter, but violence against an intimate partner was often seen as acceptable.

Cultural norms still exists for perpetrating this problem. For example, the tradition of not interfering in matters between family members. The reluctance to report rape, or to report intimate family secrets including incest or sexual abuse still exists. The media portrays domestic violence as "lover's quarrels" and domestic violence homicides-suicide as "crimes of passion" by jilted men who think, "If I can't have her, no one else will."   This "romanticizing" of domestic violence allows it to be excused or explained away – something that is not done with any other type of assault and battery.

Certain cultures, such as American Indians, believed men owned their wives and children. They treated their horses and cattle better. This changed during the mid-60s. Prior to this,

American Indian women could not be buried on their own reservation if she left her husband to marry a white man. This changed when one brave woman brought this to the world court.

It is important to acknowledge the cultural norms that victims bring with them. Norms are the agreed-upon expectations and rules by which a culture guides the behavior of its members in any given situation. Of course, norms vary widely across cultural groups. Americans, for instance, maintain fairly direct eye contact when conversing with others. Asians, on the other hand, may avert their eyes as a sign of politeness and respect. Some communities adhere to strong values of independence that prevent them from seeking help from outsiders. They do not trust people who are urban or may feel that people of color are made to adhere to a code developed through historical experiences. They have taught them not to trust whites. Elderly people have made the condition not to discuss personal issues with strangers. Therefore they resist using self-help programs or even using counselors. When people of the same-sex relationship disclosed violence they risk exposure to the social norms that condemn them because of their lifestyles.

Relationship violence is the physical, emotional and verbal abuse of one partner towards another. If you have been conditioned to keep the family secrets, then the abusers behavior is deemed acceptable. Everyone knows, everyone sees your bruises, but you stay with this man. So it is excused.

Regardless of the abusers age, it is against the law for anyone to hurt you another person, or to force someone to have sex. It is illegal to threaten with a weapon, stalk, destroy things you own, monitor your cell phone or computer.

Culturally accepted in the scene today is using the Internet and social media to spread rumors that control other people's actions. We have seen suicides and self-inflicted pain and it still continues. We watch young teenagers isolate their partners from family and friends. We see churches control religion and cultural behaviors, accepting men but not supporting the women.

We have watched financial abuse with the controlling of money or using money to threat or manipulate. We hear about sexual abuse or ignoring the partner's sexual choices through pressure, manipulation and coercion.

So, now let's look at individual questions and see how you would answer them. Have you ever used emotional, mental or verbal manipulation, humiliation, and/or threats to control your partner?

Explain how that made you feel, and how you think it made them feel

_____

_____

_____

Please explain how hitting, grabbing, pushing, shaking or restraining your partner can be confused for love or why "I'm sorry" should be enough.

_____

_____

_____

_____

_____

_____

List any sexual entitlement such touching another person without regard for their wishes and/or relationships that are inappropriate, or non-consensual at the workplace.

_____

_____

_____

_____

Have you ever told sexual jokes at an inappropriate time or place or made inappropriate comments about your partner's body or body parts?

_____

_____

_____

_____

Have you ever been a bad loser? Explain:

_____

_____

_____

_____

Do you have to win at all costs?

_____

_____

_____

Do you find that you interrupt your partner without even the consideration of what they're saying?

_____

_____

_____

_____

Looking at hostility and anger, do you have a quick temper and/or do you blame them when anything goes wrong? Do you use threats or display anger by hitting walls, yelling or throwing things?

_____

_____

_____

_____

Let's talk about your jealousy. Are you suspicious of anyone who comes near your partner? Do you have the need to know what they are talking about? When you give orders do you expect your partner immediately to follow them? List some examples below:

_____

_____

_____

_____

Do you expect that you should be forgiven as soon as you say "I'm sorry!"? Why?

_____

_____

_____

_____

_____

_____

Do you believe your partner is overly sensitive?

_____

_____

_____

_____

Do you feel that you don't deserve the wrath that you're getting?

_____

_____

_____

Do you believe that if she's overly sensitive and you ask her to do things sexually, and she doesn't want to, that it's your right; she needs to participate?

_____

_____

_____

Do you believe males and females were created certain ways, to do certain things, because they have sexual roles? List your beliefs:

_____

_____

_____

Let's talk about your past relationships. Can you discuss the last three relationships? What they were like? How long they lasted and why they broke up?

_____

_____

_____

_____

Was domestic violence or the threat of violence involved?

_____

_____

_____

_____

_____

_____

Healthy Relationships

There are different relationships that have different characteristics and we bring in different baggage. What is a healthy relationship? A healthy relationship is about learning about yourself and taking time to think about who you are and who you want to be. What are your goals and aspirations and dreams? You need to learn about building trust, affection, giving and receiving and begin to build self-esteem.

Find out what kind of person you would like to be by spending time with role models. These should be people that you believe have the qualities of a person that you want to be. This will help tremendously to re-develop your relationship; first with yourself, then with another person.

Healthy relationships support each other. That doesn't mean they enable each other. Enabling has an alternative motive. It is always there to make one person feel better than the other. Support is unconditional and Mabel Lang has an example quote: *"if I do this for you, I'm giving up so much; and then if you fail, oh my God, look what you've done to me".*

Our relationships needs to have very clear boundaries as to what everybody's position is. It may be easier to be able to talk and that's why we need honest, open and assertive, as well as have good communication. You must make your feelings clear; your partner cannot read your mind. They don't know what's in the back of your thinking process if you don't tell them!

Respecting thoughts, ideas, needs and wants of both people make relationships safe, fun and healthy. Dating and healthy marriages are when both people make decisions about relationships together. It is important to listen non-judgmentally. Give an emotional affirmation and understanding of your partner. Honesty and accountability must be a major part of this component of a good healthy relationship. Each partner accepts responsibility for themselves and for their actions.

It is important to make decisions together and respect each other's positions. It is also important to agree to disagree. Both must negotiate fairly; seeking mutual satisfaction in answers. Both must have an economic partnership, making money matters the work of two equal parts. Both share responsibility; the house, the children, mutually agreeing on projects that impact the family's existence. Parental responsibilities must be shared, being a positive role model.

Domestic Violence and Substance Abuse

While substance abuse is not cause of domestic violent there is a statistical correlation between the two issues. Studies on the method frequently indicate high rates of alcohol and other drugs used by the aggressor during the abuse. Not only do batterers tend to abuse drugs and alcohol but domestic violence also increases the probability that the victim will uses alcohol and drugs to cope with the abuse the issue of domestic violence. Substance use and domestic violence can be co-occurring and at times should be treated simultaneously

Domestic violence and drug alcohol addiction frequently occur together but no evidence suggests a causal relationship between substance abuse and domestic violence.

Substance abuse treatment will not cure abusive behavior.

Women who are abused are 15 times more likely to abuse alcohol and nine times more likely to use drugs.

In 2002, the Department of Justice found that 36% of victims in domestic violence programs also have substance use problems. This is from the National Coalition against Domestic Violence.

87% of domestic violence program directors agree that risk of intimate partner violence increases when both partners are using drugs or alcohol.

The National Center for Addiction and subsidies found that 69% of women in treatment for substance abuse say they were sexually abused as children.

The U.S. Department of Justice found that 61% of domestic violence offenders also have substance use problems.

Domestic Violence cases where a partner has alcohol abuse problems, often try to justify their violence as being drunk. This is a way to control the victim.

A survey by public child welfare agencies found that as many as 80% of children in abusive cases are associated with use of alcohol and drugs.

Stop the behavior! Stop saying "I'm sorry"!

Describe the behaviors that you are sick and tired of in relation to your partner:

Examples:

- Bad attitudes,
- Disrespectful speech,
- Consistently picking fights,
- Chronic anger,
- Disrespect particularly towards you and your family.
- Defiance
- Generally mean-spirited

If your partner shows these kinds of bad behaviors, then he or she is out-of-control. If you are exhibiting any of these behaviors, then you are out-of-control. Discuss:

_____

_____

_____

_____

Assertiveness skills

It still amazes me how many people still confuse being assertive with being aggressive. Have you learned the difference? For those who still haven't, I think this whole paragraph is important.

Assertiveness is a behavior or skill that helps you to communicate clearly, your feelings, needs, wants, thoughts, knowledge and the needs of others with confidence. It is meant that you are able to share your opinions without feeling self-conscious, as well as being able to express your emotions openly without judgment.

Being assertive will enable you to be clear to others how you wish to proceed in all aspects of your life. This does not need to have any control factors. It is time to destroy the confusion that people have with aggression and assertiveness.

- **Aggression** is an approach used to make you feel that you are being forced to react a certain way. You're forcing your point of view across on other people; hurting them, hurting yourself and making them resent you.
- **Assertiveness** is behavior in the skill that's going to help you set yourself apart from all the control factors in the past.

Aggressive means taking it out. Aggression is an emotion - out of control and can be very destructive; physically, emotionally and mentally. It is a state of confusion! One of the great skills of an assertive person is the ability to say "no" and to be brief and to the point. If you know an unwelcome request is coming your way, practice saying no! It's necessary for each of us to know the difference between assertiveness and aggressiveness!

Look at the body language of an aggressive person. Usually their hands are clenched, their muscles contract, their face and their body is tense, and they swing their hands. No trust! There is only control! This leads to a dangerous interaction and usually physical confrontations.

Assertiveness allows movements to be relaxed and uses open hand gestures even facial features. You know you may be firm and have direct eye contact. It's appropriate to express how you feel, it's not necessary to do it with a frown.

Aggressive behavior is about intimidation and creating fear in another person so that the aggressor can establish their own point of view. Usually, with forceful gestures and inappropriate language; all to give mixed messages and create confusion.

Assertiveness is about honesty! Show a willingness to explore other situations and perspectives. You can't do that with aggressive behavior. Encourage creativity because you're looking for an answer.

Passive-aggressive partners are about continuous mixed messages. One has to learn the differences between aggressive behavior and assertive behavior. Learn how to capture the attention of someone who doesn't particularly want to listen.

Get important information out without looking like a troublemaker and avoid frustration. Invite thoughtful and truthful answers to your questions, and be open to listen when discussed. Two way communication is a must!

Individuals with passive aggressive behavior express their anger and their hostility through indirect passive actions. Instead of saying, "I don't think it's fair, you expect me to clean the bathroom" he or she doesn't protest they just don't get around to doing it. When the partner gets mad and eventually explores the numerous frustrations, the passive aggressive partner just looks at him/her calmly making him/her feel like he crazy one and always blames someone else. A passive aggressive person can be so convincing that sometimes the partner will find themselves apologizing for getting so upset; thus the manipulation goes full circle and the spouse still has the original problem on their shoulders.

Passive aggressive spouses know the weak spots of their partner and often practice using sarcasm, remarks or gestures. That happens to me all the time. I can be sabotaged very easily by passive aggressive people when it comes to dieting, because I am so self-conscious.

On the surface, a partner may sound supportive, but he's really working to sabotage the other partner to approve his behavior. Passive aggressive individuals are resilient and blame others for the frustration and anger that follows.

So are you a passive aggressive person? Do you make snide remarks, or cynical humor commonly to tell them what you want and communicate unfairly? Explain:

_____

_____

_____

_____

Assertive Communication

- Send clear messages.
- Make complete statements and keep them brief;
- Use eye contact;
- Communicate clearly;
- Use positive body language - locate the position and posture and facial expressions as well as your hands, your arm movements; and
- Pay special attention to the tone of your voice; which can say volumes.

Learn how to listen - assertive people have developed their own listening skills. True listening is done with your heart. You can improve communication by becoming a better listener.

Start the conversation with "I feel…" rather than "you should…" Words have tremendous power to determine how other people experience us, and how they respond to us. For this reason, people with good assertive communication skills focus on problem behavior and not the character of the person that is bringing the problem. Stick to the point, don't use labels and make "I" statements, rather than "You" statements.

Acknowledge your part of the conflict. This is important! This is the whole point of denial. It is so natural to blame someone else, but remember that it took two people to get into this disagreement; especially when we are angry or in a defensive mode.

Learn how to say "no" and be respected saying no is a must. It is the way people really feel. Learning to say no will improve your leadership skills, as it would develop a better team environment for you because you will be delegating tasks. People will often surprise you when you actually say no. They feel that you have a better handle on your own wants and needs. This will help you overcome the negative feelings that you might have had before; so don't say "yes" when you mean to say "no". We don't have to make decisions based on guilt, rather than on honesty.

When you decide to do something it is then important to avoid conflict, rather than have a negative attitude. Be ready for an open discussion. Giving is best done when two people can openly discuss something. Maybe sometimes you don't say no because you think it's selfish saying no is not selfish, it's still setting a rule or boundary that applies to all types of assertive skills.

1. It is a healthier point of view when you don't say yes to something that you honestly don't believe in and this way you don't build up resentment;
2. This variation is about communicating and understanding the other person and situation. Following it up by your declining statement;

3. It is proven that if a person provides a reason for carrying out an action, the reaction is more likely to be accepted. With a *delayed* "no" you get back to them later; if it's okay to take the time and to think things out. This gives you time to think about your answer.

A *painful* "no" - is a variation of saying no that involves future pain to another person. It takes time to think for both your sakes. If you're going to say no (this is used by parents all the time) then basically it sometimes saves pain to say no now rather than prolong the decision.

The *repetitive* "no" - remember, when using body language and tips you are encouraged to maintain the same body language as other people.

There is *a respectful* "no"- first use of this, is if a person persists with the request, it is then respectfully a no variation. You do this with soft language so you don't come across as aggressive.

When you are doing something passive aggressive people don't want you to do their whole body language and attitude changes. This occurs when you don't give them the answer that they want!

What are some of your passive-aggressive behaviors?

_____

_____

_____

Now that you are practicing assertive behaviors how are you different?

_____

_____

_____

How could you improve?

_____

_____

_____

Killer Words

Tension is expected during complex arguments. When people don't fight fairly and find their partner off guard; words can cut especially deep and root. Remarks come from misguided efforts to put down another person's self-esteem and make others look bad or feel less than. Putdowns are hurtful low shots of communication that has only one goal; to insult, criticize and control another person.

Intimidation is the need to encourage their partners to focus on them, so that they can insist on putting the blame on them. This is essential when cutting remarks are an expression of anger. When you label your feelings and emotions this can help you understand each other and recognize problems.

Complaints, criticism and orders focus on others when words turn messages into attacks. Another example or danger is pushing people to do something they are reluctant to do otherwise. "I just dare you to say that again" is a good example. This erases everything that preceded it. It is especially effective when followed by an apology but still blames the other partner. Unrelated comments that are only there to rip into a person's ego are cruel and unnecessary inflictions of pain onto another. They have one goal and that is to make the person feel better about themselves at the expense of someone else. Defusing abusive behavior isn't the job of the person being abused; it is the responsibility of the perpetrator to notice what they're doing. That becomes their job. Asking questions clearly without buts and answers illuminate some of this. Do not offer solutions to other people's problems. They need to find it on their own.

So, some of the listening points that may make this easier are:

1. Make eye contact so that people understand that you're interested;
2. Show you understand by rephrasing the labeling and validating your feelings - that will make the person understand that you truly are paying attention;
3. Always check your accuracy, and know that you're answering properly or that you completely understand. Repeat what you think they said but do not disagree without thoroughly understanding the other person has reached their point. Sometimes perceptions are different;
4. Do not ever agree just to pacify the person because then you build resentments. It is okay to disagree or not to understand; and
5. Listen to feedback and validate by asked focused questions. Keep your points clear by expressing yourself in "I" statements. Avoid blaming such as: "I feel you should...", and always appreciate the other person. You don't need to jab or fixate on the negative.

Everybody has someone who gets on their nerves. It's sometimes your spouse, the boss, the kids or an adolescent with an attitude, a noisy neighbor, rude stranger or sometimes just the people in the line at the grocery store. Showing that you understand our objectives for good community and family dynamics using verbal statements are important deflections in your tone of voice. Sarcasm can only lead to more negative, passive-aggressive behavior. Show the understanding of family, and positive verbal statements.

Understanding your Family Drama

You feel that you're trapped in a web of your personal family soap opera and are unable to make a move without inviting disapproval to someone. Have you even thought of yourself as a director and that you're setting the stage for drama after drama? So what about thinking of it as your own family play, be the director of your own show. Courtship is usually very open. The beginning of a relationship between people is where they find each other, express feelings and talk about their thoughts and sometimes their bad behaviors. However, marriage and relationships are all about conflict resolution.

Arguing can be a healthy heart process. Marital conflict is about restraint and resistance to differences. Couples often alternate between periods of intense closeness.

When families become distant and divorce doesn't occur the family may get into the circle of domestic violence. This is when the drama intensifies and becomes very dark. Each character is defined in a role and each role has had the pattern of what creates the family dynamics. You can do a diagram of the drama by just outlining who, where and what. At this point I would suggest you do a family tree and draw that diagram.

Family Tree

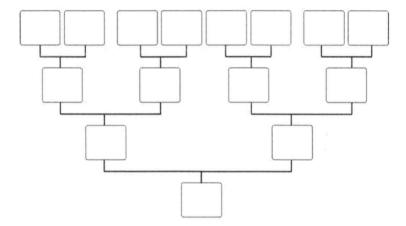

Each person has a different role in a healthy relationship. They are supposed to interact, but when one person becomes the head/director then everybody else in the drama feels that they don't have a part. That sets the stage of difference in this drama. When one is positioned in empathy, it's the complications of people. The second is the true closeness of each individual, and that means the functionality becomes less intense. The couple begins to experience closure, but one person is trying to take all the control. Individualizing display is about making decisions who's going to do what. The comfort level of each plot, of each character who rules and how the play is carried through is at this point.

I want you to draw up the family chart and then draw yourself and track yourself as a one act play; based on you and your family.

So it would have:

a beginning…a story line…a conclusion…and a lesson?

It would be important for this play to assess how your family operates by diagramming the relationship to the family, the origin of the family and interaction during this scene.

Identify the factors that contribute to the relationship problem somewhere in the act. In the first act describe the behavior that changes and how it reverses the relationships and how or if you've ever attempted to fix it. Identify the disorder, the anger in the violence; and then end it by describing how it can all be mended. The goal would be to begin active listening to cognitively learn how to behave as part of the unit. Identify gender differences if there are any.

Sometimes when designing these plays, one notices how role changing takes place. Notice that parents sometimes behave like children, and the children sometimes end up parenting.

After using different strategies, decide which are negative to begin with.

_____

_____

_____

_____

_____

_____

_____

_____

_____

_____

_____

The Relationship Worksheet

What are good qualities of my partner?

_____

_____

_____

_____

_____

What are some bad qualities of my partner?

_____

_____

_____

_____

_____

What qualities as a partner, which I think I lack?

_____

_____

_____

_____

_____

_____

What needs have I unsuccessfully tried to meet through this relationship? By my bad behaviors?

_____

_____

_____

_____

_____

_____

_____

What action would I need to take to change conflict?

_____

_____

_____

_____

What am I currently doing to fix this problem that I have with relationships?

_____

_____

_____

_____

Which problems do I need strategies for? Selfishness, jealousy, control, etc..

_____

_____

_____

Is there a lack of romance?

_____

_____

_____

_____

_____

How am I preventing the bad behavior from the past?

_____

_____

_____

_____

What strategies would make my partner like me more?

_____

_____

_____

Does my relationship need more or less distance?

_____

_____

_____

_____

_____

_____

Would I be willing to do that to please my partner and show them that I am seriously wanting to change?

_____

_____

_____

_____

_____

_____

Strategies for conflict resolution

- When angry, separate yourself from the situation and take time to cool off.
- Attack the problem not the person(s)
- Communicate your feelings assertively, not aggressively and express them without blaming.
- Accepting that the other individuals opinions may differ, don't try to force compliance with anyone else. Agree to disagree.
- Focus on the areas of common interests.
- Never jump to a conclusion that you are always right without listening to the other person's opinion. Remember when only one person's needs are satisfied in a conflict; it is not resolution and the problem will continue.
- Forget the past and stay in the present.
- Start identifying the jealousy as a negative behavior.
- Build strength without power over others; begin to thank the person for listening to you.
- Start displaying mutual respect, including the acceptance of different opinions and feelings.
- Give mutual support and encouragement in good times as well as bad times.
- Looking at the quality that both partners are on the same level, and they have the same rights; that means thinking, speaking, and making decisions.
- Trust and honesty - these are the two foundations of the strong relationship and need each other to survive.

- Good communication is the difference between swimming in clear, transparent water and swimming in gloomy, murky water.
- Enjoy each other's company and desire to set up a date night or to take time to be with each other.
- Sharing equally upon issue means sharing relationships, responsibility, chores and decisions.
- You need to respect yourself first and then expect nothing less from others.

In a healthy relationship, attention and support are equally given and both partners have the freedom to keep their individuality. They should have their own time, and their own interests. These are individual boundaries and always need to be respected.

Don't expect a partner to guess what your feelings are, or what you want. This makes things more difficult and complicated.

Relationship will not fix anyone's personal interest. Issues of like low self-esteem are not long-term anyway. Healthy relationships enhance individual lives. We all need to love and feel loved. Relationships also need to promote induced compassion and respect. It should be allowed by both partners to individually grow, be themselves, and be the best person they can be. Then they can be good to their partner as the individual grows and blooms with self-respect and happiness. They can contribute positively to the other person.

Overcoming low self-esteem requires persistent vigilance and commitment, but the rewards will reap from your efforts and are life-changing.

The freedom to ask for what you want in life, to express and open yourself to others, to create and grow together, to accept challenges without fear, and become your own person is the wisdom of growth.

- Self-talk - first thing we started a business manual, it is the inner voice that consistently judges you and everything you do. It is your own critic. When it is positive, the voice is compassionate encouraging and uplifting.
- Self-esteem – affirmations build a lot of negative core beliefs. This comes from repetitive suggestions. Take a look at what you say, and then practice what you do.
- Meditation, and then finally, the cultivation of happiness and optimism.

Ending a Relationship

Ending a relationship is never easy. Your relationship is something you have probably invested a lot of emotional energy into, and it's a letdown that things didn't turn out the way you planned. It might help to remember that you have grown from your experiences in this relationship – even from the most painful parts of it – and what you have learned from this relationship can help to make future relationship more successful. Also remember that you have the right to end a relationship any time you want to.

How do I end the relationship?

That depends. If your partner has ever been violent or threatened violence, even once, then it is very important that you do not attempt to break up until you have a safety plan in place. Work with your counselor to complete a safety plan.

If you have no concerns about your physical safety:

1. First be clear about your reasoning for breaking up, and be sure that ending the relationship is what you want to do. It's normal to feel confused at times, but never tell someone you want to break up with them as a way of manipulating them or getting them to do something you want them to do. Don't say you want to break up if you don't mean it.

What are your reasons for ending the relationship?

_____

_____

_____

_____

_____

Are you are sure that breaking up is what you want to do? Explain your reasons.

_____

_____

_____

_____

_____

_____

_____

_____

_____

_____

_____

_____

2. Choose a time when you have plenty of time to talk about your reasons for the break-up and for both of you to let out your feelings about it. (However, don't be surprised or angry if your partner does not want to talk about it too much and leaves abruptly. This is his or her way of saying she/he is overwhelmed with emotions and needs some time alone to think about it.)

This is when I will tell my partner:

_____

_____

_____

_____

_____

_____

_____

_____

_____

_____

3. Choose a quiet, private place to let your partner know
    in person that you want to end the relationship. Don't
    do it on the phone, through a friend or by letter (unless
    you are concerned about violence). Even if you're not
    concerned about violence, it's still a good idea not to be
    too isolated – be within ear shot of other people just in
    case things get out of control, but somewhere you can
    have privacy to talk and cry if necessary.

This is where I will tell my partner:

_____

_____

_____

_____

_____

_____

_____

_____

_____

4. Be clear, honest and 'firm but gentle' when telling your
partner you want to end the relationship. Don't be
wishy-washy, because it might lead your partner to
think he or she can change your mind, and it's unfair to
lead someone on like this. But don't be cruel either –
there is no reason to put your partner down or try to
make them feel bad. Use your assertiveness skills and
"I" messages.

These are the words I will use to let my partner know I want to
end the relationship:

_____

_____

_____

_____

_____

_____

_____

5. It's okay to agree to be friends, but it's a good idea to
limit your time together so you can both have time to
process your feelings and move on. And don't be
surprised if you partner does not want to be friends – it

may be too painful right now to be around you. However, even if you decide you can't be friends, you can still respect the relationship you had by being polite if you run into each other and by not bad mouthing your ex.

6. Be prepared to cope with difficult feeling about breaking up, so you don't end up going back to a relationship you really don't want to be in.

Dealing with a Breakup

If you've decided to end a relationship, it's a good idea to be prepared for your partner's reactions as well as your own feelings.

How will my partner react when I end the relationship?

There is no way to be sure, but below are some common and pretty normal reactions to a breakup. Are you prepared for them? Write how you will respond to each of the following reactions by your partner.

Disbelief, even if you think your partner should have seen it coming:

_____

_____

_____

_____

Crying:

_____

_____

_____

_____

Some degree of anger directed toward you, but no violence or threats:

_____

_____

_____

_____

Acting as if he or she doesn't care:

_____

_____

_____

_____

Making some effort to get you to change your mind, but without threats or coercion:

_____

_____

_____

_____

Denying that it is really over by saying that he or she believes you'll get back together someday without making scary threats:

_____

_____

_____

_____

Trying to hurt you back by saying mean things:

_____

_____

_____

_____

Wanting a detailed reason for the breakup and having a hard time accepting the reason you give:

_____

_____

_____

_____

Other:

_____

_____

_____

_____

Most of these reactions are using defense mechanisms – ways of protecting oneself from hurt feelings. The best way to deal with it is to just let your partner use whatever defenses she/he needs to protect him or herself at this time. Your partner's anger at you will probably go away with time. In the meantime, you should have someone you trust to talk to about your feelings.

Below are reactions to a breakup that are NOT normal or acceptable and require you to get HELP from a trusted adult or the police. Write how you will respond if your partner reacts in the following ways. If you think your partner might react in these ways, you should have a safety plan in place before breaking up.

Any violence or threats of violence:

_____

_____

_____

_____

_____

Words that scare you like "I will never let you go" or "If I can't have you no one can."

_____

_____

_____

_____

_____

_____

Threats of suicide, stated clearly like "I'll kill myself if you leave me" or implied like "I can't go on living without you."

_____

_____

_____

_____

_____

Refusing to 'let you' break up by not letting you leave, or refusing to leave you alone:

_____

_____

_____

_____

_____

Stalking you after the breakup: following you, calling constantly, or having you watched:

_____

_____

_____

_____

_____

_____

Other:

_____

_____

_____

_____

_____

_____

How will I feel after the breakup?

Below are some normal feelings you may experience, along with suggestions for how to deal with them:

Sadness and frequent crying, but his should begin to slow down after a week or two. It's okay to let yourself be sad and cry – even though you wanted the breakup, you are experiencing a real loss. One healthy way to work through your confusing feeling is to write about them in a journal. Start here by writing some of the feelings you are having while thinking about breaking up:

Feelings of loneliness and missing your partner. You should let yourself go through some of these feelings, but don't sit around feeling lonely for too long. Now is the time to re-connect with your friends and family, get involved in extracurricular activities, or get involved with a project or hobby. Write names of people or activities that can help you cope with the loneliness:

_____

_____

_____

_____

_____

_____

Guilt. There's no way to get around someone getting hurt when a relationship ends. You and your partner will both get through it and grow from the experience. Console yourself by knowing that you did the best thing for your partner by being honest and ending the relationship at the right time; it would have hurt your partner more to string him or her along. Write this sentence in the space below, and remind yourself whenever necessary "I have the right to end a relationship. I am making the best decision for me."

_____

_____

_____

_____

_____

_____

_____

_____

_____

Questioning yourself about whether you did the right thing. It is normal to have some doubts, but it not a good idea to call up your partner and tell him or her about them. This might give your partner false hope and hurt them more, or lead you both into a painful 'on again – off again' cycle. The best thing is to talk about these doubts with someone in your support system and remind yourself of all of the reasons you made the decision to breakup in the first place.

Who will you talk to? _____

What are the biggest reasons for your decision to end the relationship?

_____

_____

_____

_____

_____

_____

_____

_____

Other:

_____

_____

_____

_____

_____

_____

_____

_____

_____

_____

_____

_____

_____

Below are some more serious reactions to a breakup that you could experience. These reactions mean that you need help from a counselor or doctor. List the people or organizations you will go to for help if you experience each problem:

Feelings of extreme depression and loneliness that do not go away after a short period

_____

_____

_____

_____

_____

Thoughts of hurting or killing yourself

_____

_____

_____

_____

_____

_____

Loss or gain of more than a few pounds

_____

_____

_____

_____

_____

_____

Use of drugs or alcohol as a way of dealing with pain

_____

_____

_____

_____

_____

_____

_____

Other

_____

_____

_____

_____

_____

_____

_____

_____

Orders of Protection

Getting an order of protection (or protective order) is one step you can take to put a stop to abuse or harassment. It is not a guarantee of safety, but it can send a serious message to your abuser that you are not willing to put up with abuse.

What is an order of protection?

It is a legal order from a judge that sets strong limitations on the abusers contact with you. Every state is different but in many states an order of protection can do the following things:

Order the abuser to stay away from you. It may say the abuser cannot come within a certain distance of you, your family, your home, your job or school. It may also say the abuser cannot call you, send you mail or write you notes.

Order the abuser not to abuse you. Some types of orders of protection do not make the abuser stay away from you, but say the abuser cannot physically hurt you or verbally abuse you.

Order the abuser to move out if you live together. You an even request that a police officer come to your home when the abuser comes to get his/her personal belongings.

Orders the abusers to join a counseling or educational program for abusers

Give you temporary custody of any children you have with the abuser, and order visits with the children be supervised by a social worker if the children have also been abused.

How do I get an order of protection?

You have to apply for an order of protection in court – Family, Criminal or Supreme Court, depending on the situation. Usually, you can go to a family court if you are/were married or have a child together. Otherwise you will have to go to criminal or supreme court. Here are some steps you should talk:

Notify the police during or immediately after an incident or abuse or harassment. This will help build your case in court. If the police are involved, write the names of the responding officers here:

_____

_____

_____

_____

_____

Gather evidence of the abuse. Have a friend take a picture if you have any injuries and get written statements from any witnesses. List evidence here:

_____

_____

_____

_____

_____

Call a domestic violence or victim advocate agency to get advice. Many agencies have legal counselors who can tell you the specifics about orders of protection in your state, tell you which court to go to, accompany you to court, and provide free legal representation if necessary. If you are a minor, they can also tell you whether you have to have a parent involved in order to get an order of protection.

The agency you can call and its phone number:

_____

_____

Complete the forms and file for the order of protection at the appropriate court. You will have to write down details of the abuse, with dates and places. A counselor from the domestic violence services agency or the court clerk can help you. An emergency order of protection can be put in place immediately and you will be given a hearing date.

Write the locations of your local Family, Criminal and Supreme Courts here:

Family Court: _____

Criminal Court: _____

Supreme Court: _____

Go to the court hearing and tell your story to the judge. Be sure to have a supportive person with you. The abuser will probably be there any may try to upset or intimidate you. Make sure you get a certified copy of your order of protection.

After getting the Order of Protection:

- Carry a copy of the order of protection with you at all times.
- If the abuser violates the order, report it to the police immediately.
- Do not make contact with the abuser.
- Continue to follow your safety plan. There are risks involved in getting an order of protection because it may make the abuser angry and more dangerous. Even through the abuser can be arrested if she/he violates the order, the abuser may still try to hurt you.
- Safety Plan

What did you get out of the book overall?

_____

_____

_____

_____

_____

_____

_____

_____

_____

_____

_____

_____

_____

_____

What did you think of this program?